T0184004

Lecture Notes in Computer Science   **11470**

Commenced Publication in 1973
Founding and Former Series Editors:
Gerhard Goos, Juris Hartmanis, and Jan van Leeuwen

More information about this series at http://www.springer.com/series/7409

Vijay Gadepally · Timothy Mattson
Michael Stonebraker · Fusheng Wang
Gang Luo · George Teodoro (Eds.)

Heterogeneous Data Management, Polystores, and Analytics for Healthcare

VLDB 2018 Workshops, Poly and DMAH
Rio de Janeiro, Brazil, August 31, 2018
Revised Selected Papers

 Springer

Editors
Vijay Gadepally
Massachusetts Institute of Technology
Lexington, MA, USA

Timothy Mattson
Intel Corporation
Hillsboro, OR, USA

Michael Stonebraker
Massachusetts Institute of Technology
Cambridge, MA, USA

Fusheng Wang
Stony Brook University
Stony Brook, NY, USA

Gang Luo
University of Washington
Seattle, WA, USA

George Teodoro
University of Brasília
Brasilia, Brazil

ISSN 0302-9743   ISSN 1611-3349   (electronic)
Lecture Notes in Computer Science
ISBN 978-3-030-14176-9   ISBN 978-3-030-14177-6   (eBook)
https://doi.org/10.1007/978-3-030-14177-6

Library of Congress Control Number: 2019932781

LNCS Sublibrary: SL3 – Information Systems and Applications, incl. Internet/Web, and HCI

This Springer imprint is published by the registered company Springer Nature Switzerland AG
The registered company address is: Gewerbestrasse 11, 6330 Cham, Switzerland

Preface

In this volume we present the accepted contributions for the VLDB conference workshops entitled Polystore and Other Systems for Heterogeneous Data (Poly 2018) and the 4th International Workshop on Data Management and Analytics for Medicine and Health Care (DMAH 2019) held in Rio De Janeiro, Brazil, with 44th International Conference on Very Large Data Bases during August 27–31, 2018.

Poly 2018 Overview

Enterprises must deliver data management solutions for large, heterogeneous datasets often composed of disparate data with queries constructed from a variety of programming models. A "one size fits all" mentality simply will not work in these cases. Parallel database management systems (DBMSs) help with performance and federated DBMSs support heterogeneity, but no single engine can support these complex datasets for any but the simplest problems.

In response, new multi-DBMS systems such as Polystore systems have been proposed. These systems combine individual DBMSs, each suited to the needs of a portion of the dataset, into a single system. They are designed to support heterogeneous datasets but do so in a way that exposes the complete functionality and programming models of underlying DBMSs.

Poly 2018 was a workshop designed to bring together leading researchers and practitioners and focused on growing a larger and more diverse research agenda around data system solutions for heterogeneous data.

DMAH 2018 Overview

The goal of the workshop is to bring researchers from the cross-cutting domains of research including information management and biomedical informatics. The workshop aims to foster exchange of information and discussions on innovative data management and analytics technologies. We encourage topics that highlight the (a) end-to-end applications, systems, and methods addressing problems in health care, public health, and everyday wellness and (b) integration with clinical, physiological, imaging, behavioral, environmental, and "omics" data, as well as the data from social media and the Web. Our hope for this workshop is to provide a unique opportunity for the mutual benefit and informative interaction between information management and biomedical researchers from the interdisciplinary fields.

January 2019

Vijay Gadepally
Timothy Mattson
Michael Stonebraker
Fusheng Wang
Gang Luo
George Teodoro

Organization

Poly 2018

Workshop Chairs

Vijay Gadepally	Massachusetts Institute of Technology, USA
Timothy Mattson	Intel Corporation
Michael Stonebraker	Massachusetts Institute of Technology, USA

Program Committee

Edmon Begoli	Oak Ridge National Laboratory, USA
Rada Chirkova	North Carolina State University, USA
Amarnath Gupta	University of California San Diego, USA
Bill Howe	University of Washington, USA
Jeremy Kepner	Massachusetts Institute of Technology, USA
David Maier	Portland State University, USA
Samuel Madden	Massachusetts Institute of Technology, USA
Ratnesh Sahay	NUI Galway, Ireland
Nesime Tatbul	Intel Corporation, USA
Kristin Tufte	Portland State University, USA
Timothy Weale	Department of Defense, USA

DMAH 2018

Workshop Chairs

Fusheng Wang	Stony Brook University, USA
Gang Luo	University of Washington, USA
George Teodoro	University of Brasilia, Brazil

Program Committee

Jesús B. Alonso-Hernández	Universidad de Las Palmas de Gran Canaria, Spain
Thomas Brettin	Argonne National Laboratory, USA
J. Blair Christian	Oak Ridge National Laboratory, USA
Alba Cristina M. A. Melo	Universitat Politècnica de Catalunya, Spain
Dejing Dou	University of Oregon, USA
Alevtina Dubovitskaya	École polytechnique fédérale de Lausanne, Switzerland
Peter Elkin	University at Buffalo, USA
Zhe He	Florida State University, USA
Guoqian Jiang	Mayo Clinic, USA
Jun Kong	Emory University, USA
Tahsin Kurc	Stony Brook University, USA
Ulf Leser	Humboldt-Universität zu Berlin, Germany

Yanhui Liang	Google Research, USA
Gang Luo	University of Washington, USA
Fernando Martin-Sanchez	Weill Cornell Medicine, USA
Jorge Munoz-Gama	Pontificia Universidad Católica de Chile, Chile
Casey Overby Taylor	Johns Hopkins University, USA
Maristela Terto De Holanda	University of Brasília, Brazil
George Teodoro	University of Brasília, Brazil
Fusheng Wang	Stony Brook University, USA
Hua Xu	University of Texas Health Science Center at Houston, USA

Data-Driven Genomic Computing: Making Sense of the Signals from the Genome (Keynote Paper)

Stefano Ceri

Dipartimento di Elettronica,
Informazione e Bioingegneria Politecnico di Milano, Milano, Italy
stefano.ceri@polimi.it

Abstract. Genomic computing is a new science focused on understanding the functioning of the genome, as a premise to fundamental discoveries in biology and medicine. Next Generation Sequencing (NGS) allows the production of the entire human genome sequence at a cost of about 1000 US $; many algorithms exist for the extraction of genome features, or *signals*, including peaks (enriched regions), variants, or gene expression (intensity of transcription activity). The missing gap is a system supporting data integration and exploration, giving a *biological meaning* to all the available information; such a system can be used, e.g., for better understanding how genetic or epigenetic features influence cancer development.

The GeCo Project (Data-Driven Genomic Computing, ERC Advanced Grant, 2016–2021) has the objective or revisiting genomic computing through the lens of basic data management, through models, languages and instruments, focusing on genomic data integration. Starting from an abstract model, we developed a system that can be used to query processed data produced by several large Genomic Consortia, including Encode and TCGA; the system employs internally the Spark engine, and prototypes can already be accessed from PoliMi servers, from Cineca or from FireCloud (Broad Institute). During the five-years of the ERC project, the system will be enriched with data analysis tools and environments and will be made increasingly efficient. Among the objectives of the project, the creation of an "open source" repository of public data, available to biological and clinical research through query languages, web services, and search interfaces.

Contents

Poly 2018

FastDAWG: Improving Data Migration in the BigDAWG Polystore System

Xiangyao Yu[1(✉)], Vijay Gadepally[2], Stan Zdonik[3], Tim Kraska[1],
and Michael Stonebraker[1]

[1] Massachusetts Institute of Technology, Computer Science and Artificial Intelligence
Laboratory, Cambridge, USA
yxy@mit.edu
[2] Massachusetts Institute of Technology, Lincoln Laboratory, Lexington, USA
[3] Computer Science Department, Brown University, Providence, USA

Abstract. The problem of data integration has been around for
decades, yet a satisfactory solution has not yet emerged. A new type
of system called a polystore has surfaced to partially address the integration problem. Based on experience with our own polystore called Big-
DAWG, we identify three major roadblocks to an acceptable commercial
solution. We offer a new architecture inspired by these three problems
that trades some generality for usability. This architecture also exploits
modern hardware (i.e., high-speed networks and RDMA) to gain performance. The paper concludes with some promising experimental results.

Keywords: Polystore · BigDAWG · Migration · RDMA

1 Introduction

The database landscape has been plagued for decades by problems of data integration. Operational data is stored in multiple heterogeneous database management systems (DBMSs) each of which may differ in their data model, their
vendor, or their schema. Typically, the component systems run on different
machines adding communication problems to this nightmare. How can a user
extract and combine information from multiple heterogeneous sources? Most
systems have tried to solve this problem in its full generality, by integrating
arbitrary databases. But what if we could simplify the notion of what can be
integrated in a way that is still useful and that addresses some of the long-time
impediments to wide-spread adoption? The architecture presented in this paper
attempts to do just that.

A number of recent collection of papers popularized the notion of polystores [5,7,8,11,18]. The concept was to allow K islands of information each
of which supports a common data model and a common island query language
along with a candidate set of database engines. Examples include a relational
island, an array island, and a key-value island. An individual DBMS, call it D,
would join an island by constructing a wrapper that maps between the island

© Springer Nature Switzerland AG 2019
V. Gadepally et al. (Eds.): Poly 2018/DMAH 2018, LNCS 11470, pp. 3–15, 2019.
https://doi.org/10.1007/978-3-030-14177-6_1

query language and the local query language of D and a local-cast that converts D's data representation to the standard island format. In addition, there is an an island-cast from each island to every other island (very often, direct casts are made between particular engines of interest). Hence, when system A needs to send data to system B, then A converts its data to standard island format, an island-cast is applied to get to the other island representation, and then finally the data is converted to the local dialect via a local-cast. For more information consult the individual papers that discuss the components of the middleware in detail [4,6,9,14].

We have implemented this island concept in a system called BigDAWG. At present, we have two islands in operation, a relational one with Postgres, MySQL, and Vertica as members and an array island composed of SciDB. We have identified the following problems with our initial architecture:

1. **Learning multiple query languages is a daunting task.** Our previous proposal assumed that a BigDAWG programmer would know multiple query languages. In practice, this is a lot to ask. Most programmers have a main language in which they are competent. A realistic polystore proposal should not require a multi-lingual facility.
2. **Data movement is too slow.** Moving one record at a time using an insert in SQL is exceeding slow. Even connecting to the bulk load facility of the various systems is quite slow. We need a faster way to move data between islands.
3. **Wrappers are inefficient and hard to write.** The idiosyncrasies of the various query languages make wrappers tedious to write. Also, different type systems, treatment of nulls, integrity constraints, and the complexity of SQL just make matters worse. To add MySQL to the BigDAWG island took multiple months of effort. We need a simpler architecture that makes it easier to add new DBMSs to a polystore system.

In this paper, we propose a new polystore architecture that addresses all three concerns above. Section 2 presents a simpler overall architecture which does not require a user to learn multiple query languages and effectively addresses Challenge 1 above. Section 3 continues with a data movement system using networks with remote direct memory access (RDMA) supports and solves Challenges 2 and 3. Section 4 shows experimental results that make us optimistic about the success of this new architecture. Finally, Sect. 5 discusses some previous work, Sect. 6 talks about future work, and Sect. 7 concludes the paper.

2   A New Polystore Architecture

One issue with the current BigDawg system is that a user has to learn the query languages of multiple systems in order to run queries across them. The architecture proposed in this section requires a user to learn only one query language which will be translated to different systems, which effectively solves Challenge 1 discussed in the previous section.

We assume that a user has a main query language and most of his data is in systems that support some dialect of his main query language. Hence, an analyst might know an array query language, and a business intelligence expert would know some relational query language, such as Postgres or Vertica or Redshift. We will term this system as the user's **main** system.

Most sophisticated systems support the notion of **foreign** objects; for example, RDBMSs support the notion of external tables. We assume that all foreign objects (e.g., arrays, graphs) will be specified using the foreign object interface of the main system. We require this external interface to be extended with simple notions of indexing, so the query optimizer of the main system can do a complete query plan for any user query in the dialect of the main system. This query plan will be executed locally until foreign objects must be dealt with.

Assume the main system is relational. In this case, assume joins are coerced to run locally. Hence, the operation that is associated with an external table is a predicate and perhaps a projection. The one-table query is the result of pushing down all predicates and collecting them into a single query with the combined predicate.

Listing 1 shows an example of a query Q executed over two machines. Table R1 resides on the main system and table R2 is an external table residing on a different machine. In BigDAWG, query Q is broken down into three subqueries, Q1, Q2, and Q3, as shown in Listing 2. At the local machine, Q1 filters table R1 and stores the results into a temporary table T1. Meanwhile at the remote machine, Q2 filters table R2 and stores the results into a temporary table T2. After both filtering operations finish, BigDAWG migrates T2 from the remote machine to the local machine and performs the join locally.

Listing 1. Example Query Execution.

```
Q:   SELECT *
     FROM R1 , R2
     WHERE R1.A1=a AND
           R2.A1=b AND
           R2.A2=R1.A2
```

Listing 2. Query Q is broken down into subqueries Q1, Q2, and Q3.

```
Q1:  SELECT *      // filter R1 locally
     INTO T1
     FROM R1
     WHERE R1.A1 = a

Q2:  SELECT *      // filter R2 remotely
     INTO T2
     FROM R2
     WHERE R2.A1 = b

Q3:  SELECT *      // migrate T2 and perform the join locally
     FROM T1 , T2
     WHERE T1.A2 = T2.A2
```

The data movement discussed in the next section deals with the remote subquery (Q2) of the example above. A filtered table is returned to the main system which is stored and query execution continues. Hence, the data for all joins and aggregates can be fetched by pushing the predicates to the remote node. In this case, the entire query semantics is that of the main system.

3   Data Movement and Semantic Transformations

In this section, we propose an RDMA-based data movement design that addresses Challenges 2 and 3 discussed in Sect. 1. Specifically, Sect. 3.1 describes how datatype conversion works in the new architecture. Section 3.2 discusses how the system uses RDMA to accelerate data transfer and datatype transformation. Section 3.3 shows the execution of an example query. Finally, Sect. 3.4 compares the proposed data movement strategy with data migration solution in the current BigDAWG system.

3.1   Semantic Transformations

In this section, we describe the required steps in manipulating data across systems. Consider a main system M and a second system S. If a user wishes to interact with an object in the second system, he must enter an external object schema into the catalog at M. Thus, when the query execution engine needs data from S, it will look it up in M's catalog where it will find the external object definition. The data conversion logic will be included in the definition.

Assuming a polystore system that supports a relational database, an array store, a graph database, and a key-value store, the data conversion logic for each type of main system is discussed below:

Relational Database: A key-value store, a graph database, and an array store can all be "table-ized" in a straightforward way and be queried using SQL. Hence, it is easy for the owner of any of these systems to export a collection of tables, whose schema information can be used to access remote objects by entering it into remote catalogs.

Array Store: Relational tables are a special case of arrays. A graph store can easily export an incidence matrix and a node matrix. Similarly, a key-value store is a degenerate array.

Graph Database: Each tuple in a relational database can be considered a node of a graph and the foreign key relationship can be considered an edge of the graph. Similarly, a collection of key-value stores and arrays can be considered separate nodes in a graph.

Key-Value Store: A table can be exported as multiple key-value stores with each attributed exported as a key-value pair. An array or a graph database can be table-ized and then exported the same way.

As a result, **data wrappers** at this level are straightforward to construct. Most systems support the notion of predicates so a predicate on the main system can usually be converted straightforwardly to one on S, so predicates can be pushed into the remote system. Of course M and S may have different semantics for nulls and operators on single objects. Hence, pushing predicates has to be optional.

3.2   RDMA-Based Data Movement

We assume that all nodes are connected by networks with remote direct memory access (RDMA) support. RDMA allows a computer to directly access data in a remote computer's main memory without the intervention of the remote CPUs or the operating system (OS). Compared to traditional TCP/IP networks, RDMA can provide an order of magnitude lower latency and higher network bandwidth [3], making it a promising technology to replace TCP/IP based networks in small to medium sized computer clusters.

Besides high bandwidth and low latency, the next generation of InfiniBand network interface controller (NIC) is equipped with embedded compute capability (e.g., Mellanox BlueField SmartNIC integrates the NIC with ARM processors [2] and the Innova Flex adapters integrate the NIC with FPGA [1]). As a result, type conversion can be done in the processor within the NIC, thereby not requiring CPU involvement. Null conversion can be similarly accomplished. We first discuss the protocol for local execution of query Q with potentially remote data:

The site M sends an RPC request over RDMA to S to fetch remote object O. We use the term object to mean any collection data type (e.g., relation, array, graph) that is supported by S. Site S does the appropriate casting to the data model of M as noted above and returns a set of locations in S's memory where the result is located. M then directly reads the memory locations on S using RDMA and continues with the local query plan.

If a predicate P is being pushed, then the RPC request is P(O). In this case, S does casting plus filtering and returns a collection of memory locations as above.

3.3   An Example of Query Execution

Consider a simplified version of the query example presented in Sect. 2. To understand the proposed architecture, we use an example of two relational tables, R1 and R2, located on two nodes, main system and second system, respectively. The coordinator node (which can be co-located with the main system) is responsible for receiving client queries and dispatching them to other nodes. When a query, such as `select * from R1,R2 where R1.id=R2.id` is received, the coordinator breaks the query into two pieces, similar to the breakdown in Listing 2, and dispatches it to the two systems for execution. Figure 1 describes the flow of messages for this example.

When the coordinator receives the query from the client, it first instructs the second system to do a part of the query locally (`select * from R2 into tmp`).

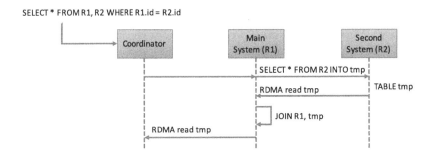

Fig. 1. An example query executed over two systems, main and second systems, with tables R1 and R2 respectively.

In this example, `tmp` is the location in the second system's memory that can be directly accessed by the main system through RDMA. Once this is complete, the main system is notified and performs the join of table R1 and table `tmp` locally. Finally, the results are sent back to the coordinator and the client.

In the case of two systems with dissimilar organizations (e.g., arrays or key-value stores), we assume that the remote systems (the second system in the above example) can be table-ized (i.e., we can consider the object foreign to the main system as a table). When there are dissimilar datatypes the above message between the main and remote systems will need to include information about how the type conversion is to be performed. The processor within the NIC can then perform the type conversion.

3.4   Comparison with Writing BigDAWG Connector

We believe that the proposed system can significantly reduce the amount of effort to integrate a new database system. Adding a new database engine to BigDAWG is a non-trivial task. As described in [19], there are a number of steps to be followed to add a new system (within an existing island). First, the developer must define a connection to the database. With relational systems, one can leverage a JDBC driver. The classes for the new database engine must then be generated. Next, a query generator is required that can translate one query language to another. In the case of different datatypes, some common representation must be defined. Once the engine definitions are complete, islands are modified in order to "see" this new engine. Assuming that queries will move data from one system to another, developers need to write export and load classes that can be used for migration. Again, this needs to take datatype conversion into account. Next, migrators are needed for all possible migrations. New migrators are registered in the middleware. Finally, catalog entries are required in the BigDAWG middleware. For MySQL and Vertica, adding each new engine was on the order of 2000 lines of code (each).

In short, adding a new engine to a system such as BigDAWG requires three major development efforts: (1) Connections, (2) Query generation/data conversion and (3) Migration. We believe that the proposed architecture can greatly simplify this process. By removing the need for users to translate queries from one global query language to a local query, we drastically simplify the query generation step from the description above. Additionally, writing custom data migrators between each system can be time consuming and difficult. Our proposed system relies on the well-defined RDMA protocol that can be used on a variety of interconnects.

4 Performance Analysis

4.1 Experimental Setup

In this section, we look at the relative performance of using RDMA vs. TCP/IP for data movement. We use predicted performance when comparing against the BigDAWG migrator.

The experiments in this section are performed on two machines, each with an Intel Xeon CPU E5-2660 v2 processor and 256 GB of main memory and runs Ubuntu 14.04.1. Both machines are equipped with a Mellanox Connect IB EDR NIC, which supports a theoretical bandwidth of 100 Gigabit per second. Each machine is also equipped with an Ethernet NIC that supports a theoretical bandwidth of 1 Gigabit per second.

For the BigDAWG experiments, we installed BigDAWG v0.1 [8] on both servers. Each server runs PostgreSQL [16] as the native database system.

4.2 RDMA Vs. TCP

We now compare the performance of RDMA with TCP/IP over the same Infini-Band network. In this case, TCP is implemented using IP over InfiniBand (IPoIB). As discussed in Sect. 3.2, one advantage of RDMA over TCP is the lower network latency due to bypassing the network stack. This is shown in Fig. 2 where we measure the network latency of both RDMA and TCP at different message sizes.

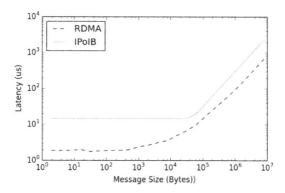

Fig. 2. Network latency with different message sizes.

With small messages, the latency of a TCP message stays constant at $14\,\mu s$, which is primarily the time to process the message in the operating system. RDMA, in contrast, incurs only $1.9\,\mu s$ latency with small messages. This is because RDMA queries do not require the involvement of the OS and only minor CPU computation is required at the client side. As the message size increases, the latency for both RDMA and TCP increases. But the latency of RDMA remains lower than that of TCP.

4.3   InfiniBand Vs. Ethernet

In this experiment, we compare the network bandwidth of InfiniBand and Ethernet. The results are shown in Fig. 3. With both network settings, the bandwidth consumption increases as messages get larger, until the bandwidth saturates when the message size reaches 2 KB. Regardless of the message size, the bandwidth of InfiniBand is around 2 orders of magnitude higher than that of Ethernet. This matches the theoretical bandwidth gap between these two types of networks (i.e., 1 Gigabit vs. 100 Gigabit).

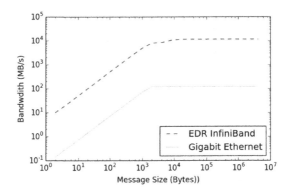

Fig. 3. Network bandwidth of InfiniBand and Ethernet with different message sizes.

4.4   BigDAWG Comparison

In this section, we investigate the performance bottleneck of BigDAWG and study how much performance improvement RDMA can bring to BigDAWG. To perform this study, we deployed two PostgreSQL tables, S at the local machine and R at the remote machine. Both tables have the same schema:

Table S s_key: integer, s_value: char (1000)
Table R r_key: integer, r_value: char (1000)

Each table contains one million rows which corresponds to roughly 1 GB of storage. The BigDawg system runs the following query over tables S and R where table S is on the main server and table R is on the remote server.

```
Query Q1:
    SELECT * from S, R
    WHERE S.s_key = R.r_key
```

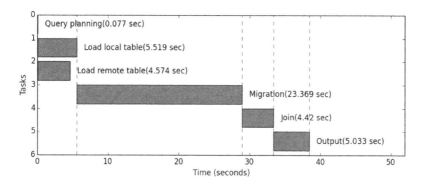

Fig. 4. The runtime breakdown of Query Q1 running on BigDawg.

Within BigDAWG, the query is broken down into three subqueries: (1) selecting the local table S, (2) selecting the remote table R and performing the migration, and (3) performing the join locally. The breakdown of execution time of Q1 is shown in Fig. 4. The majority of the execution time is spent on the migration process, namely, migrating one table from the remote machine and perform the join operation locally. After integrating RDMA into BigDAWG, this portion of execution time can be largely eliminated, leading to about 3× performance improvement.

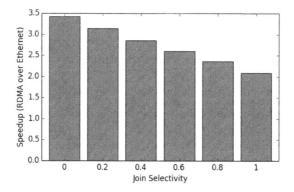

Fig. 5. Predicted speedup of BigDawg when replacing Ethernet with RDMA.

In Fig. 5, we demonstrate the performance improvement of BigDAWG when using RDMA as the selectivity of the join operation changes from 0 to 1. As the selectivity increases, the performance gain of using RDMA decreases. This is because higher selectivity leads to a larger joined table. Therefore, the portion of execution time spent on the join operation increases and the portion of time spent on migration decreases, limiting the potential improvement of RDMA which can accelerate only the migration but not the join.

4.5   Alternate Architecture and Proof of Concept

Many relational systems support the notion of a foreign table. An alternate architecture uses the concept of a foreign table on S. In this model, we can design a foreign data wrapper that can communicate with the node containing table R. The wrapper is used to define server connections, fetch/update data, and return to the executor. When a query is issued that requires data from R, the foreign data wrapper can fetch this remote data via an RDMA connection. The architecture of Sect. 3 leverages RDMA as a generalized migrator for polystore systems. This alternate architecture, while likely requiring increased developer effort, can reduce latency, improve query planning and optimization and can be used to largely hide the details of data movement from the end-user.

To demonstrate the viability of this RDMA-based join, we wrote a simple program to manually perform the join using RDMA and compare its performance to a local join. In this experiment, we used two tables S and R that have the same schema and size as in Sect. 4.4 where each row in table S joins with exactly one row in table R. For the local join, both tables reside on the same machine which performs a hash join. For the distributed join, the host machine builds a hash table using the local table, and then uses one-sided RDMA read operations to load individual records from the second table over the network and performs the join operation.

Table 1. Execution time of local Join vs. RDMA-based remote join.

	Local join	Remote join
Execution time	0.798 s	0.806 s

Table 1 shows the runtime of both the local join and the RDMA join. Overall, the RDMA join is only 1% slower than the local join, although 1 GB of data is transferred over the network during that period of time. For this type of data intensive query, the computation is the high pole in the tent and RDMA does not limit the system performance at all. Note that the performance number in Table 1 is much better than the performance number measured on PostgreSQL. This is because the hand-optimized join code does not have some overhead in PostgreSQL.

5 Previous Work

The notion of making database systems that interoperate has a long history. In the early 1980s the topics of multi-databases and federated systems were the focus of much research [10,13,15]. The high-level vision of these systems was very much like the concept of a polystore, but the implementation challenges were different.

First, a multi-database was built from a loosely-coupled collection of computers that communicate via TCP. Queries that required a lot of very expensive data motion, typically made the system unusable. Second, The multi-database system needed to be capable of integrating any data model and complete with any queries making interoperability a difficult task. Foreign database schemas were converted first to a common intermediate representation and then translated to the target system's schema/model which was complex and slow.

We address the data movement problem by using RDMA to make remote data access competitive in speed to local RAM. We address the complexity issue by limiting the models that can interoperate. We show that we can cover the common cases even with limited models.

More recently, a number of polystore systems have been developed to address the downsides of multi-databases; examples include BigDAWG [5,7], CloudMD-sQL [12], Myria [18], and Apache Drill [11]. While these systems all have different query interfaces and heterogeneous execution strategies [17], all of them used software-based data wrappers and migration policies. The RDMA based fast migration solution that we propose in this paper is able to benefit all of these systems above.

6 Future Work

Compared to BigDAWG, one limitation of FastDAWG is that a query is executed only on the main system—the other systems in the polystore handle data conversion and predicates, but not query execution. BigDAWG, in contrast, can execute different parts of a query using different systems, thereby potentially achieves better overall performance. While a FastDAWG user can still choose the main system for maximal performance, the level of flexibility is more limited. In practice, however, we believe the majority of most queries are optimized by running on a single system, in which case BigDAWG and FastDAWG will have similar execution plans. We plan to study the performance implication of FastDAWG by comparing its performance to BigDAWG on a variety of queries.

This paper has demonstrated the performance potential of FastDAWG using relational database systems. As future work, we plan to study how data type conversion and predicates can be pushed down to the new-generation of RDMA hardware. Hopefully, we can demonstrate the simplicity and performance improvement of this design.

7   Summary

We have described a new polystore architecture that addresses three shortcomings that we observed in our own polystore called BigDAWG, They are (1) the need to learn multiple query languages, (2) the data movement is too slow, and (3) wrappers are inefficient and hard to write. We make a conscious decision to limit interoperability between systems in order to make the system easier to use. We believe that our choice for how to maintain this balance is a sweet-spot. Our next step is to follow this up with some real-world deployments.

References

1. Innova-2 Flex Programmable Network Adapter (2018). https://goo.gl/xNzVD1
2. Mellanox BlueField SmartNIC (2018). https://goo.gl/dic6HH
3. Binnig, C., Crotty, A., Galakatos, A., Kraska, T., Zamanian, E.: The end of slow networks: it's time for a redesign. Proc. VLDB Endow. **9**(7), 528–539 (2016)
4. Chen, P., Gadepally, V., Stonebraker, M.: The BigDAWG monitoring framework. In: 2016 IEEE High Performance Extreme Computing Conference (HPEC), pp. 1–6. IEEE (2016)
5. Duggan, J., et al.: The BigDAWG polystore system. ACM SIGMOD Rec. **44**(2), 11–16 (2015)
6. Dziedzic, A., Elmore, A.J., Stonebraker, M.: Data transformation and migration in polystores. In: 2016 IEEE High Performance Extreme Computing Conference (HPEC), pp. 1–6. IEEE (2016)
7. Elmore, A., et al.: A demonstration of the BigDAWG polystore system. Proc. VLDB Endow. **8**(12), 1908–1911 (2015)
8. Gadepally, V., et al.: BigDAWG version 0.1. In: 2017 IEEE High Performance Extreme Computing Conference (HPEC), pp. 1–7. IEEE (2017)
9. Gupta, A.M., Gadepally, V., Stonebraker, M.: Cross-engine query execution in federated database systems. In: 2016 IEEE High Performance Extreme Computing Conference (HPEC), pp. 1–6. IEEE (2016)
10. Hammer, M., McLeod, D.: On database management system architecture. Technical report, Massachusetts Institute of Technology Cambridge Lab for Computer Science (1979)
11. Hausenblas, M., Nadeau, J.: Apache drill: interactive ad-hoc analysis at scale. Big Data **1**(2), 100–104 (2013)
12. Kolev, B., et al.: Design and implementation of the CloudMdsQL multistore system. In: CLOSER: Cloud Computing and Services Science, vol. 1, pp. 352–359 (2016)
13. McLeod, D., Heimbigner, D.: A federated architecture for database systems. In: Proceedings of the National Computer Conference, 19–22 May 1980, pp. 283–289. ACM (1980)
14. She, Z., Ravishankar, S., Duggan, J.: BigDAWG polystore query optimization through semantic equivalences. In: 2016 IEEE High Performance Extreme Computing Conference (HPEC), pp. 1–6. IEEE (2016)
15. Sheth, A.P., Larson, J.A.: Federated database systems for managing distributed, heterogeneous, and autonomous databases. ACM Comput. Surv. (CSUR) **22**(3), 183–236 (1990)

16. Stonebraker, M., Rowe, L.A.: The Design of Postgres, vol. 15. ACM, New York City (1986)
17. Tan, R., Chirkova, R., Gadepally, V., Mattson, T.G.: Enabling query processing across heterogeneous data models: a survey. In: 2017 IEEE International Conference on Big Data (Big Data), pp. 3211–3220. IEEE (2017)
18. Wang, J., et al.: The Myria big data management and analytics system and cloud services. In: CIDR (2017)
19. Yu, K., Gadepally, V., Stonebraker, M.: Database engine integration and performance analysis of the BigDAWG polystore system. In: 2017 IEEE High Performance Extreme Computing Conference (HPEC), pp. 1–7. IEEE (2017)

Multi-model Database Management Systems - A Look Forward

Zhen Hua Liu[1], Jiaheng Lu[2(✉)], Dieter Gawlick[1], Heli Helskyaho[2,3],
Gregory Pogossiants[4], and Zhe Wu[1]

[1] Oracle Corporation, Redwood City, USA
[2] University of Helsinki, Helsinki, Finland
Jiaheng.lu@helsinki.fi
[3] Miracle Finland Oy, Helsinki, Finland
[4] Soulmates.ai, Pasadena, USA

Abstract. The existence of the variety of data models and their associated data processing technologies make data management extremely complex. In this paper, we envision a single Multi-Model DataBase Management Systems (MMDBMS) providing declarative accesses to a variety of data models. We briefly review the history of the evolution of the DBMS technology to derive requirements of MMDBMSs and then we illustrate our ideas of building MMDBMSs satisfying those requirements. Since the relational algebra is not powerful enough to provide a mathematical foundation for MMDBMSs, we promote the category theory as a new theoretical foundation, which is a generalization of the set theory. We also suggest a set of shared data infrastructure services among data models to support "Just-In-Time" multi-model data access autonomously.

1 Introduction – Why MMDBMS?

Here is a short history of databases: Initially, database management systems supported the hierarchical and the network model (e.g., IBM's IMS and GE's IDS respectively). These databases evolved very fast and developed the core infrastructures, such as journaling, transactions, locking, 2PC (group and fast commit), recovery, restart, fault tolerance, high performance, TP-monitors, messaging, main storage databases, and much, much more. We still use these concepts today. In the 80' and 90', these databases were widely replaced by the relational database management systems (RDBMS). The main argument is its solid theoretical foundation: set based relational data model and declarative query language (SQL) based on abstract algebra over set processing.

However, the demands to simplify the interaction between applications and databases with simple storage and querying interfaces are not always possible using only the relational model. Object databases ODBMS (Object Database Management Systems) filled this gap by providing easy access to objects with object-oriented programming languages. With additional OO features in RDBMSs, ORDBMSs are able to support many domain data types, such as text, spatial, and images data. Interestingly, the last decade has witnessed the re-emergence of hierarchical data models in the form of XML and JSON data and the re-emergence of the network data model in the form of RDF semantic graph and property graph data. This has led to native XML, JSON,

V. Gadepally et al. (Eds.): Poly 2018/DMAH 2018, LNCS 11470, pp. 16–29, 2019.
https://doi.org/10.1007/978-3-030-14177-6_2

graph database systems and ORDBMSs providing XML, JSON, RDF and graph data support via SQL/XML, SQL/JSON standards and ongoing standard development to provide graph access via SQL. More applications are adopting graph modelling and graph query since graphs provide a flexible way to structure application data and adapt them dynamically to changes [15, 27, 29]. The source of graph data could come from relational, XML, or JSON that exist in the different databases [17].

The history of the database evolution has shown that new applications often require new data models leading to extended infrastructure of DBMSs with new query languages over these new data models. One existing solution is the polyglot persistency approach, which leverages numerous DBMSs to support different data models and integrates them programmatically at the application layer. The biggest issue of polyglot persistency is that the combined DBMSs is neither declarative nor unified. It leaves database application to procedurally join data among multiple data models and manually transform among data model instances. Instead of putting the burden on applications, it is more desirable to have a unified single DBMS [16], which hides the complexity of multiple data models by providing declarative approach of querying multi-model data instances and just-in-time data model transformation.

In this position paper, we advocate a multi-model database management system (MMDBMS) that has the ability to incorporate any data model and allows users to manipulate all data models declaratively. Users are able to explore the real power of an MMDBMS by leveraging its ability to autonomously transform data from one data model to another. MMDBMSs allow data providers and data consumers to look at the same data using different models depending on their most effective view. MMDBMSs accomplish these data model transformation autonomously on behalf of users.

We argue that the design of a full-fledged MMDBMS requires a more powerful mathematical foundation. The last few decades have witnessed a tremendous success of RDBMSs leveraging the relational algebra as theoretical foundation and therefore limiting this foundation to relational data. We recognize the same data can be represented relationally, hierarchically, graphically and are thus queryable by SQL, XQuery, Property-Graph Query Language respectively. Therefore, we feel the need of having a new theoretical foundation to provide transparent data model and query language transformations among those data models and languages. In other words, MMDBMSs require a powerful mathematical foundation to reason about declarative data model transformation among multiple data models. In this paper, we promote category theory [5, 14] shall be able to play the role of the new mathematical foundation to reason declarative construction and transformations among various data models.

In addition, this paper describes a set of shared data infrastructure services. The shared services not only include essential common data services, such as transaction, recovery, security, high availability but also include integrating artificial intelligence to provide "Just-In-Time" data model access and telemetry service to promote multi-model situation awareness service [4].

Organization. The remainder of this paper is structured as follows: Sect. 2 introduces the preliminaries on categories and examples of model transformation. Section 3 presents category theory as the mathematical foundation for MMDBMS. Section 4 illustrates MMDBMS infrastructure services. Section 5 shows related work and Sect. 6 concludes the paper.

2 Preliminaries on Categories and Model Transformation

The category theory exists since 1940 and has been successfully used in many mathematical, physical and computer science areas. Recently, researchers have applied it to the databases area (e.g. the functorial query language in [9–11, 18]). In this section, we review the concept of *category*, *functor* and give an example to perform cross-model transformation between relation and JSON data.

Definition 1 [19]. *A **category** consists of a collection of objects, a collection of morphisms, so that:*

- *Each morphism has specified domain and codomain objects; the notation f: X → Y signifies that f is a morphism with domain X and codomain Y.*
- *Each object has a designated identity morphism: X → X.*
- *For any pair of morphisms f, g, there exists a composite morphism whose domain is equal to the domain of f and whose codomain is equal to the codomain of g.*

Definition 2 [19]. *A **functor** F: C → D, between categories C and D, consists of the following data:*

- *An object $F_C \in D$, for each object $c \in C$,*
- *A morphism F: $F_C \to F_{C'} \in D$, for each morphism f: $c \to c' \in C$, so that the domain and codomain of F are, respectively equal to F applied to the domain or codomain of f.*

Each category can be considered as a collection of objects with some relations between them, expressed by "*morphisms*" – special form of describing relation dependency of the objects. One category could be mapped to some other by "*functors*". Mapping category C to D means mapping objects in such a way that relationship between mapped objects in D will be inducted by the corresponded relation in C. With category theory, MMDBMSs can be considered as a container that hosts multiple data sets of different data models as multiple different categories.

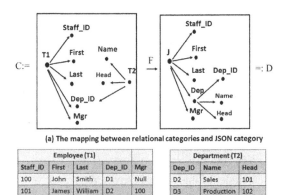

(a) The mapping between relational categories and JSON category

Employee (T1)						Department (T2)		
Staff_ID	First	Last	Dep_ID	Mgr		Dep_ID	Name	Head
100	John	Smith	D1	Null		D2	Sales	101
101	James	William	D2	100		D3	Production	102

(b) Two example tables with data instances

Fig. 1. A functor F: C → D from the schema of relation to that of JSON

In particular, a functor F: C → D of database schemas is a mapping that takes vertices in C to vertices in D and arrows in C to arrows or paths (a sequence of arrows) in D. For example, in Fig. 1, each of the six leaf vertices: *Staff_ID*, *First*, *Last*, *Dep_ID*, *Name*, *Head* in C is mapped to the vertex in D of the same label. This mapping is not necessarily bijective (e.g. the vertex of *Dept* in D cannot map to any vertex in C). Based on this mapping, we will discuss in turn three functors on the level of data instances in Example 1–3, which transform JSON instances to relational instances and vice versa, illustrated in Table 1.

Table 1. Illustration of data instance transformations induced by three functors.

Category operations	Symbol	Database operations
Pullback	Δ_F: *J-inst* → *R-inst*	JSON to relation
Right Pushforward	$\prod_F$: *R-inst* → *J-inst*	Relation to JSON by inner-join
Left Pushforward	$\sum_F$: *R-inst* → *J-inst*	Relation to JSON by outer-join

*Example 1 (**Pullback**). We explore the pullback functor Δ_F by applying it to a JSON file depicted in* Fig. 2. *This operation splits the JSON document into two tables.*

In the next two examples, we will explore the right and left pushforward functors induced by Fig. 1.

*Example 2 (**Right Pushforward**). We explore the right pushforward functors $\prod_F$ by applying on two tables in* Fig. 1(b). *The JSON file is described in* Fig. 2. *The JSON file can be considered as the inner-join of two relational tables* (Fig. 3).

```
{ Staff: { "Staff_ID": "100", "First": "John", "Last": "Smith", "Mgr": Null
    "Dept": { "Dep_ID": "D1", "Name": "CEO", "Head": "100"} },
      { "Staff_ID": "101 ", "First": "James ", "Last": "William ", "Mgr": "100"
      "Dept": { "Dep_ID": "D2", "Name": "Sales", "Head": "101",}},
        { "Staff_ID": "102", "First": "Sophia", "Last": "Davis", "Mgr": "100"
        "Dept": { "Dep_ID": "D3", "Name": "Production", "Head": "104", }
          }
}
```
(a) JSON file

Employee (T1)						Department (T2)		
Staff_ID	First	Last	Dep_ID	Mgr		Dep_ID	Name	Head
100	John	Smith	D1	Null		D1	CEO	100
101	James	William	D2	100		D2	Sales	101
102	Sophia	Davis	D3	100		D3	Production	104

(b) Two relational tables after pull-back

Fig. 2. Example JSON file and the tables after pull-back operations

*Example 3 (**Left Pushforward**). In this example, we explore the left pushforward functor. Instead of being an inner-join, as in the case of above, the JSON file is formed by the union of two tables. In order to deal with the fact that the record do not have department information, the respective value are skolemized. In other words, the cell is simply added by a new "variable".*

```
{ Staff: {"Staff_ID": "101", "First": "James", "Last": "William", "Mgr": "100"
    "Dept": { "Dep_ID": "D2", "Name": "Sales", "Head": "101" }
        }
}
```

(a) Right Pushforward

```
{ Staff: { "Staff_ID": "100", "First": "John", "Last": "Smith", "Mgr": Null
    "Dept": { "Dep_ID": "D1", "Name": "D1 _Name", "Head": "D1 _Head "} },
        { "Staff_ID": "101 ", "First": "James ", "Last": "William ", "Mgr": "100"
    "Dept": { "Dep_ID": "D2", "Name": "Sales", "Head": "101",}},
        { "Staff_ID": "D3_Staff", "First": "D3_First", "Last": " D3_Last", "Mgr": "D3_Mgr"
    "Dept": { "Dep_ID": "D3", "Name": "Production", "Head": "102", }
        }
}
```

(b) Left Pushforward

Fig. 3. JSON files after Right Pushforward and Left Pushforward functors

As shown in the above example, based on category schema and functor mapping, a relational model can be created on top of a hierarchical XML or JSON object. Conversely, a hierarchical model can be created on top of relational rows to access relational object. Therefore, category theory builds the mathematical foundation for the transformation of data instances between different models, which will be further elaborated in the following sections.

3   MMDBMS Framework and Category Theory

Building RDBMSs based on the abstract/set algebra as theoretical foundation has been a tremendous success. The ORDBMS technology is a subsequent successful engineering framework to enable RDBMS to accommodate object data. However, an ORDBMS by itself is not a MMDBMS since MMDBMSs require an improved mathematical foundation to reason about a declarative data model transformation among multiple data models, something not covered by the relational or object-relational algebra. To facilitate transformations among multiple data models, we argue that the category theory [5, 14, 19] is a more appropriate theoretical foundation for MMDBMS. In this section, we will discuss query transformation, view processing, in-memory processing in MMDBMSs and their potential connections to the category theory.

3.1   Query Transformation

MMDBMS enables a query over one data model to be transparently rewritten into an equivalent query over another data model. For example, given the property graph defined in Fig. 4, one can run various graph queries (e.g. shortest path). We investigate the following two graph queries (GQ1 and GQ2) in the context of MMDBMS.

Table 2. Graph and relational model transformations

Description	Graph query (PGQL v1.1)	Equivalent SQL query
Find a department D1's head and all individuals who report directly or indirectly to D1's head	*GQ1: PATH fp AS ()-[e: Mgr]-> ()* *SELECT emp* *MATCH (emp)-/:fp+/->(h)-[e1:Head]-> (d WITH Dep_ID="D1")*	*WITH g(Staff_ID, First, Last, Dep_ID, Mgr, Depth) AS (SELECT Staff_ID, First, Last, Dep_ID, Mgr, 1 as Depth FROM T1 UNION all SELECT T1.Staff_ID, T1.First, T1.Last, T1.Dep_ID, g.Mgr, 1+g.Depth as Depth FROM g, T1 where T1.Mgr=g.Staff_ID) SELECT g.Staff_ID FROM g WHERE Mgr is not null and Mgr in (SELECT Head FROM T2 WHERE T2. Dep_ID='D1')*
Find a complete list of departments that an employee John and his whole team belong to	*GQ2: PATH fp AS ()-[e: Mgr]-> ()* *SELECT DISTINCT d* *MATCH (d) < -[e1: Dept]-(emp) -/:fp +/-> (j WITH First = "John")*	*WITH g(Staff_ID, First, Last, Dep_ID, Mgr, 1 as Depth) AS (FROM Staff_ID, First, Last, Dep_ID, Mgr, 1+g.Depth as Depth FROM T1 UNION all FROM T1.Staff_ID, T1.First, T1.Last, T1.Dep_ID, g.Mgr, g.Depth as Depth from g, T1 where T1.Mgr=g.Staff_ID) SELECT DISTINCT Dep_ID FROM g WHERE Mgr=(SELECT T1.Staff_ID FROM T1 WHERE T1.First='John')*

Assume the graph data stays in the underlying relational base tables T1, T2, shown in Fig. 1. The two declarative graph PGQL queries (Property Graph Query Language, see specifications in [22]) in Table 2 are created on top of T1 and T2. Table 2 also shows equivalent SQL implementations using a recursive WITH clause.

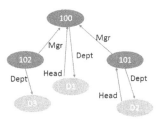

Fig. 4. An example of property graph

Category theory enables query rewriting crossing different data models. In particular, we consider each model data-set of a MMDBMS as a category and declare one or many functors to transform objects from one category to another through query languages. Further, a natural transformation provides a way of transforming one functor into another while respecting the internal structure (i.e., the composition of morphisms) of the categories involved. Hence, a natural transformation can be considered a "morphism of functors". Sometimes two quite different constructions yield the "same" result; this is expressed by a natural isomorphism between the two functors. Therefore, the transformation between functors can be employed to investigate the equivalence between queries with different models.

3.2   Multi-model Data View Processing

A view is nothing but a query. However, a view bridges the gap between how data is logically organized from the perspective of users and how the data is physically organized from the perspective of the underlying DB system. In MMDBMSs, a view is also a simple way to virtually access one data model on top of another via declarative data model transformation. **This is the power of MMDBMSs, which allows an application to store data in one data model and later query the same data by another application using a different data model via defining multi-model data views.** Thus, multi-model data view realizes the genuine value of MMDBMS which enables data applications requiring different data models to share the same MMDBMS and rely on MMDBMS to transparently provide different access views of the same data adaptive to each data application's requirement.

For example, JSON documents and XML documents are based on hierarchical data models. However, JSON and XML documents can be viewed relationally by decomposing the hierarchy into set of rows and columns. This is achieved by defining XMLTABLE() or JSON_TABLE() view on top of the native storage of XML or JSON documents to view the XML and JSON content relationally. Similarly, contents in a set of relational tables can be weaved constructively to create hierarchical model through SQL/XML and SQL/JSON generation function. Therefore XML view or JSON view can be achieved by defining SQL/XML and SQL/JSON generation function on top of the relational tables. In general, when transformation functions are defined to convert data between different data models, views can be defined to use the transformation function to present desired data model even though the underlying storage of the data may not be in that data model physically. Using relational tables and JSON files in Figs. 1 and 2, Table 3 shows SQL/JSON views for constructing relational data model from JSON data model and construct JSON data model from relational model.

Table 3. JSON and relational model transformations

Description	Query
Q1- Construct JSON view from relational content	*CREATE JSON_VIEW AS* *SELECT JSON { "Staff" : { "STAFF_ID" : e.staff_id,* *"First" : e.first, "Last" : e.last, "Mgr" : e.mgr,* *{ "Dept" : { "Dept_ID" : d.dept_id, "Names" : d.name,* *"Head" : d.head}}}* *FROM Employee e, department d* *WHERE e.dep_id=d.dep_id*
Q2 - Construct relational view of employee from JSON	*CREATE EMPLOYEE_REL_VIEW AS* *SELECT *** *FROM JSON_VIEW f, JSON_TABLE (f.Staff* *COLUMNS (Staff_ID, First, Last, Mgr)*
Q3 - Construct relational view of department from JSON file	*CREATE DEPARTMENT_REL_VIEW AS* *SELECT *** *FROM JSON_VIEW f, JSON_TABLE(f.Dept* *COLUMNS (Dep_ID, Name, Head)*

One approach to improve query over such multi-model view is to through query rewrite technique by leveraging the underlying algebraic property of the transformation functions among different data models. For example, relational predicates over XMLTABLE() or JSON_TABLE() views can be written into XPATH/JSON PATH predicates directly navigating the native hierarchical storage of the underlying XML or JSON data [2]. Inversely, XPATH/JSON path query over the views constructed via SQL/XML or SQL/JSON generation functions over relational tables can be written into relational predicate over the underlying relational table storage [2, 13]. Table 4 shows applying query rewrite transformation for Q2 and Q3 of Table 3. The intermediate JSON view don't need to be physically materialized.

Table 4. Query rewrite transformation results

Description	Query
Q2	SELECT Staff_id, First, Last, Mgr FROM Employee
Q3	SELECT Dep_ID, Name, Head FROM Department

Providing view update capability is feasible provided that transformation function is reversible. The MMDBMS can manage a set of built-in transformation functions between different models and understand the reversibility of the transformation function so that it can automatically determine if the view is updatable. For views that are not updatable systematically due to lack of inverse function, instead-of-update trigger can be supplied by users to deal with ad-hoc update. Therefore, the category theory can be used to reason about view updatability when a natural transformation is reversible. An MMDBMS optimizer manages a set of transformation algebraic rules between different models for query optimization and rewrite and understand the reversibility of the algebraic transformations for view update feasibility.

3.3   Multi-model In-memory Processing

The classical RDBMS technology assumes the data layout on disk is the same as the one cached in the buffer cache. However, the use of columnar main-memory structures has revolutionized this model [3]. By decoupling the storage format from their in-memory data format, MMDBMSs shall decide how to provide fast in-memory access for multi-model data. There is probably no single best storage format for a data model instance to satisfy all the workload requirements. Using functors and natural transformation in the category theory, MMDBMSs may autonomously rearrange and cache data in a different format as compared to the format stored on disk. MMDBMSs need not to lock down an optimized universal way of storing multi-model data and yet being able to provide 'Just-In-Time' data model access through materializing data model instances in alternative forms in NVRAM or RAM.

When the query over multi-model view is complex enough so that it is not feasible to do such query rewrite, for example, performing arbitrary directional path navigations in a hierarchical tree model, then materialized multi-model view technique can be used. The materialized view performs the actual transformation of the data into the physical model to run the query. In classical RDDBMS, materialized view has to be persistent, an in-memory only materialized view is a good option for MMDBMS to have because in-memory materialized view can be populated to speed up query without incurring the overhead of persistency management. Furthermore, the in-memory transformation can be implemented in background without delaying or blocking the foreground DML operations on the original base data. This is in the same way as how in-memory columnar population of the on-disk row format serves a good alternative to persistently migrating from row storage format to columnar storage format [6]. Rather than attempting to determine a best storage format of data upfront to satisfy potentially all workload, in-memory materialized view provides a flexible mechanism to decouple the storage format of data in view from the base table. In this way, neither the system nor the users need to lock down one way of storing and indexing the data. Applying this idea to RDBMS, users may have columnar physical storage with row oriented views materialized in memory or may have row oriented physical storage with columnar view materialized in memory.

In summary, MMDBMS shall use meta-algebra among data model instances to decide whether and when to materialize data model instances physically or in memory or to leave it as a logical entity to avoid materialization cost while providing good access performance. This is the key to integrate in-memory query processing with MMDBMS.

3.4 Multi-model Security Access via View

Just as classical RDBMS, view serves as an effective mechanism to enforce data security. In classical RDBMS, security can be enforced at table level, row level, column level via column projection and row filtering criteria declared declaratively by users. In MMDBMS, we shall be able to leverage view to enforce data security. Although MMDBMS has concept of table as collection and documents in a collection as a row so that inter-document security can be enforced just as relational DB case, the intra-document security enforcement is not a clear cut as the document does not have concept of column. However, we shall still be able to leverage the concept of view to enforce the intra-document security. For example, a view using XPATH to project a set of XML fragments within an XML document can be used to define part of an XML document that access is granted or revoked. Users may not be granted any privilege to access the base table or collection, however, they are granted access to views defined using document filter and projection to define fine-grained security access privilege.

3.5 Multi-model with Flexible Schema

In MMDBMS that aligns with the idea of data first/schema later or never, there is another creative usage of view in MMDBMS. It allows system and users to use adaptive schema concept [1] to access the data. The key to provide adaptive schema access is to leverage view. For example, in a heterogeneous collection of semi-structured documents, the underlying semi-structured data have loose structures so that defining a full schema over the semi-structured data could result in a very large sparse schema with many choices and uncertainties. Such full schema may not be practically useful for query analysis. Therefore, multiple views with various degrees of exposure of the underlying semi-structure data can be provided to users for their query use cases. In this way, users and their applications are not required to lock down one schema of the data using classical E-R design resulting a set of physically materialized tables but rather may have multiple logical flexible schemas, each of which represents certain way of viewing and accessing the data [23]. The underlying data may be stored natively in user input format as the source of the truth. There are many views defined in the system. Some of the views are virtual that require on-the-fly query rewrite to push the access to the underlying storage data. Other views are materialized persistently or computed and populated on-demand in-memory to speed up query access. The advantage of supporting multi-view approaches is that there are no schema evolution and physical data migration issues that classical RDBMS with fixed schema has. This is because there is only one source of truth using the original data directly from the import of the user without using any physical schema to shred the original data. All views are secondary whose content are always re-computable from the original physical data based on the schema that the system and user agree upon [23]. Through automatic schema derivation efforts by the MMDBMS system, users have tremendous flexibility to pick and choose views needed for their current applications and are able to keep evolving their view definition without physically migrating the storage data.

3.6   Application of Inverted Index in MMDBMS

Borrowed from the idea from IR inverted index on full text search, MMDBMS may extend the inverted index to a universal index that indexes not only full text content, but also other multi-model data instances and their schema. The inverted index in MMDBMS is model-context-aware schema and data search. The advantage of such inverted search index is that users do not need to know what to index in advance yet still enjoy high performance for an explorative type of queries. For example, searching keywords from inverted index shows the occurrence of the keywords under different data models: keywords within XML documents or JSON objects under a hierarchical path, within graph structures inside a graph traversal path, or within relational rows under a specific set of columns. From the search result of a multi-model context aware inverted index, users can then use model domain specific index to further narrow down the search and query criteria.

The existing ORDBMS supports domain index as a way to index domain specific data. MMDBMS inherits the domain index approach. However, a new usage of domain index is that it can be used as a secondary index after general inverted index. Furthermore, just as in RDBMS, conventional B+ tree index scan might be slower than in-memory columnar scan for an unselective query. Similar investigation needs to be carried out to evaluate if in-memory scan in MMDBMS is compatible with adaptive domain index for different kinds of multi-model data.

3.7 Benefits of MMDBMS Users

We summarize two main benefits for MMDBMS users:

- **Flexible data models.** In a MMDBMS, there is no primary data model. It does not matter that the data are initially defined with hierarchical data model or relational model or graph model etc. It will be easy for users to start the operation with one model and later add and incorporate new data models as their use cases demand. Users are able to incorporate multiple data models into a single MMDBMS and manage them in a holistic way.
- **Transparent cross-model query transformation and rewriting.** All query languages are equal in MMDBMSs. Each data model may have its own domain-specific declarative query and modification language. User applications may initially start with one data model language to access one data model. However, as they start to manage multiple data models and try to transform, join and mix data models in MMDBMSs, MMDBMSs understand the connections among these data models and their respective languages so that it can transparently do query transformation and rewriting among different data model languages on behalf of applications. The genuine value of MMDBMSs is that they allow many data applications to share one DBMS and on-demand declaratively transform from one data model to another. It is the MMDBMS's (not users') responsibility to optimize and execute inter-data model queries and modification requests.

3.8 Limitation of Category Theory

Some logical limitation of Category Theory has been pointed by Jean–Yves Girard [24], renowned logician in Proof Theory area. Girard considered the notion of equivalence in Category Theory to be too strict "up to isomorphism". Therefore, he wrote, the Category Theory can't operate with other, more complicated equality forms, in-particular in novel logic theory [25, 26]. However, right now we are far away from such problems in our MMDBMS approach.

4 Infrastructure Services – Ecosystem for MMDBMS

MMDBMSs need to provide a set of common services that can be used by the different models. This section describes some of these key services:

- **Atomicity:** Databases allow users to bundle requests; this is the well-known transaction support. The fundamental idea is that if a transaction is unable to complete there will not be any trace of that transaction in the database and if it succeeds, everything is committed permanently. To achieve this any required database object has to be isolated from other transactions progressing in parallel and changes are not visible until a transaction completes successfully. However, this basic (ACID) model has significant limitations in respect to functionality, performance and scalability. A well-known technology is to use escrow technology, which supports parallel updates for commutative operations that are commonly frequently available for inventory management. Additionally, weaker models exist for those applications that can tolerate relaxed support; e.g., BASE. MMDBMSs need to support a wide range of models and therefore support different levels of atomicity for different data models and different use cases. The level of atomicity should be able to be tuned differently for different data models and use cases based on their requirements both manually and automatically.

- **Fault resilience for recovery and provenance:** Fault resilience is a service to capture information to recover from any error and avoid any loss of data while supporting atomicity. Implementing fault resilience for an MMDBMS is challenging but it should be done better than with a polyglot solution due to its single integrated backend. The requirements for fault resilience can be different for diverse data models and use cases. It should be able to be tuned both manually and automatically.

- **Telemetry:** This service will provide a base for a wide range of data capturing and analysis services in MMDBMS. The basic usage is to understand the system behavior for a wide range of perspectives; e.g., understanding and debugging functionality and performance, understanding usage patterns, and billing. A more advanced usage is to identify abnormal behavior in real time. Multi-model data can be analyzed in real time and/or externalized for provenance and offline-analysis. For this service, MMDBMSs should be able to be more adaptive and flexible, such as adaptive in-memory processing, adaptive universal multi-model indexing, and adaptive view processing via query rewrite or in-memory materialization and adaptive schema view for just-in-time semi-structured data in-memory processing.

- **Machine Learning:** MMDBMSs will use machine learning on top of telemetry Data to understand user's data application so that it can recommend suitable data model for applications. As applications evolve different data model might become appropriate. MMDBMSs will autonomously build the appropriate data model just-in-time to better serve users. At a more advanced level, telemetry and machine learning can also identify abnormal behavior such as faulty sensors, as well as assets and system components.

5   Related Work

A multi-model data management system is designed to address the variety challenge of a complex world. In general, there exist two solutions: (i) polyglot persistence and (ii) multi-model database.

The history of polyglot persistence may trace back to the federation of relational engines or distributed DBMSs, which was studied in depth during the 1980s and early 1990s. Polyglot persistence approach is similar to the use of mediators in early federated database systems. Recently, some research groups have been working on polyglot persistence platforms. For example, Musketeer [6] provides an intermediate representation between applications and data processing platforms and has the merit of proposing an optimizer for the supported applications and platforms. DBMS+ [7] is another work that aims at embracing several processing and storage platforms for declarative processing. BigDAWG [8] has recently been proposed as a federated system that enables users to run their queries over multiple vertically integrated systems such as column stores, NewSQL engines, and array stores.

The second approach is to develop MMDBMSs to support multiple data models against a single, integrated backend, while meeting the growing requirements for scalability and performance. However, as far as our knowledge, there exist very few research works [12, 20, 21, 28] on the theories and algorithms of MMDBMS. Paper [20] illustrates the query compilation technique for logical and physical design in data management that is relevant to query processing over multiple physical data models in MMDBMS. Paper [21] has introduced the concept of "meta-model" as a framework for defining different data models and specifying translations schema among data models. In this paper, we make the contributions by showing the benefit of leveraging category theory as new theoretical foundation in MMDBMS. We suggest a new mathematical foundation, which not only can capture relational model and relational algebra but also be able to capture many other data models and their algebra, so that the meta-connections among data models and their algebra are transparent from their data applications.

6 Conclusion and Future Work

In this paper, we have discussed the challenges supporting the "Variety" of data; we are advocating an MMDBMS technology with category theory as mathematical foundation. We envision leveraging category theory for multi-model query transformation, viewing processing, in-memory processing and adaptive schema. We also propose a set of shared data infrastructure services in MMDBMS to support "Just-In-Time" multi-model data access autonomously.

Exciting follow-up research can be centered on an in-depth research of category theory into MMDBMS. Of foremost importance is to chart the natural transformation among multiple models to enable transparent cross-model query processing and rewriting. Another of our efforts is aimed at the potential impact of the interplay between category theory and machine learning algorithms on an autonomous data model selection and accesses.

Acknowledgement. Jiaheng Lu is partially supported by the Academy of Finland (No. 310321).

References

1. Spoth, W., et al.: Adaptive schema databases. In: CIDR (2017)
2. Liu, Z.H., Gawlick, D.: Management of flexible schema data in RDBMSs-opportunities and limitations for NoSQL. In: CIDR (2015)
3. Lahiri, T., et al.: Oracle database in-memory: a dual format in-memory database. In: Data Engineering (ICDE) (2015)
4. Gawlick, D., Chan, E.S., Ghoneimy, A., Liu, Z.H.: Mastering situation awareness: the next big challenge? ACM SIGMOD Rec. **44**(3), 19–24 (2015)

5. Spivak, D.I.: Database queries and constraints via lifting problems. Math. Struct. Comput. Sci. **24**(6) (2014)
6. Grosvenor, M.P., Clement, A., Hand, S.: Musketeer: all for one, one for all in data processing systems. In: EuroSys, pp. 1–16 (2015)
7. Lim, H., Han, Y., Babu, S.: How to fit when no one size fits. In: CIDR (2013)
8. Elmore, A., et al.: A demonstration of the BigDAWG polystore system. Proc. VLDB Endow. **8**(12), 1908–1911 (2015)
9: Schultz, P., et al.: Algebraic databases. CoRR abs/1602.03501 (2016)
10. Fleming, M., Gunther, R., Rosebrugh, R.: A database of categories. J. Symb. Comput. **35**, 127–135 (2002)
11. Wisnesky, R., Spivak, D.: A functorial query language. Presented at Boston Haskell (2014). http://categoricaldata.net/fql/haskell.pdf
12. Abiteboul, S., et al.: Research directions for principles of data management (Abridged). SIGMOD Rec. **45**(4), 5–17 (2016)
13. Liu, Z.H., et al.: Towards a physical XML independent XQuery/SQL/XML engine. PVLDB **1**(2), 1356–1367 (2008)
14. Michael, B., Charles, W.: Category Theory for Computing Science. Reprints in Theory and Applications of Categories, vol. 22 (2012)
15. Yan, Da, et al.: Big graph analytics platforms. Found. Trends Databases **7**(1–2), 1–195 (2017)
16. Lu, J., Holubová, I.: Multi-model data management: what's new and what's next? In: EDBT 2017, pp. 602–605 (2017)
17. World Wide Web Consortium (W3C). https://www.w3.org/
18. Wisnesky, R., Spivak, D.I., Schultz, P., Subrahmanian, E.: Functorial data migration: from theory to practice. CoRR abs/1502.05947 (2015)
19. Riehl, E.: Category Theory in Context. Courier Dover Publications, Mineola (2017)
20. Toman, D., Weddell, G.E.: Fundamentals of Physical Design and Query Compilation. Synthesis Lectures on Data Management. Morgan & Claypool Publishers, San Rafael (2011)
21. Atzeni, P., Torlone, R.: A metamodel approach for the management of multiple models and translation of schemes. Inf. Syst. **18**(6), 349–362 (1993)
22. Property Graph Query Language 1.1 Specification. http://pgql-lang.org/spec/1.1/
23. Liu, Z.H., Hammerschmidt, B.C., McMahon, D., Liu, Y., Chang, H.J.: Closing the functional and performance gap between SQL and NoSQL. In: SIGMOD Conference 2016, pp. 227–238 (2016)
24. Girard, J.-Y.: Locus solum: from the rules of logic to logic of rules. Math. Struct. Comput. Sci. **11**(3), 301–506 (2001)
25. Girard, J.-Y.: From foundations to ludics. Bull. Symb. Log. **9**(2), 131–168 (2003)
26. Lecomte, A.: Meaning, Logic and Ludics. Imperial College Press, London (2011)
27. Liu, Y., et al.: ProbeSim: scalable single-source and top-k SimRank computations on dynamic graphs. PVLDB **11**(1), 14–26 (2017)
28. Lu, J.: Towards benchmarking multi-model databases. In: CIDR (2017)
29. Chen, J., et al.: Big data challenge: a data management perspective. Front. Comput. Sci. **7**(2), 157–164 (2013)

Progressive Interactions Between Data Sources

Ben McCamish$^{(\boxtimes)}$ and Arash Termehchy

Oregon State University, Corvallis, OR, USA
{mccamisb,termehca}@oregonstate.edu

Abstract. Queries submitted by the user to their local database may require the DBMS to retrieve additional information from another DBMS. This is traditionally done through mappings, which can be quite costly. We have modeled the process of achieving these mappings as a communication game between multiple DBMSs. One DBMS will attempt to communicate what data it desires from the other DBMS using a common language. Thus, the DBMSs will use this game to facilitate communication in order to successfully build a mapping between them. We give an overview of our system and discuss the challenges presented.

Keywords: Entity matching · Schema mappings · Game theory · Reinforcement learning

1 Introduction

To better satisfy the users' information needs, a data management system (DBMS) should often use data stored in external data sources in its domain of interest. It may also require data that is in another format, but not remote. Each data source may represent information in a distinct form. For example, different databases may use different schemas to store information or refer to the same domain entity differently. Hence, DBMS has to translate the input user query to a query that is understandable by the external data sources, get the results, aggregate the external results with its own local results, and returned the aggregated answers to the user. This process is traditionally performed via *mappings* between the local and external data sources [1]. Well-known examples of such mappings are *schema mappings* that establish relationships between schema elements in multiple data sources. That is, a mapping allows for one data source to map its own entities to entities in a remote data source.

Mappings provide powerful abstractions and simplify communication between data sources. However, it takes a significantly long time and a great deal of financial resources and manual labor to develop mappings [2]. As the underlying data sources evolve, one has to spend time and effort to update and repair their associated mappings. Hence, it is difficult and costly to scale the data integration systems to cover a large number of local databases. Mapping developers must also have access to the content and schemas of the underlying

© Springer Nature Switzerland AG 2019
V. Gadepally et al. (Eds.): Poly 2018/DMAH 2018, LNCS 11470, pp. 30–38, 2019.
https://doi.org/10.1007/978-3-030-14177-6_3

data sources in their entirety to create correct mappings. Such an access is *not* often possible as many databases may be available only via query interfaces. For instance, many Web data sources can be accessed only via restricted keyword or form-based query interfaces and/or API calls [6].

To address the aforementioned limitations, we propose a new approach to constructing mappings between data sources progressively via sending queries between data sources. The user submits queries to her own local database. The local data source finds the tuples that satisfy the user's query in the local database. Then, it formulates a query in a common query language that is supported and understandable by other data sources, in particular keyword queries, based on the input user query and its local results and sends the query to other data sources. The local DBMS does *not* need to know the schema of other data sources to formulate the keyword queries. Each data source returns some results to the local DBMS. The local DBMS aggregates and shows the final results to the user. Because keyword queries are inherently vague, the external data sources may return non-relevant tuples to the user query and/or do *not* return all the relevant tuples they contain. Moreover, since the local DBMS does *not* know the structure of the data stored in the external data sources completely, it may *not* accurately aggregate them with its own results. The local DBMS leverages user feedback on the returned results to learn and progressively improve its query formulation and result aggregation strategies. Since external data sources often support feedback on their returned results, the local DBMS also propagates the user feedback to the other data sources so they revise their own strategy of understanding and answering keyword queries. In this framework, a query over the local DBMS is *mapped* to a query over the external data source using the query reformulation strategy of the local DBMS and the (keyword) query answering strategy of the external data source. In a conceptual level, one may view this interaction is a collaborative game between some potentially rational agents that interaction and revise their communication strategy based on the success of previous communications [3,4].

Our method builds on and extends current ideas on pay-as-you-go and human-in-the-loop approaches to data integration [2,5] by using interactive communication in a common and possibly vague query language between data sources to build mappings. Since data sources communicate using a common query language, this method has the potential to be used for integrating structured and semi-structured data. This method may *not* create an accurate mapping due to the vagueness of the common query language and inaccurate initial aggregations of the results. Our goal is to ensure that with minimal user feedback, the data sources improve the accuracy of their mapping over time in a reasonable pace. The design of the system is inspired by the theory of natural language creation and evolution [4]. It is believed that a natural language does *not* have a single inventor and is created gradually by interactive communication of humans via sending utterances and receiving feedback. Since this approach has been obviously successful in creating mutually understandable communications, we believe that our proposed method is promising for pay-as-you-go data integration and communication. In the rest of the paper, we overview the elements of our proposed method and discuss its challenges.

2   Framework

In this section we will describe our framework. We model the mapping between two different DBMSs as an interactive and collaborative game. We have used a similar framework in our previous work modeling the interaction between users and DBMSs [3]. The goal of this game is to facilitate successful communication between two different DBMSs. One DBMS wishes to find content in another DBMS that might be similar to its own data in order to integrate and combine the two datasets to answer the users initial query. For this work, we restrict ourselves to the case of entity resolution, where one DBMS wishes to find tuples in other databases that might contain the same content conceptually. The DBMSs may be written in conflicting languages, making knowing how to query the other impossible. Often databases can only be accessed through the deep web, requiring the use of restricting forms or ambiguous keyword queries. We examine the case where the common means of communication between the two DBMSs is keyword queries. Thus the DBMS wishing to find relevant information in another DBMS may attempt to access it through the keyword query interface.

Consider Tables 1(a) and (b), each are an instance of the databases for different companies. Company A wishes to see how their prices compare to the prices of Company B for the same items. However, both databases store the information with different names and IDs. Thus, Company A is going to have to learn how to properly query the database in Company B in order to find updated prices for similar products in the future. For the remainder of the paper we assume that there are two different DBMSs, one with a sender strategy and another with a receiver strategy. However, it is quite intuitive to expand this model to an infinite number of DBMSs, all with either both strategies or a single one. Figure 1 illustrates how this system would like with the two DBMSs described above. The remainder of this section will cover the details of each of the components depicted in this figure.

2.1   Entity

An *entity* is the tuple(s) that a DBMS wishes to communicate to another DBMS. In more general terms, the entity is a query in the language that the DBMS follows. If the sender contains a DBMS that is written in SQL, then the entities would be SQL queries. Likewise, if the receiver contains a DBMS with a Datalog database, then the entities would in turn be Datalog queries. For the remainder of this paper, however, we consider an entity to be a set of tuples from the respective DBMS.

Example 1. Consider the database instance and entities illustrated in Tables 1(a) and 2(a) respectively. If the sender had the entity e_1, then it would attempt to communicate this entity to the other DBMSs in the game. There would be similar entities for the receiver, with regards to its database.

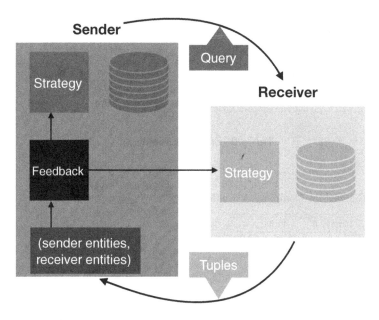

Fig. 1. Example framework for two databases, one with a sender strategy the other with a receiver strategy

2.2   Query

A *query* is the chosen information that a DBMS uses to communicate its entity to other databases. Often the complete interface of a database is not available. Most of the data available through the web is stored on the deep web, thus requiring the use of limited methods of access. That is, in order to communicate with other DBMSs, we may have use some sort of form or limited interface in order to access the database. One most common form of limited communication that is available to many types of databases is the use of keyword queries. Keyword queries, while vague, are used as the common language and means of querying other databases. We may not wish to send an unlimited number of keyword queries, due to limits in communication or the interface. Thus, the queries that are sent to other databases is some finite set of keywords.

Example 2. Again, consider the database instance, entities, and queries illustrated in Tables 1(a), 2(a), and 2(b) respectively. Suppose that the entity of the DBMS is still e_1. Thus the queries available are q_1, q_2, q_3, each constructed from features, which will be explained later.

2.3   Sender Strategy

The *sender strategy* reflects how entities are conveyed to other DBMS using queries. Since the entities are queries in a language that may be foreign to other

Table 1. Two database instances of relations Company A and Company B

(a) Company A

Product_ID	Product_Name	Price
1	Water	12.99
2	Soda	5.99

(b) Company B

Product_ID	Product_Name	Price
3	H2O	2.99
4	Pop	13.99

Table 2. Entities and queries

(a) Entities for Company A Sender

Entity#	Entity
e_1	1 Water 12.99
e_2	2 Soda 5.99

(b) Queries for Company A Sender

Query#	Query
q_1	'1 Water'
q_2	'1 12.99'
q_3	'Water 12.99'
q_4	'2 Soda'
q_5	'2 5.99'
q_6	'Soda 5.99'

Table 3. Sender and receiver strategies

(a) Sender strategy profile

	q_1	q_2	q_3	q_4	q_5	q_6
e_1	0.25	0.25	0.5	0	0	0
e_2	0	0	0	0.33	0.33	0.34

(b) Receiver strategy profile

	e_1	e_2
q_1	1	0
q_2	0.5	0.5
q_3	0.75	0.25
q_4	0	1
q_5	0.5	0.5
q_6	0.25	0.75

DBMSs, they must be communicated in a way that is understood by every DBMS. We assume there are $0 \le i \le n$ entities. For each entity there are $0 \le j \le m$ queries available. We call the sender strategy S, where S is a $n \times m$ row-stochastic matrix.

First the DBMS picks an entity e_i that it wishes to find some similar data in a remote DBMS. This entity is determined by receiving a query from the user. Once the query from the user has been received, it can be used to determine what tuples will be contained in this entity. Once an entity has been selected, the query q_j is chosen to send to another DBMS. Thus, the probability of sending query q_j for entity e_i is $S_{i,j}$. A particular query has a probability associated with it given the entity. However, in practice the queries are constructed from various components which we refer to as features. These will be discussed in Sect. 3.1.

2.4   Receiver Strategy

The other type of strategy that a DBMS can have would be that of the *receiver strategy*. The receiver strategy takes as input a query from the sender and then decides what entity of its own it should return. There are $0 \leq j \leq m$ queries that the receiver can get as input. It is not necessary for the receiver to know all the queries that it may receive before interaction takes place. Instead these queries are added to the strategy as the interaction proceeds. For each query received there are $0 \leq \ell \leq o$ entities. We refer to the receiver strategy as R, where R is a $m \times o$ row-stochastic matrix. Thus the probability of returning entity r_ℓ when query q_j is received is $R_{\ell j}$.

Entities are the queries written in the local query language, thus returning simply the entity would not be beneficial to the sender. The sender may not understand the entity or the proper interface to run the query over the receiver's database may be unavailable. Thus, the receiver instead returns the tuples that it receives from running its entity over its own database. These tuples may be returned in the form of plain text or in a common format that both the sender and receiver understand.

Example 3. Consider the database instance of Company B in Table 1(b). The receiver strategy for this DBMS is illustrated in Table 3(b), where r_1 and r_2 are the first and second tuples in the instance respectively. The queries received on the receiver strategy do not need to be known ahead of time. Instead, when a new query is received, then a new entry is added into the strategy. This prevents unnecessary communication beforehand. In our example, we can assume that the receiver has seen all the queries available to the sender and has some probabilities for the tuples to return. For instance, if the receiver gets query q_2, then it will return r_1 or r_2 with equal probability.

2.5   Feedback

Next, we compute the expected payoff of the players. We call the set of a sender and receiver strategy a *strategy profile*. The expected payoff for both players with strategy profile (S,R) is shown in Eq. 1. The probability of the sender picking an entity to send a query for is represented with π. The feedback function y is the feedback that the sender and receiver strategy receive after one single interaction.

$$u_y(S, R) = \sum_{i=1}^{m} \pi_i \sum_{j=1}^{n} S_{ij} \sum_{\ell=1}^{o} R_{j\ell} \, y(e_i, r_\ell), \qquad (1)$$

The feedback module of our system is a "black box" in the sense that any form of a feedback function can be used here. The first approach would be to use an oracle that is able to determine with utter certainty whether e_i and r_ℓ match. This oracle function would take the two sets of tuples as input and be able to determine with perfect accuracy if these are proper matches. However, an oracle is not always available and one must construct other methods of conducting feedback.

This oracle in the system can also be viewed as a user in practice. The user would give feedback to the system letting it know whether the communication between the sender and receiver was a success, based on the query they initially submitted to the sender. However, it is unreasonable to ask the user to give feedback on every single interaction. It would be better if the user could give feedback at a much reduced rate. We must examine alternative methods of receiving feedback in order to supplement or reduce the amount of user feedback required.

3   Methodology

A single interaction consists of the following. We do not have an actual user involved to decide the entities for the sender and give feedback. Thus we pick entities for the sender with equal probability. The feedback is determined by our oracle, knowing the true mapping and letting the sender and receiver know whether their communication was successful or not with either a reward of 1 or 0 respectively.

1. The sender will decide on which entity e_i to send a query for.
2. Based on the strategy of S, the sender will send a query q_j with probability S_{ij}.
3. The receiver will receive the query q_j and pick entity r_ℓ to return with probability $R_{j\ell}$.
4. Since the sender may not understand the entity of the receiver, the entity r_ℓ chosen by the receiver will be queried over the receiver's database. Then the tuples returned from the entity r_ℓ will be returned to the sender.
5. The sender, upon receiving the tuples from the receiver, will evaluate how well the tuples match. It compares the entity it chose at the beginning of the interaction s_i and the tuples returned from the receivers entity r_ℓ. To do this, the sender uses the feedback function $y(e_i, r_\ell)$.
6. Once the feedback has been calculated from $y(e_i, r_\ell)$, the sender will communicate the feedback to the receiver and each will update their strategies appropriately.

3.1   Feature Construction

A query is composed of multiple features, such that $q = f_1, f_2, \ldots, f_x$. Consider the entity e_1 in Table 2(a). Assuming that we set the length of each query to consist of 2 features, then the possible queries that could be sent for this entities are q_1, q_2, q_3 illustrated in Table 2(b). This is assuming that the features are constructed using 1-grams. It is possible to create a variety of features to compose and send to the receiver. For the current work, we only consider n-grams as features.

3.2   Reinforcement

Once the sender has received tuples from the receiver strategy it can then evaluate how well those tuples match its own entity. Since the goal of the entire communication game is to find tuples in other databases that sufficiently match the tuples in its own database, the better the returned tuples match with the entity, the higher the reward should be. We use our extension of Roth and Erev that was used in previous work [3]. The following equations are for the sender strategy. The same update algorithm can be applied to the receiver side.

We keep a reward matrix for each strategy. If entity e_i was selected and expressed with query q_j, then the reward matrix would be updated as illustrated in Eq. 2.

$$G_{ij}(t+1) = G_{ij}(t) + y(e_i, r_o) \qquad (2)$$

We currently employ an oracle to determine the value of $y(e_i, r_o)$. If e_i is a match to r_o, then $y(e_i, r_o) = 1$, otherwise 0. To update the actual strategy of the sender or receiver, we use the reward matrix values. This update occurs after every interaction if the value of the reward matrix to be updated has changed. The sender strategy is updated as shown in Eq. 3 using the reward matrix from Eq. 2.

$$S_{ij}(t+1) = \frac{G_{ij}(t+1)}{\sum\limits_{j'}^{m} G_{ij'}(t+1)} \qquad (3)$$

The strategy update in Eq. 3 occurs for every query in the strategy. This way, if the reward matrix was increased for the query sent, that query will have its probability increased while all other queries will have their probabilities implicitly decreased.

4   Open Problems

There has been some research investigating how keyword queries over multiple data sources can successfully integrate data. However, their model assumes that the data is available to all parties, which is not always feasible. Thus interacting and learning over time with other data sources becomes necessary in order to find the data desired. We wish to extend our model for the case where not all DBMSs are capable of learning. Most modern data sources are capable of accepting feedback, specifically from clicks. In the current model, the user is able to provide feedback every interaction. However, this is not always feasible as many interactions may be necessary for an effective mapping to surface. Therefor, we wish to determine alternative methods of giving feedback to the system. Without constraints on what information is exchanged between data sources, one may extract and send all features. This is not feasible, as sending too much information often leads to noisy and ineffective queries. However, sending too little information can inhibit learning as there might not be enough information to facilitate learning. We wish to examine the problem of query construction and communication between the data sources.

References

1. Bernstein, P., Melnik, S.: Model management 2.0: manipulating richer mappings. In: SIGMOD (2007)
2. Franklin, M.J., Halevy, A.Y., Maier, D.: A first tutorial on dataspaces. PVLDB **1**(2), 1516–1517 (2008). http://www.vldb.org/pvldb/1/1454217.pdf
3. McCamish, B., Ghadakchi, V., Termehchy, A., Touri, B., Huang, L.: The data interaction game. In: Proceedings of the 2018 International Conference on Management of Data, pp. 83–98. ACM (2018)
4. Nowak, M.A., Krakauer, D.C.: The evolution of language. Proc. Nat. Acad. Sci. **96**(14), 8028–8033 (1999)
5. Yan, Z., Zheng, N., Ives, Z.G., Talukdar, P.P., Yu, C.: Actively soliciting feedback for query answers in keyword search-based data integration. In: Proceedings of the VLDB Endowment. vol. 6, pp. 205–216. VLDB Endowment (2013)
6. Zhang, N., Das, G.: Exploration of deep web repositories. PVLDB **4**(12), 1506–1507 (2011). http://www.vldb.org/pvldb/vol4/p1506-zhang-tutorial3.pdf

TDM: A Tensor Data Model for Logical Data Independence in Polystore Systems

Eric Leclercq$^{(\boxtimes)}$ and Marinette Savonnet

LE2I EA 7508 - University of Bourgogne, 20178 Dijon, France
{eric.leclercq,marinette.savonnet}@u-bourgogne.fr

Abstract. This paper presents a Tensor Data Model to carry out logical data independence in polystore systems. TDM is an expressive model that can link different data models of different data stores and simplifies data transformations by expressing them by means of operators whose semantics are clearly defined. Our contribution is the definition of a data model based on tensors for which we add the notions of typed schema using associative arrays. We describe a set of operators and we show how the model constructs take place in a mediator/wrapper like architecture.

Keywords: Polystore · Data model · Logical data independence · Tensor

1 Introduction and Motivations

In a globalized economy, driven by digital technologies, data become an element of added value and wealth. Beyond the volume, data are also more and more diverse in their production mode and use. All sectors of the economy are undergoing a deep transformation of their business. Banks must be able to trace and detect potential risks for their clients, to predict evolution of stock markets. Retail must be able to optimize tour management using historical data deliveries. In the energy sector, the implementation of remote control tools, smart-grids can be used to optimize and adapt networks delivery to users needs. In the environmental sector, data can be used to detect pollution phenomena, anticipate the risks of flooding. In marketing, social networks data are used to discover communities, opinion leaders or to detect and study the propagation of fake news.

All these domains use data grounded in different models such as complex networks, times series, grids, cubed sphere, multi-layer networks, etc. In order to study these data in depth, i.e. to go through data, information and knowledge layers, several analyses are made. Analyses usually require to use data from different sources in an integrated way and are performed by algorithms which have different theoretical foundations such as graph theory, linear algebra, statistical models, Markov models and so on. For example, many algorithms for detecting communities use a graph represented as an adjacency matrix associated with a random walk or a density measure. Recommendation systems built

© Springer Nature Switzerland AG 2019
V. Gadepally et al. (Eds.): Poly 2018/DMAH 2018, LNCS 11470, pp. 39–56, 2019.
https://doi.org/10.1007/978-3-030-14177-6_4

with machine learning techniques frequently use linear algebra such as singular value decomposition (SVD) [5] and/or alternating least squares (ALS) [53]. To develop predictive models that determine relationships between graph entities, identify behaviors or detect anomalies or events in time series, statistical models such as covariance matrix are needful.

Furthermore, subjects or goals of modern data-intensive applications are not always well-defined. This is especially true when the aim of analyses is scientific research or when the phenomenon being analyzed is poorly understood. These characteristics are not typically observed in Business Intelligence where enterprise data semantics is usually well-defined. For example, there is no ambiguity about a person who is a customer and about its features. However, in a more general context, a single algorithm is not enough to analyze data and to ensure the veracity of the results. For example, social scientists will gather a set of results from different community detection algorithms applied on Twitter data to establish a body of evidence and then conduct a qualitative study.

Anyway, forcing varied data to fit into a single database could lead to performance problems and be a hindrance to setting up analyses. As stated by Stonebraker in [47,48] "one size fits all" is not a solution for modern data-intensive applications. Likewise Ghosh explains in [19], storing data the way it is used in an application simplifies programming and makes it easier to decentralize data processing. For these reasons, a number of research projects are shifting the focus to build system on multiple data stores using multiple data models.

In-database analysis is another important issue as it can reduce complex and costly data transformations (i.e. features selection, export and convert data) before applying analysis algorithms. Recent algorithms are rarely implemented in DBMS and matrix operations and associated factorizations [23,38] are not directly supported by traditional storage systems. For graph analysis tools, only a few NoSQL systems like Neo4j support a small set of algorithms[1]. However, Neo4j does not allow to manage very large amount of data with attributes as the column-oriented systems would do [24]. The situation is almost similar for machine learning algorithms and tools. Only some recent systems such as Vertica[2] or SciDB[3] support standard machine learning algorithms as black-box. On the other hand some tool-boxes such as TensorFlow[4], Theano[5], Keras[6] or MLlib in Apache Spark[7] have been developed to design machine learning tools using data structures close to algorithms. As a result these systems require to develop complex, hard to reuse and often error-prone programs for loading and transforming data [1,22].

---

[1] https://neo4j.com/developer/graph-algorithms/.
[2] https://www.vertica.com/product/database-machine-learning/.
[3] https://www.paradigm4.com/.
[4] https://www.tensorflow.org/.
[5] http://deeplearning.net/software/theano/.
[6] https://keras.io/.
[7] https://spark.apache.org/mllib/.

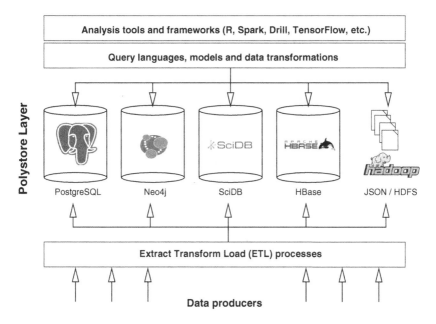

Fig. 1. Outline of the approach

We propose to revisit logical data independence in the context of polystore to develop an approach close to in-database analysis that integrates analysis tools such as Spark, R, Drill, TensorFlow in a loosely coupled architecture. Our approach allows users to quickly feed algorithms with data coming from several databases by reducing models and data transformations (Fig. 1).

The remainder of the paper is organized as follows. While Sect. 2 discusses about multi-paradigm storage systems, Sect. 3 presents the tensor based data model and its operators. Section 4 describes the software architecture and different experiments and results obtained in TEP 2017 project which studies the use of Twitter during the French presidential election in 2017.

2   Related Works on Multi-paradigm Storage Systems

The problem of accessing to heterogeneous data sources has been addressed for many years by research communities in schema integration and multi-database system [44]. Big Data oriented storage systems like HDFS and NoSQL systems, which have been mature for several years, have changed the heterogeneous data access issues [17]. As a result, several research projects have been inspired by previous works on distributed databases [44] in order to take advantage of a federation of specialized storage systems with different models[8]. Multi-paradigm data storage relies on multiple data storage technologies, chosen according to

---

[8] http://wp.sigmod.org/?p=1629.

the way data is used by applications and/or by algorithms [45]. The problem is magnified by some other facts: (1) NoSQL systems do not always have a well-established separation between logic model and physical model; (2) to achieve flexibility new systems do not necessarily provide a well-defined schema.

2.1   A Taxonomy

In [49] authors propose a survey of such systems and a taxonomy in four classes:

- **federated database systems** as collection of homogeneous data stores and a single query interface;
- **polyglot systems** as a collection of homogeneous data stores with multiple query interfaces;
- **multistore systems** as a collection of heterogeneous data stores with a single query interface;
- **polystore systems** as a collection of heterogeneous data stores with multiple query interfaces.

In order to have more significant groups of systems we adopt a slightly different classification that replaces federated database systems by a more specific class of pragmatic systems using a common query language. So, our updated classification is based on models and languages by: (1) considering multi-database query language approach [40] instead of federated systems to better represent the autonomy of data sources and existing enterprise-oriented systems; (2) replacing homogeneity of data model systems by isomorphic models[9], for example for JSON and the relational model [9,15] and; (3) instead of using query interface or query engine terms as a criterion we prefer query language. According to these criteria our classification is (Table 1): multi-database query language (unique language), polyglot system including data models isomorphic to relational model (with multiple languages), multistore, and polystore. For each of these classes we describe some of the most significant representative systems.

Table 1. Classification of multi-paradigm storage approaches

Model	Language	
	Single	Multiple
Single or isomorphic	Multibase	Polyglot
Multiple	Multistore	Polystore

---

[9] To be isomorphic two data models must allow two way transformations at the structure level but also support equivalence between sets of operators. For example graph data model and relational data model are not isomorphic because relational data model with relational algebra do not support directly transitive closure.

2.2 Representative Systems

Spark SQL[10] is the major representative of multidatabase query language. It allows to query structured data from relational-like data sources (JDBC, JSON, Parquet, etc.) in Spark programs, using SQL. Apache Drill[11] is similar to Spark without having a very large support of analysis algorithms as Spark does with MLlib and GraphX.

According to our classification, CloudMdsQL [35] is more a polyglot system than a multistore system as suggested by the title of one of their articles published before the first taxonomy proposal. CloudMdsQL is a functional SQL-like language, designed for querying multiple data store engines (relational or column-store) within a query that may contain sub-queries to each data store's native query interface. SQL++ which is a part of the FORWARD platform[12], is a semi-structured query language that encompasses both SQL and JSON [41,42].

HadoopDB [2] coupled to Hive[13] is a multistore, it uses the map-reduce paradigm to push data access operations on multiple data stores. D4M (Dynamic Distributed Dimensional Data Model) [29] is a multistore that provides a well founded mathematical interface to tuple stores. D4M allows matrix operations and linear algebra operators composition and applies them to the tuple stores. D4M reduces the autonomy of data stores to achieve a high level of performance [30].

The BigDAWG system [16, 18] is a polystore allowing to write multi-database queries with reference to islands of information, each corresponding to a type of data model (PostgreSQL, SciDB and Accumulo). Myria [52] supports multiple data stores as well as different data computing systems such as Spark. It supports SciDB for array processing, RDBMS, HDFS. The RACO (Relational Algebra COmpiler) acts as a query optimizer and processor for MyriaL language. Myria also supports user data functions in different other languages such as Python. Morpheus [3] is a polystore approach, implemented using Apache Spark, that focuses on Cypher query language instead of SQL and takes advantage of graph analysis algorithms implemented in Neo4j.

2.3 Discussion

Polystores are designed to make the best use of the data models, combining systems by unification with language. Tool-box approaches (TensorFlow, Theano) use data structures close to algorithms but they do not supply storage mechanism. The MLog system [39] is an hybrid approach which defines a tensor data model with operators and study optimization techniques for queries over TensorFlow.

Several kinds of data analytics platforms have also been defined in the last few years [46]. They are usually an aggregation of existing technologies and can be

---

[10] https://spark.apache.org/sql/.
[11] https://drill.apache.org/.
[12] http://forward.ucsd.edu/.
[13] https://hive.apache.org/.

classified in computation-centric architecture or data-centric architecture. Two main typical architectures are data analytics stacks and data lakes.

New data analytics stacks have emerged as infrastructure for giving access to data stores and enabling data processing workflows. The Berkeley Data Analytics Stack (BDAS) from the AMPLAb project[14] is a multi-layer architecture that provides multiple storage layer (multistore) using Alluxio[15] and data processing using Apache Spark ecosystem.

The IT industry uses the metaphor of data lake to define shared data environment consisting of multiple repositories. A data lake provides data to a variety of processing systems including streaming. The solutions are mature and there are products on the market such as Microsoft Azure Data Lake[16], IBM data lake[17]. Alluxio included in BDAS is also a data lake system.

The ANSI/SPARC architecture [12] characterizes classical data management systems (relational, object-oriented) from a logical point of view by proposing a 3-layer decomposition that reflects the abstraction levels of data: (i) the external data schemata describe the different external views over data dedicated to end-users or applications; (ii) the logical or conceptual schema describes entities and relationships among them, including integrity constraints and (iii) the physical schema describes the storage and the organization of data. As for operating systems or network protocols, Härder and Reuter [20, 21] have proposed a decomposition of the functional architecture of a DBMS in 5 layers: (i) file management that operates on blocks and files, (ii) propagation controls that define and manage segments and pages, (iii) records and access path management that works on access path and physical records, (iv) record oriented navigational access that describes records, sets, hierarchies and (v) non-procedural or algebraic access that defines tuples, relations, views and operators for logical schema description and data retrieval. But most of RDBMS rather use less layer following System R [6] which defines two layers: (1) the Relational Storage System (RSS) with a Relational Storage Interface (RSI) which handles access to tuples and manages devices, space, allocation, storage buffers, transaction consistency and locking as well as indexes; (2) the Relational Data System (RDS) with a Relational Data Interface (RDI) provides authorization, integrity enforcement, and support views of data as well as a definition, manipulation and query language. The RDS also maintains the catalogs of names to establish correspondences with internal names in RSS.

NoSQL systems, beyond their models differences, exhibit a common characteristic with respect to the architecture: the external and logic levels disappear [50]. As a consequence the applications are close to the physical level with no real logical independence between programs and data. Moreover, due to the nature of schema-less NoSQL systems, the source code contains implicit assumptions about the data schema. These drawbacks make it difficult to set up a data cura-

---

[14] https://amplab.cs.berkeley.edu/software/.
[15] http://www.alluxio.org/.
[16] https://azure.microsoft.com/en-us/services/data-lake-analytics/.
[17] https://www.ibm.com/analytics/data-lake.

tion process. The ingestion phase can be done quite easily (i.e. a feature puts forward by data lake vendors) but the data transformation, schema integration, data cleaning and entity consolidation are heavily hindred by the lack of logical and external schemata.

Our approach is a top-down approach that favors the notion of model and applications in contrast to bottom-up approaches that are guided by performance and query optimization. The Tensor Data Model acts as views over data sources, and aims at quickly feed algorithms with data coming from several sources by reducing models and data transformations. Our focus is on the theoretical foundation of the model and the algebraic structures of its operators before studying their implementation. It is obvious that these two points of view must be studied jointly to build an operational system.

3   Core Concepts of TDM

This section addresses the definition of a Tensor Data Model (TDM), starting with the tensor mathematical object, we add it the notion of typed schema using associative arrays and we define a set of data manipulation operations. We also study mappings between TDM and others data models.

Tensors are very general abstract mathematical objects which can be considered according to various points of view. A tensor can be seen as a multi-linear applications, as the result of the tensor product, as an hypermatrix. We will use the definition of a tensor as an element of the set of the functions from the product of N sets $I_j, j = 1, \ldots, N$ to $\mathbb{R} : \boldsymbol{\mathcal{X}} \in \mathbb{R}^{I_1 \times I_2 \times \cdots \times I_N}$, N is the number of dimension of the tensor or its order or its mode. In a more general definition, a tensor is a family of values indexed by N finite sets. A tensor is often treated as a generalized matrix, 0-order tensor is a scalar, 1-order one is a vector, 2-order one is a matrix, tensors of order 3 or higher are called higher-order tensors.

Tensor operations, by analogy with the operations on matrices and vectors, are multiplications, transpose, unfolding or matricization and factorizations (also named decompositions) [13,34]. The most used tensor products are the Kronecker product denoted by $\otimes$, Khatri-Rao product denoted by $\odot$, Hadamard product denoted by $\circledast$, external product denoted by $\circ$ and n-mode denoted by $\times_n$.

In the rest of the article, we use the boldface Euler script letters to indicate a tensor $\boldsymbol{\mathcal{X}}$, boldface capital letters $\mathbf{M}$ for matrices, boldface lowercase letters to indicate a vector $\mathbf{v}$, and an element of the tensor or a scalar is noted in italic, for example x_{ijk} is ijk-i-th element of 3-order tensor $\boldsymbol{\mathcal{X}}$.

3.1   TDM's Data Model

In TDM, tensor dimensions and values are represented by associative arrays. In the general case, an associative array is a map from a key space to a value space and can be implemented using hash table or tree.

Definition 1 (Associative Array). *An associative array is a map that asso-ciates keys to values as $A : K_1 \times \cdots \times K_N \to \mathbb{V}$ where $K_i, i = 1, \ldots, N$ are the sets of keys and $\mathbb{V}$ is the set of values.*

The definition given in [27] restricts $\mathbb{V}$ to have a semi-ring structure and the associative array to have a finite support. In TDM we use associative arrays in three different cases.

First, we use different associative arrays denoted by $\mathbf{A}_i$ for $i = 1, \ldots, N$ to model dimensions of a tensor $\mathcal{X}$, in this case the associative array has only one set of keys associated with integers $\mathbf{A}_i : K_i \to \mathbb{N}$ and $\mathbf{A}_i$ represents bijective functions. For example $\mathbf{A}_1 : String \to \mathbb{N}$ associates integers to users names. Their values are obtained by native queries sent to storage systems.

Second, at a lower level, an associative array can be used to represent the values of a sparse N-order tensor by associating compound keys from dimensions to values (real, integer) $\mathbf{A}_{vst} : K_1 \times \cdots \times K_N \to \mathbb{V}$.

Third, for tensors with non numerical values, two associative arrays are used as an indirection, one to map keys dimensions to a set integer keys ($\mathbf{A}_{vst}$) and another one to map the integer keys to non-numeric domains values (one integer is associated with each different value).

Definition 2 (Named Typed Associative Array). *A named and typed asso-ciative array of a tensor $\mathcal{X}$ is a triple $(Name, \mathbf{A}, T_A)$ where $Name$ is a unique string which represents the name of a dimension, $\mathbf{A}$ is the associative array, and T_A the type of the associative array i.e. $K \to \mathbb{N}$.*

The signature of a named typed associative array is $Name : K \to \mathbb{N}$. The schema of a named typed associative array is $(Name : Dom_{\mathbf{A}})$, its set of key values is noted $Name.Keys$.

Definition 3 (Typed Tensor). *A typed tensor $\mathcal{X}$ is a tuple $(Name, D_A, V, T)$ where $Name$ is the name of the tensor, D_A is a list of named typed associative arrays i.e., one named typed associative array per dimension, V is an associative array that stores the values of the tensor and T is the type of the tensor, i.e. the type of its values.*

The schema of a tensor is the concatenation of $Name : T$ with the schema of all elements of D_A. For example if a tensor represents the hashtags of tweets published by a user during an hour, the schema will be $(UHT : \mathbb{N}, U : String, H : String, T : Integer)$. A TDM schema is a set of typed tensors schema.

If we consider the representation of tensor values, V handles the sparsity of tensors. Sparse tensors have a default value (e.g. 0) for all the entries that not explicitly exist in the associative array. Associative array refers to the gen-eral mathematical concept of map or function, as we want to conform to the separation of logical and physical levels, the associative arrays in the model are abstract data types that can be implemented using different representation tech-niques as well as for the tensor values. For example Kuang et al. [36] describe a unified tensor model to represent unstructured, semi-structured, and struc-tured data and propose a tensor extension operator to represent various types of data as sub-tensors merged into a unified tensor. Lara [25, 26] proposes a logical model and an algebra using associative array (called associative table) with a set of operations to unify different data models such as relational, array and key-value. The authors show how to use Lara as middleware algebra, their approach is directed towards operators translation and optimization. However their model is not very suitable for expressing high-level data transformations as tensors can do with their capacity of modeling complex relationships (i.e. not only binary).

3.2   Translating TDM's and Other Models

In this section we establish mappings between TDM and other data models with the assumption that associative arrays are invariant to permuting keys.

1. a relation R is a set of tuples $(v_1, v_2, \ldots, v_k)$, where each element v_j is a member of a domain Dom_j, so the set-theoretic relation R is a subset of the cartesian product of the domain $Dom_1 \times Dom_2 \times \cdots \times Dom_k$. We can write a typed tensor $\mathcal{X}$ using the name of each associative array in D_A as domain $Dom_i, i = 1, \ldots, N$ for R and by adding an attribute whose domain is the name of the tensor. The values of a tuple are those corresponding to keys of each D_A associated with the values of $\mathcal{X}$. The names of D_A form a compound key for R. The reverse mapping from a relation R to typed tensors produces a set of tensors $\mathcal{X}_i$ where the dimensions are the n attributes that are the key of R and for the $k - n$ remaining attributes we create a tensor for each. The keys of each D_A are formed of the different values of each attribute domains.
2. most of key-value stores save data as ordered $(key, value)$ pairs in a distributed hash table [7]. As typed tensor schema and its values are described by associative arrays there is a straight mappings between this type of NoSQL store and Tensor Data Model.
3. a column store system, like Vertica or Cassandra, uses a relational-like schema so their mapping to Tensor Data Model is the same as for relation.
4. a graph $G = (V, E)$, where V is the set of vertices and $E \subset V \times V$ the set of edges, can be represented by its adjacency or incidence matrices i.e. a 2-order tensor. Matrices can also represent oriented, weighted graphs. For multigraph, i.e. graph with different types of links for which $E = \{E_1, E_2, \ldots, E_k\}$ is partitioned set of edges, can be modeled by a 3-order tensor where one dimension is used to specify the different edges types. Moreover, multi-layer network [32] is defined as $GM = (V, E, L)$ where $V = \{V_1, V_2, \ldots, V_n\}$ is a partitioned set of nodes, $E = \{E_1, E_2, \ldots, E_k\}$ is partitioned set of edges, with $E \subseteq V \times V$ and $E_i \subseteq V_l \times V_m$ for $i \in \{1, \ldots, k\}$ and $l, m \in \{1, \ldots n\}$. L is a partitioned set of layers, $L = \{L_1, L_2, \ldots, L_p\}$ where $L_i \subseteq E$, with $L_i \cap L_j = \emptyset, \forall i, j$ modeling the dimensions. The construction of a tensor $(2(p+1)$ order) for multi-layered networks is given in [14, 32]. Hypergraphs are also taken in consideration in [32] that shows their mapping to tensors. Graph databases handle in different way theoretical models of graphs [4] most of them except maybe the nested-graph can be generalized by multi-layer graph and specified by tensors.

All the above models are structurally equivalent to TDM. The most appropriate storage system can be chosen based on the nature of the data and the cost models associated with the operations to be favored. Moreover, in specific cases part of data can be duplicated. We have studied some real examples of such equivalences in [37].

3.3   TDM's Operators

To carry out a wide range of queries it should possible to define several of the standard operators from relational algebra in terms of tensor operations. In [26,27] the authors define a model and operators over associative arrays to unify relational, arrays, and key-value algebras. Our operators are defined to provide programmers with a logical data independence layer i.e. to bridge the semantic gap between analysis tools and storage systems. Our set of operators works on typed tensors at two different levels: at the associative array level and at the tensor value level. We focus on the following subset of operators on typed tensors: selection, projection, union, intersection, join and some analytic operators such as group by and tensors decomposition.

Data Manipulation Operators

Projection operators are the usual operators of tensor algebra. A fiber of a tensor $\mathcal{X}$ is a vector obtained by fixing all but one $\mathcal{X}$'s indices: $\mathcal{X}_{:jk}$, $\mathcal{X}_{i:k}$ and $\mathcal{X}_{ij:}$. Fibers are always assumed to be column vectors, similar to matrix rows and columns. A slice of a tensor $\mathcal{X}$ is a matrix obtained by fixing all but two of $\mathcal{X}$'s indices: $\mathcal{X}_{i::}$, $\mathcal{X}_{:j:}$ et $\mathcal{X}_{::k}$. A project operator can be generalized by using the mode-n product $\times_n$ (mode-n product behavior is detailed in [34]).

Definition 4 (Project). *The projection of a N-order typed tensor $\mathcal{X}$ on one or more mode, noted as $\Pi_{mode}(expr)$, where $mode = 1, \ldots, N$ and expr is an equality between the name of an associative array and a constant value, reduces the dimensions of the tensor to the selected ones.*

The project operator can be computed by using the n-mode product with a boolean vector that contains 1 for the elements of the mode(s) to retain: $\mathcal{X} \times_n \mathbf{b}$. For example, consider a 3-order tensor, $\mathcal{X}_1$, with dimensions users, hashtags and time used to store the number of times a hashtag is used in tweets by a user per time slice. The number of each hashtag used by a user u_i, for all time slices is a 2-order tensor such as: $\mathcal{X}_2 = \mathcal{X}_1 \times_1 \mathbf{b}$ with $b_i = 1, b_j = 0, \forall j \neq i$.

A selection operator can be defined on two levels: (1) on the values contained in the tensor or (2) on the values of the dimensions i.e. typed associative arrays $\mathbf{A}_i, i = 1, \ldots, N$.

Definition 5 (Select on tensor values). *The operator $\sigma_{expr}\mathcal{X}$ selects values of the tensor which satisfy expr and produces a new tensor with the same schema. The connectors allowed in expr are $\wedge, \vee$ and $\neg$, the binary operators are $\{<, \leq , =, \neq, \geq, >\}$. The implicit left operand is a variable (values of $\mathcal{X}$), the right one is a constant.*

For example $\sigma_{[>10]}\mathcal{X}$ produces a new tensor (user, hashtag, time) with users that have published one or more tweets during time slice using more than 10 times the same hashtag.

Definition 6 (Restriction on dimensions values). *The operator* $\rho_{expr}\mathcal{X}$ *restricts the tensor shape by selecting some values of the dimensions contained in the propositional formula expr. The connectors allowed in expr are* $\land$, $\lor$ *and* $\neg$, *the binary operators are* $\{<, \leq, =, \neq, \geq, >\}$, *the terms or variables are the sames of the associative arrays corresponding to dimension.*

The schema of a tensor is not affected by the restriction operator nor the schema of its typed associative arrays. The following example selects hashtags used by the user $u1$ for time slices between 18-03-08 and 18-02-28, from the tensor $\mathcal{X}$:

$$\rho_{[U = \text{'}u1\text{'} \land T \geq \text{'}18\text{-}02\text{-}28\text{'} \land T \leq \text{'}18\text{-}03\text{-}08\text{'}]}\mathcal{X}$$

Definition 7 (Union). *The union of two typed tensors* $\mathcal{X}_1$ *and* $\mathcal{X}_2$ *having the same schema, noted* $\cup_\theta$, *where* $\theta \in \{+, -, \times, \div, max, min\}$ *is a typed tensor* $\mathcal{X}_3$ *with the same schema,* $\mathcal{X}_3.D_{A_i}.Keys = \mathcal{X}_1.D_{A_i}.Keys \cup \mathcal{X}_2.D_{A_i}.Keys$, *for* $i = 1, \ldots, N$. *Values of* $\mathcal{X}_3$ *are values from* $\mathcal{X}_1$ *and* $\mathcal{X}_2$ *except for keys in common for which the operator* θ *is applied.*

Definition 8 (Intersection). *The intersection of two typed tensors* $\mathcal{X}_1$ *and* $\mathcal{X}_2$ *having the same schema, noted* $\cap_\theta$, *where* $\theta \in \{+, -, \times, \div, max, min\}$ *is a typed tensor* $\mathcal{X}_3$ *with the same schema,* $\mathcal{X}_3.D_{A_i}.Keys = \mathcal{X}_1.D_{A_i}.Keys \cap \mathcal{X}_2.D_{A_i}.Keys$, *for* $i = 1, \ldots, N$. *Values of* $\mathcal{X}_3$ *are values associated to common keys of each dimension on which the operator* θ *is applied.*

Definition 9 (Join). *The join of two typed tensors* $\mathcal{X}_1$ *and* $\mathcal{X}_2$ *having at least one common dimension, noted* $\bowtie_\theta$ *is a typed tensor* $\mathcal{X}_3$ *which schema is the union of the two sets of dimension. The keys retained in the common dimensions are those satisfying the operator* θ, *where* $\theta \in \{<, \leq, =, \neq, \geq, >\}$.

Analytical Operators

Group by like operations [33,43] can be defined on typed tensors applying aggregation function with selection of tensor dimension values to aggregate.

Definition 10 (Aggregation). *The aggregation applied on a typed tensor* $\mathcal{X}$ *is noted* $\mathcal{F}_{expr}(assoc)$ *where expr is a list of expressions of the op(name) where op* $\in$ $\{SUM, AVG, COUNT, MIN, MAX\}$ *and name is the name of an associative array in* D_A, *assoc is a list of names of associative arrays in* D_A. *The aggregation operator applies operators on specified dimensions for equals values of keys to produce a typed tensor with a schema specified by assoc.*

This operator is useful to transform typed tensor to time series for example to obtain the total number of each hashtag used during each time slice.

Tensor decompositions such as CANDECOMP/PARAFAC (CP), Tucker, HOSVD are used to perform dimensionality reductions and to extract latent

relations [34]. Since tensor representations of data are multiple and their semantics are not explicit, the results of tensor decompositions are complex to interpret. Research in applied mathematics is important, it concerns the problems of
robustness, remote calculations and value reconstruction [8, 10, 28]. To develop an
in-database approach, the cost models of the manipulation and analysis tensors
operators must be studied carefully in regards to sparsity.

4   Architecture and Experiments

We validate our approach by a *proof-of-concept*, showing polystore architecture
with real data from a multi-disciplinary project (TEP 2017) involving collaborations with communication scientists. The main research objective of TEP 2017
is to study the dynamics of political discourse on Twitter during the French
Presidential election in March–May 2017.

The architecture set up to carrying out the experimentation includes a polystore built on the top of PostgreSQL, HDFS, and Neo4j and three analysis
frameworks R, Spark and TensorFlow. The data set is a tweets corpus captured during the period from 2017-02-27 to 2017-05-18. The data set contains
49 million tweets emitted by more than 1.8 million different users using $288, 221$
different hashtags. Of the 49 million tweets, 36 million are retweets. Raw data
are stored in JSON file format in HDFS (720Go), most important attributes
of tweets are stored in a relational database (PostgreSQL) in a unique table
(50Go), in another database with a normalized schema (55Go), links between
entities (tweets, users, hashtags) are stored in Neo4j (23Go).

The abstraction layer is developed using R and Spark connectors. Associative arrays are implemented using RDD and dataframes. More details on the
architecture (Fig. 2) are given in [37].

In order to study the possible influence of robots on the circulation of viral
tweets, we sought to detect robots among Twitter accounts which had retweeted
at least 1,000 times over the period between the two rounds of this election (from
23rd April until 7th May 2017), reducing the corpus of 49M of tweets to one
thousand. In order to reduce the number of accounts to analyze, only accounts
having tweeted more the 100 times in the 2-weeks period are retained. 1,077
accounts are selected in this way. This corresponds to the hypothesis that robots
are tweeting intensively during these final period of the election campaign. A
second hypothesis is that robots does not tweet in hazard so we extract hashtags
contained in these tweets. We built a 3-order tensor modelling these accounts
A, the hashtags H and the time T (2-weeks period). We got a tensor containing
potentially $1, 077 \times 568 \times 336$ items. The tensor construction from the relational
data requires approximately 15 SQL lines and less of 5 min including a few
seconds for the associative arrays. TensorFlow is used as reference for simulating
a traditional framework without a polystore connection using data exchange
with file and data transformation programs. Around a hundred lines of complex
SQL queries are required to produce a tensor for TensorFlow.

We performed a CP decomposition to reduce the user space based on their
behavior, it produces n groups of three 1-order tensors, here vectors A, H, T. We

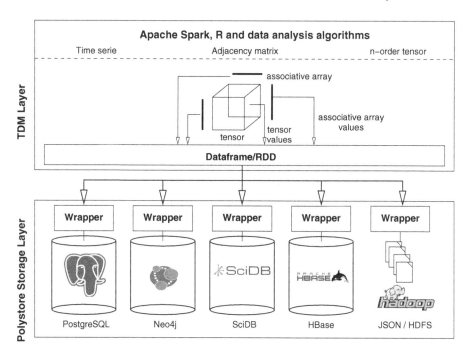

Fig. 2. Architecture of the polystore system using TDM

then apply the k-means clustering algorithm to identify groups of users having similar behavior in the time. A k-means algorithm applied to this data determines 4 groups of users: a group of one account previously detected as a robot and suspended by Twitter, a group of three accounts, a group of about thirty accounts and a last group containing other users. The group of three accounts, revealed after manual study, to be linked (same behavior and hashtags) and assisted by an algorithm that retweets messages against the Macron candidate. Each tweeted between 1,000 and 1,800 times during the period with a vast majority of retweets.

We also used the Louvain algorithm [11] to detect accounts which retweet or are retweeted frequently by the other accounts and which tend to share the same retweets. The retweet graph represented by its adjacency matrix is obtained from a 3-order tensor $(AAT : \mathbb{N}, A : String, A : String, T : Integer)$. The result of the CP decomposition is confirmed (Fig. 3): yellow community corresponds to the user detected as robot, pink community corresponds to the group of three users and others (blue and green communities) are the users of the third group. The biggest nodes are accounts from the 4 clusters obtained by the CP decomposition and k-means.

Fig. 3. Communities obtained from retweet graph (Color figure online)

Our result is consistent with the use of OSoMe API Botometer[18] which provides an overall probability score that an account studied is automated. It uses 1,150 criteria and machine learning techniques to calculate the probability [51]. The group of about thirty accounts comprises more than half users with a probability of being a robot greater than 0.42 (Fig. 4). But we note that the values of the probabilities were not enough significant to detect robots during the studied period. One of the assumptions is that it is hybrid accounts of users assisted by algorithms. However, simple criteria such as the maximum number of tweets published in one hour make it possible to unambiguously find some accounts with automated behavior, confirmed by the manual study.

---

[18] https://botometer.iuni.iu.edu/.

from_user	user_id	nbrt	nbrtjour	nbtweetp2	proba	retrycount	maxrateh	htnb	cluster
Manuel Hollande	639	1073	76	1078	0.66	1	113	155	1
Macron Jamais	622	1481	105	1706	0.61	1	88	242	1
Degage Hollande	277	1394	99	1464	0.66	0	118	189	1
	724	1594	113	5688	0.5	0	188	276	3
	933	3405	243	3727	0.31	1	149	512	4
	477	2037	145	2370	0.39	0	96	437	4
	761	2254	161	2263	0.3	1	93	381	4
	1071	2289	163	2538	0.39	2	153	387	4
	197	1988	142	2415	0.37	0	75	274	4
	932	1967	140	2041	0.35	0	90	372	4
	158	1932	138	1951	0.38	0	149	308	4
	1070	1814	129	1820	0.54	0	174	177	4
	979	1472	105	2396		9	133	236	4
	712	1365	97	1428	0.48	0	131	231	4
	968	4513	322	4558	0.39	1	214	598	4
	248	6466	461	6672	0.5	0	141	869	4
	345	6134	438	6549	0.34	0	242	911	4
	446	5228	373	5336	0.34	0	120	722	4
	112	1291	92	1395	0.69	0	95	125	4
	834	7001	500	7105		8	106	1090	4
	877	1223	87	1243	0.42	4	114	241	4
	324	1108	79	1111	0.4	0	147	108	4
	347	3525	251	3908	0.49	0	79	136	4
	896	1509	107	1509	0.62	0	201	212	4
	191	3337	238	3361	0.27	0	129	505	4
	172	2917	208	2954	0.3	0	140	459	4
	644	3431	245	3431	0.42	1	124	285	4
07 mai 2017	2	7233	516	7233		8	516	1822	6
(28 rows)									

Fig. 4. Results given by Botometer (column with label proba) and cluster number obtained by the CP decomposition (column with label cluster)

5 Conclusion

In this article we described a Tensor Data Model for polystore systems and studied its ability to generalized several kinds of models such as relational, column, key-value, graph (including multi-layer graphs). Using associative array we defined schema, manipulation and analytics operators. We are working on an implementation of each operator in Spark and R.

We defined a set of real experiments with Twitter data to evaluate the ease of use of the operator toolkit and the performance of the architecture. We detected the possible influence of robots on the circulation of viral tweets. Our results have been validated by researchers in communication science. The experiments demonstrated the TDM capabilities according to the ease of data transformations in analyses.

Our short term future work will be on the storage of tensor as materialized views in SciDB through a matricization process [31]. As there is multiple ways of doing matricization, one must be chosen according to the privileged operators and it should be necessary to specify normal forms to guide matricization.

References

1. Abo Khamis, M., Ngo, H.Q., Nguyen, X., Olteanu, D., Schleich, M.: In-database learning with sparse tensors. In: Proceedings of the 35th ACM SIGMOD/PODS Symposium on Principles of Database Systems, pp. 325–340. ACM (2018)
2. Abouzeid, A., Bajda-Pawlikowski, K., Abadi, D., Silberschatz, A., Rasin, A.: HadoopDB: an architectural hybrid of mapreduce and DBMS technologies for analytical workloads. Proc. VLDB Endow. **2**(1), 922–933 (2009)
3. Allen, D., Hodler, A.: Weave together graph and relational data in apache spark. In: Spark+AI Summit. Neo4j (2018). https://vimeo.com/274433801

4. Angles, R.: A comparison of current graph database models. In: 2012 IEEE 28th International Conference on Data Engineering Workshops (ICDEW), pp. 171–177. IEEE (2012)
5. Arora, S., Ge, R., Moitra, A.: Learning topic models-going beyond SVD. In: 2012 IEEE 53rd Annual Symposium on Foundations of Computer Science (FOCS), pp. 1–10. IEEE (2012)
6. Astrahan, M.M., et al.: System R: relational approach to database management. ACM Trans. Database Syst. (TODS) **1**(2), 97–137 (1976)
7. Atikoglu, B., Xu, Y., Frachtenberg, E., Jiang, S., Paleczny, M.: Workload analysis of a large-scale key-value store. In: ACM SIGMETRICS Performance Evaluation Review, vol. 40, pp. 53–64. ACM (2012)
8. Austin, W., Ballard, G., Kolda, T.G.: Parallel tensor compression for large-scale scientific data. In: 2016 IEEE International Parallel and Distributed Processing Symposium, pp. 912–922. IEEE (2016)
9. Baazizi, M.A., Lahmar, H.B., Colazzo, D., Ghelli, G., Sartiani, C.: Schema inference for massive JSON datasets. In: Extending Database Technology (EDBT), pp. 222–233 (2017)
10. Battaglino, C., Ballard, G., Kolda, T.G.: A practical randomized CP tensor decomposition. arXiv preprint arXiv:1701.06600 (2017)
11. Blondel, V.D., Guillaume, J.L., Lambiotte, R., Lefebvre, E.: Fast unfolding of communities in large networks. J. Stat. Mech: Theory Exp. **2008**(10), P10008 (2008)
12. Brodie, M.L., Schmidt, J.W.: Final report of the ANSI/X3/SPARC DBS-SG relational database task group. ACM SIGMOD Rec. **12**(4), 1–62 (1982)
13. Cichocki, A., Zdunek, R., Phan, A.H., Amari, S.: Nonnegative Matrix and Tensor Factorizations: Applications to Exploratory Multi-way Data Analysis and Blind Source Separation. Wiley, Hoboken (2009)
14. De Domenico, M., et al.: Mathematical formulation of multilayer networks. Phys. Rev. X **3**(4), 041022 (2013)
15. DiScala, M., Abadi, D.J.: Automatic generation of normalized relational schemas from nested key-value data. In: Proceedings of the 2016 International Conference on Management of Data, pp. 295–310. ACM (2016)
16. Duggan, J., et al.: The BigDAWG polystore system. ACM SIGMOD Rec. **44**(2), 11–16 (2015)
17. Franklin, M., Halevy, A., Maier, D.: From databases to dataspaces: a new abstraction for information management. ACM SIGMOD Rec. **34**(4), 27–33 (2005)
18. Gadepally, V., et al.: The BigDAWG polystore system and architecture. In: IEEE High Performance Extreme Computing Conference (HPEC), pp. 1–6 (2016)
19. Ghosh, D.: Multiparadigm data storage for enterprise applications. IEEE Softw. **27**(5), 57–60 (2010)
20. Haerder, T., Reuter, A.: Principles of transaction-oriented database recovery. ACM Comput. Surv. (CSUR) **15**(4), 287–317 (1983)
21. Härder, T.: DBMS architecture-the layer model and its evolution. Datenbank-Spektrum **13**, 45–57 (2005)
22. Hellerstein, J.M., et al.: The MADlib analytics library: or MAD skills, the SQL. Proc. VLDB Endow. **5**(12), 1700–1711 (2012)
23. Hogben, L.: Handbook of Linear Algebra. Chapman and Hall/CRC, Boca Raton (2013)
24. Hölsch, J., Schmidt, T., Grossniklaus, M.: On the performance of analytical and pattern matching graph queries in Neo4j and a relational database. In:

EDBT/ICDT 2017 Joint Conference: 6th International Workshop on Querying Graph Structured Data (GraphQ) (2017)

25. Hutchison, D., Howe, B., Suciu, D.: Lara: a key-value algebra underlying arrays and relations. arXiv preprint arXiv:1604.03607 (2016)

26. Hutchison, D., Howe, B., Suciu, D.: LaraDB: a minimalist kernel for linear and relational algebra computation. In: Proceedings of the 4th ACM SIGMOD Workshop on Algorithms and Systems for MapReduce and Beyond, pp. 2–12. ACM (2017)

27. Jananthan, H., Zhou, Z., Gadepally, V., Hutchison, D., Kim, S., Kepner, J.: Polystore mathematics of relational algebra. In: IEEE International Conference on Big Data (Big Data), pp. 3180–3189, December 2017. https://doi.org/10.1109/BigData.2017.8258298

28. Kang, U., Papalexakis, E., Harpale, A., Faloutsos, C.: GigaTensor: scaling tensor analysis up by 100 times - algorithms and discoveries. In: Proceedings of the 18th ACM SIGKDD International Conference on Knowledge Discovery and Data Mining, KDD 2012, pp. 316–324. ACM (2012)

29. Kepner, J., et al.: Dynamic distributed dimensional data model (D4M) database and computation system. In: IEEE International Conference on Acoustics, Speech and Signal Processing (ICASSP), pp. 5349–5352. IEEE (2012)

30. Kepner, J., et al.: Achieving 100,000,000 database inserts per second using Accumulo and D4M. In: High Performance Extreme Computing Conference (HPEC), pp. 1–6. IEEE (2014)

31. Kim, M.: TensorDB and tensor-relational model (TRM) for efficient tensor-relational operations (2014)

32. Kivelä, M., Arenas, A., Barthelemy, M., Gleeson, J.P., Moreno, Y., Porter, M.A.: Multilayer networks. J. Complex Netw. **2**(3), 203–271 (2014)

33. Klug, A.: Equivalence of relational algebra and relational calculus query languages having aggregate functions. J. ACM **29**(3), 699–717 (1982)

34. Kolda, T.G., Bader, B.W.: Tensor decompositions and applications. SIAM Rev. **51**(3), 455–500 (2009)

35. Kolev, B., Bondiombouy, C., Valduriez, P., Jiménez-Peris, R., Pau, R., Pereira, J.: The CloudMdsQL multistore system. In: Proceedings of the International Conference on Management of Data (SIGMOD), pp. 2113–2116 (2016)

36. Kuang, L., Hao, F., Yang, L.T., Lin, M., Luo, C., Min, G.: A tensor-based approach for big data representation and dimensionality reduction. IEEE Trans. Emerg. Top. Comput. **2**(3), 280–291 (2014)

37. Leclercq, E., Savonnet, M.: A tensor based data model for polystore: an application to social networks data. In: Proceedings of the 22nd International Database Engineering and Applications Symposium (IDEAS), pp. 1–9. ACM, New York (2018)

38. Leskovec, J., Rajaraman, A., Ullman, J.D.: Mining of Massive Datasets. Cambridge University Press, Cambridge (2014)

39. Li, X., Cui, B., Chen, Y., Wu, W., Zhang, C.: MLog: towards declarative in-database machine learning. Proc. VLDB Endow. **10**(12), 1933–1936 (2017)

40. Litwin, W., Abdellatif, A., Zeroual, A., Nicolas, B., Vigier, P.: MSQL: a multi-database language. Inf. Sci. **49**(1–3), 59–101 (1989)

41. Ong, K.W., Papakonstantinou, Y., Vernoux, R.: The SQL++ unifying semi-structured query language, and an expressiveness benchmark of SQL-on-Hadoop, NoSQL and NewSQL databases. Technical report, UCSD (2014)

42. Ong, K.W., Papakonstantinou, Y., Vernoux, R.: The SQL++ query language: configurable, unifying and semi-structured. Technical report, UCSD (2015)

43. Özsoyoğlu, G., Özsoyoğlu, Z.M., Matos, V.: Extending relational algebra and relational calculus with set-valued attributes and aggregate functions. ACM Trans. Database Syst. **12**(4), 566–592 (1987)

44. Özsu, M.T., Valduriez, P.: Principles of Distributed Database Systems. Springer, Heidelberg (2011). https://doi.org/10.1007/978-1-4419-8834-8

45. Sharp, J., McMurtry, D., Oakley, A., Subramanian, M., Zhang, H.: Data Access for Highly-Scalable Solutions: Using SQL, NoSQL, and Polyglot Persistence. Microsoft Patterns & Practices, 1st edn. (2013)

46. Singh, D., Reddy, C.K.: A survey on platforms for big data analytics. J. Big Data **2**(1), 8 (2015)

47. Stonebraker, M., et al.: One size fits all? Part 2: benchmarking results. In: Proceedings of CIDR (2007)

48. Stonebraker, M., Cetintemel, U.: "One size fits all": an idea whose time has come and gone. In: Proceedings of 21st International Conference on Data Engineering, ICDE 2005, pp. 2–11. IEEE (2005)

49. Tan, R., Chirkova, R., Gadepally, V., Mattson, T.G.: Enabling query processing across heterogeneous data models: a survey. In: IEEE International Conference on Big Data (Big Data), pp. 3211–3220. IEEE (2017)

50. Vargas-Solar, G., Zechinelli-Martini, J.L., Espinosa-Oviedo, J.A.: Big data management: what to keep from the past to face future challenges? Data Sci. Eng. **2**(4), 328–345 (2017)

51. Varol, O., Ferrara, E., Davis, C.A., Menczer, F., Flammini, A.: Online human-bot interactions: detection, estimation, and characterization. In: Proceedings of the Eleventh International Conference on Web and Social Media (ICWSM), pp. 280–289 (2017)

52. Wang, J., et al.: The Myria big data management and analytics system and cloud services. In: CIDR (2017)

53. Zhou, Y., Wilkinson, D., Schreiber, R., Pan, R.: Large-scale parallel collaborative filtering for the netflix prize. In: Fleischer, R., Xu, J. (eds.) AAIM 2008. LNCS, vol. 5034, pp. 337–348. Springer, Heidelberg (2008). https://doi.org/10.1007/978-3-540-68880-8_32

Sketching Data Structures for Massive Graph Problems

Juan P. A. Lopes[1(✉)], Fabiano S. Oliveira[2], Paulo E. D. Pinto[2],
and Valmir C. Barbosa[1]

[1] Federal University of Rio de Janeiro, Rio de Janeiro, Brazil
{jlopes,valmir}@cos.ufrj.br
[2] State University of Rio de Janeiro, Rio de Janeiro, Brazil
{fabiano.oliveira,pauloedp}@ime.uerj.br

Abstract. In this work, we explore the application of sketching data structures to solve problems in graphs that do not fit entirely in memory. These structures allow compact representations of data, admitting some probability of failure. We aim at the implicit representation and dynamic connectivity problems. Our contributions include two new probabilistic implicit representations, one that uses Bloom filters and allows representing sparse graphs with $O(|E|)$ bits, and another that uses MinHash sketches and represents trees with $O(|V|)$ bits. We also describe a variant of an ℓ_0-sampling sketch that allows proving a tighter upper bound on the failure probability of sampling.

Keywords: Sketching data structures · Graphs · Stream algorithms

1 Introduction

Sketching data structures allow the representation of data in a compact fashion, often in sublinear space with respect to the original data. The interest in these data structures has increased in recent years, as a direct consequence of the emergence of applications that deal with large volumes of streaming data. In these applications, it is often necessary to answer queries quickly, which is infeasible by simply querying over stored data due to high latency. Be that as it may, such volumes do not generally fit into memory in the first place. Sketching data structures offer a good compromise for many applications, allowing less memory and CPU usage at the cost of decreased accuracy.

In this work, we survey some sketching data structures and their applications to massive graph problems. In Sect. 2, we describe the application of Bloom filters and MinHash sketches to the implicit graph representation problem [16], one of them representing trees with better space complexity than the optimal deterministic representation. In Sect. 3, we detail two variants of a sketch to solve the ℓ_0-sampling problem, which can be used to determine dynamic connectivity in n-vertex graph streams using $O(n \log^3 n)$ bits [1,13].

© Springer Nature Switzerland AG 2019
V. Gadepally et al. (Eds.): Poly 2018/DMAH 2018, LNCS 11470, pp. 57–67, 2019.
https://doi.org/10.1007/978-3-030-14177-6_5

2   Probabilistic Implicit Graph Representations

An *implicit graph representation* is a vertex labeling scheme that allows testing the adjacency between any two vertices efficiently by just comparing their labels [9,15,16]. More formally, given a graph class $\mathcal{C}$ with $2^{\Theta(f(n))}$ graphs with n vertices, a representation is said to be *implicit* if

1. it is *space-optimal*, that is, it requires $O(f(n))$ bits to represent graphs in $\mathcal{C}$;
2. it *distributes information evenly* among vertices, that is, each vertex is represented by a *label* using $O(f(n)/n)$ bits;
3. the *adjacency test is local*, that is, when testing the adjacency of any two vertices, only their labels are used in the process.

According to this definition, the *adjacency matrix* is an implicit representation of the class containing all graphs, because there are $2^{\Theta(n^2)}$ graphs on n vertices and the adjacency matrix can represent them using $\Theta(n^2)$ bits. On the other hand, for m the number of edges, the *adjacency list* is not an implicit representation, because it requires $\Theta(m \log n)$ bits to represent the same graph class, which may require $\Theta(n^2 \log n)$ bits in the worst case (e.g., for complete graphs). In contrast, an adjacency list is space-optimal to represent trees, as $O(m \log n) = O(n \log n)$ for trees and there are $2^{\Theta(n \log n)}$ trees on n vertices, but still it is not an implicit representation because it does not distribute information evenly: each tree vertex may use $\Theta(n \log n)$ bits to represent its adjacency in an adjacency list (e.g., the center vertices of stars).

In [11], the concept of *probabilistic implicit graph representations* was explored, extending the concept of implicit representations by relaxing one of the properties: the adjacency test is *probabilistic*, meaning that it has a constant probability of resulting in false negatives or false positives. A 0% chance of false positives and negatives implies an ordinary implicit representation. The main benefit of probabilistic representations is the ability to trade accuracy for memory, that is, to achieve more space-efficient representations by allowing some incorrect results in adjacency tests. We present two novel probabilistic implicit representations, each based on a distinct sketching data structure.

2.1   Representation Based on Bloom Filters

The Bloom filter is a data structure that represents a set $S' \subseteq S$ and allows testing elements for set membership with some probability of false positives, but no false negatives [2]. A Bloom filter consists of an array M of m bits and k pairwise independent hash functions, $h_i : S \rightarrow [1, \ldots, m]$ for $1 \leq i \leq k$. The insertion of an element x is performed by computing k hash values, $h_1(x), \ldots, h_k(x)$, and setting these indices in the array to 1, that is, $M[h_i(x)] \leftarrow 1$ for all $1 \leq i \leq k$. The membership query for some element x is done by verifying whether all bits in positions given by the hash values are 1, that is, by verifying whether $M[h_i(x)] = 1$ for all $1 \leq i \leq k$. If at least one bit is 0, then x is certainly not in the set. If all bits are 1, it is assumed that the element is in the set, although this may not be the case (a false positive). The probability of a false positive when n elements are already stored (event FP) can be determined from the probability of collisions in all k hash values, that is,

$$\Pr[\mathrm{FP}] = \Pr\left[\bigwedge_{1 \leq i \leq k} M[h_i(x)] = 1\right] = \left(1 - \left(1 - \frac{1}{m}\right)^{kn}\right)^k \approx \left(1 - e^{-kn/m}\right)^k.$$

Defining $q = m/n$, that is, q as the ratio between the size of M in bits and the number of stored elements, it is possible to show that the probability of false positives is minimized when $k \approx q \ln 2$, so $\Pr[\mathrm{FP}] \approx (1 - e^{-\ln 2})^{q \ln 2} \approx 0.6185^q$. Thus, for example, setting the dimension of M to 10 bits per element and using 7 hash functions, it is possible to estimate set membership with less than 1% of false positives.

Bloom filters are commonly used in database systems, both to avoid the attempt to fetch non-existing data and to optimize communication costs in distributed joins. In summary, Bloom filters are useful in contexts where the performance gain in negative queries makes up for the cost of false positives.

Bloom filters can also be used in implicit graph representations, as follows. For each vertex, a Bloom filter is created using some constant number of bits per element (say, 10 bits), representing the set of vertices adjacent to it. The set of Bloom filters of all vertices constitutes a probabilistic implicit representation. This representation requires $\Theta(\sum_{v \in V(G)} d(v) = 2m)$ bits to represent any graph, which makes it equivalent to the adjacency matrix in the worst case (e.g., for complete graphs). However, this representation has better space complexity for sparse graphs than the deterministic one. In fact, it is better for any graph having $m = o(n^2)$. Also, it has the property of not allowing false negatives in adjacency tests. That is, it will never fail to report an existing edge, although it may report the existence of non-existing edges with a small probability.

The theoretical predictions about this representation were verified through two practical experiments. These experiments aimed to validate the rate of false positives as the graph's density $(2m/(n^2 - n))$ or the number of bits per edge (q) changed while keeping other parameters fixed (results are shown in Fig. 1).

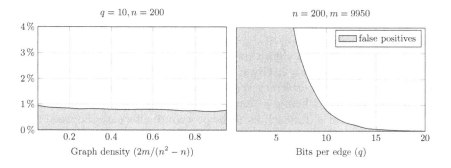

Fig. 1. Rate of false positives.

2.2   Representation Based on MinHash

MinHash is a sketching data structure that represents sets $A, B \in \mathcal{S}$ and allows estimating their Jaccard coefficient, $J(A, B) = \frac{|A \cap B|}{|A \cup B|}$ [3]. The estimation is done by computing a signature (a k-tuple of hash values) for each set $S \in \mathcal{S}$, using k pairwise independent hash functions $h_1, \ldots, h_k$. Each element in the signature is given by $h_i^{\min}(S) = \min\{h_i(x) : x \in S\}$, $1 \le i \le k$. The probability of two sets A and B having a common signature element can be shown to be equal to their Jaccard coefficient, that is, $\Pr[h_i^{\min}(A) = h_i^{\min}(B)] = J(A, B)$, $1 \le i \le k$. Given two sets A, B, let X_i denote the Bernoulli random variable such that $X_i = 1$ if $h_i^{\min}(A) = h_i^{\min}(B)$, or $X_i = 0$ otherwise. The set $\{X_1, \ldots, X_k\}$ consists of an independent set of unbiased estimators for $J(A, B)$, in such a way that increasing k decreases the estimator variance. The error bounds for the estimation of $J(A, B)$ can be proved using the Chernoff inequalities. In particular, to achieve an error factor of θ with probability greater than $1 - \delta$, k should be chosen such that $k \ge \frac{2+\theta}{\theta^2} \ln(2/\delta)$.

MinHash's original motivation remains its most useful application, detecting plagiarism. It is possible to evaluate the similarity of two documents by only comparing their MinHash signatures in constant time. It can also be used in conjunction with HyperLogLog [7] to estimate the cardinality of set intersection without having both sets in the same machine [12].

In the context of graphs, we introduced a probabilistic implicit representation based on MinHash in which the main idea is, for any graph $G = (V, E)$ in a class $\mathcal{C}$ and for some pair of constants $0 \le \delta_A < \delta_B \le 1$, to find representing sets $S_v \ne \emptyset$ for every $v \in V$ such that the following two conditions hold: (i) $J(S_u, S_v) \ge \delta_B$ if and only if $(u, v) \in E$, and (ii) $J(S_u, S_v) \le \delta_A$ if and only if $(u, v) \notin E$. Therefore, no pairwise Jaccard coefficient of representing sets should lie within the interval (δ_A, δ_B). This way, the adjacency (u, v) could be tested by determining $J(S_u, S_v)$ and comparing it with δ_A and δ_B. We use MinHash to provide not the exact values, but estimates of the Jaccard coefficients. Therefore, the actual idea to test adjacency is to assume that $(u, v) \in E$ if $J(S_u, S_v) > \delta$ for some $\delta_A \le \delta \le \delta_B$. Note that only the signatures of the representing sets must be stored, requiring a constant number of elements. Furthermore, those signatures can be represented with a constant number of bits [10], and therefore a representation based on MinHash requires $O(n)$ bits to represent any class for which such representing sets exist.

In [11], we presented an algorithm to build such representing sets for trees with $\delta_A = 1/3$ and $\delta_B = 1/2$. Given a tree T, the construction is performed recursively starting at an arbitrary vertex v, with S_v being defined with ℓ arbitrary distinct elements, where $\ell = \min\{2^r : r \in \mathbb{N} \mid 2\Delta(T) \le 2^r\}$. Transforming T into a tree rooted at v, for each level the procedure alternates between choosing S_u as a subset of S_p (*selection* phase) and choosing S_u as a superset of S_p (*extension* phase), where p is the parent of u in T. Figure 2 exemplifies this construction.

The selection phase is done as follows. For a set $S_p = \{a_1, \ldots, a_x\}$, $x/2$ subsets $U_1, \ldots, U_{x/2}$ are selected from it, each with $x/2$ elements, such that each

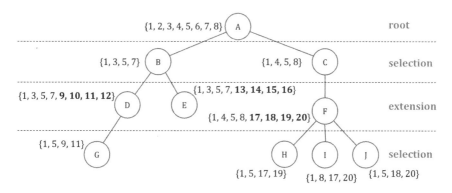

Fig. 2. Example of representing sets for a given tree.

pair of subsets has $x/4$ elements in common. This way, $J(U_i, U_j) = 1/3$ for $1 \leq i < j \leq x/2$ and $J(U_i, S_p) = 1/2$ for $1 \leq i \leq x/2$. Thus, each child of p must be assigned a distinct U_i as its representing set. The efficient implementation of this selection procedure is based on the representation by a binary string u_i, with length $x/2$, of a subset $U_i \subset S_p$, such that if the jth bit of u_i has value b, then a_{2j-1+b} belongs to U_i. The generation of the strings that represent $U_1, \ldots, U_{x/2}$ can be achieved iteratively, starting from a 1×1 matrix and, at each step, fourfolding the current matrix with negated bits in the lower right quadrant. This is illustrated in Fig. 3 for $S_p = \{1, \ldots, 8\}$. The extension phase is done through the inclusion of $|S_p|$ unique elements from the already defined representing sets.

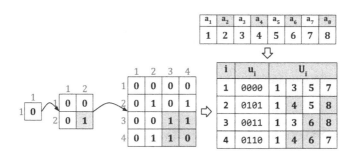

Fig. 3. Example of a subset selection for $S_p = \{1, \ldots, 8\}$.

The MinHash signatures are then computed for the representing sets and used as labels for the corresponding vertices. As this labeling scheme requires only $O(n)$ space to probabilistically represent trees, a class with $2^{\Theta(n \log n)}$ graphs on n vertices, such a probabilistic representation has better space complexity than the optimal deterministic representation.

The theoretical predictions about this representation were verified through three practical experiments. The experiments aimed to validate the rate of false positives and negatives as we change the evaluation threshold (δ), the number of vertices in the graph (n), and the signature size (k), while keeping the other parameters fixed. The results are shown in the Fig. 4.

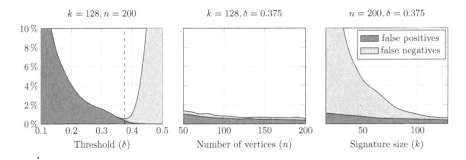

Fig. 4. Rate of false positives and negatives.

2.3   Considerations on Bipartite Graphs

In [16], it is shown that any hereditary graph class with $2^{\Theta(n^2)}$ members of n vertices should entirely include either the bipartite, co-bipartite, or split graphs. Also, it is possible to transform any graph $G = (V, E)$ into a bipartite graph $G' = (V', E')$ such that $V' = \{v_1, v_2 \mid v \in V\}$, and $E' = \{(u_1, v_2), (v_1, u_2) \mid (u, v) \in E\}$. Any efficient representation of G' can be used to efficiently represent G. This makes the search for a probabilistic representation of bipartite graphs specially appealing. However, we proved the non-existence of some representations. For example, it is impossible to construct a MinHash-based representation with $\delta_A = 0.4$ and $\delta_B = 0.6$ for a graph as simple as the complete bipartite $K_{3,3}$ [11]. Our proof is based on the formulation of a corresponding integer linear programming problem, which turns out to be infeasible. This suggests that further investigation concerning this probabilistic implicit graph representation is that of characterizing the class of graphs that are amenable to it.

3   Graph-Streams Connectivity

In many real applications, graphs are not static entities. Instead, it is often the case that edges and vertices are added and removed with high frequency. The study of fully dynamic graph algorithms is already well established [6,13], but the recent explosion in the scale of graphs has encouraged further research into algorithms that require sublinear space to compute queries on them. In this work, we present two variants of an ℓ_0-sampling sketch, a data structure that allows the sampling of edges in graph cut-sets and can be used to determine dynamic graph connectivity using $O(n \log^3 n)$ bits.

3.1 ℓ_0-sampling Sketch

The ℓ_0-sampling problem consists in sampling a nonzero coordinate from a dynamic vector $\boldsymbol{a} = (a_1, \ldots, a_n)$ with uniform probability. This vector is defined in a turnstile model, which consists of a stream of updates $S = \langle s_1, s_2, \ldots, s_t \rangle$ on $\boldsymbol{a}$ (initially $\boldsymbol{0}$), where $s_i = (u_i, \Delta_i) \in \{1, \ldots, n\} \times \mathbb{R}$ for $1 \leq i \leq t$, meaning an increment of Δ_i units to a_{u_i}. It is desirable that such sample be produced in a single pass through the stream with sublinear space complexity. The challenge arises from the fact that, since Δ_i can be negative and hence some updates in the stream may cancel others, directly sampling the stream may lead to incorrect results. In order to achieve sublinear space complexity in a single pass, an ℓ_0-sampling algorithm must represent $\boldsymbol{a}$ through a sketch.

In [5], a seminal sketch-based algorithm for the ℓ_0-sampling problem was introduced. The algorithm uses a universal family of hash functions to partition the vector $\boldsymbol{a}$ into $O(\log n)$ subvectors with exponentially decreasing probabilities of representing each element of $\boldsymbol{a}$. It is proved that there is a constant lower bound on the probability that at least one of those subvectors has exactly one nonzero coordinate. Through a procedure called 1-*sparse recovery*, which stores $O(\log n)$ bits for each subvector, it is possible to recover such coordinate. Considering that the probability of failure has a constant upper bound, running $O(\log(1/\delta))$ independent instances of the algorithm can ensure a success probability of at least $1 - \delta$. The total space complexity of this algorithm is $O(\log^2 n \log(1/\delta))$. Further studies show stronger results by relaxing assumptions on the hash functions used [8,14]. Nevertheless, they keep the same worst-case space complexity. In fact, any algorithm that performs ℓ_0-sampling in a single pass should require $\Omega(\log^2 n)$ bits in the worst case [8]. This holds even if the algorithm allows a relative error of ϵ and a failure probability of δ.

1-Sparse Recovery Procedure. A vector is 1-*sparse* when it has a single nonzero coordinate. A 1-sparse recovery procedure allows deciding whether a vector $\boldsymbol{a}$ is 1-sparse, and recover the only nonzero coordinate from it. Note that while $\boldsymbol{a}$ is expected to be 1-sparse at the time of a successful recovery, it may have any number of nonzero coordinates before that. This procedure is a building block for many ℓ_0-sampling algorithms. Here we present a false-biased randomized variant that handles cases where $\boldsymbol{a}$ has negative values [4]. It begins by choosing a sufficiently large prime $p \leq n^c$, for some constant $c > 1$, and a random integer $z \in \mathbb{Z}_p$. Then, iterating through all $s_i = (u_i, \Delta_i) \in S$, three sums are computed:

$$b_0 = \sum_{i=1}^{t} \Delta_i, \qquad b_1 = \sum_{i=1}^{t} \Delta_i u_i, \qquad b_2 = \sum_{i=1}^{t} \Delta_i z^{u_i} \mod p.$$

If $\boldsymbol{a}$ is 1-sparse, it is easy to see that the nonzero coordinate i can be recovered as $i = b_1/b_0$, with $a_i = b_0$. However, verifying that $\boldsymbol{a}$ is 1-sparse requires more effort.

Theorem 1. *If $\boldsymbol{a}$ is 1-sparse, then $b_2 \equiv b_0 z^{b_1/b_0} \mod p$. Otherwise, $b_2 \not\equiv b_0 z^{b_1/b_0} \mod p$ with probability at least $1 - n/p$.*

Proof (sketch). If $\boldsymbol{a}$ is 1-sparse, with a nonzero coordinate i, it is trivial to see that $b_2 \equiv a_i z^i \mod p$. Otherwise, $b_2 \equiv b_0 z^{b_1/b_0} \mod p$ may still hold if z is a root in $\mathbb{Z}_p$ of the polynomial $p(z) = b_0 z^{b_1/b_0} - \sum \Delta_i z^{u_i}$. As $p(z)$ is a degree-n polynomial, it has at most n roots in $\mathbb{Z}_p$. Therefore, given that z is chosen at random, the probability of a false recovery is at most n/p. □

This 1-sparse recovery procedure stores z, b_0, b_1, and b_2. Assuming that every a_i is limited by a polynomial in n, the total space required is $O(\log n)$ bits.

Algorithm. Here, two variants of the same ℓ_0-sampling sketch are presented. Both variants define $\boldsymbol{a}^{(1)}, \boldsymbol{a}^{(2)}, \ldots, \boldsymbol{a}^{(m)}$ subvectors of $\boldsymbol{a}$. For all $1 \leq j \leq m$, each $a_i \neq 0$ has a $1/2^j$ probability of being *present* at $\boldsymbol{a}^{(j)}$, that is, $a_i^{(j)} = a_i$ with probability $1/2^j$, otherwise $a_i^{(j)} = 0$. To decide whether $a_i^{(j)}$ is present, we draw a hash function $h_j : \{1, \ldots, n\} \to \{0, \ldots, 2^m - 1\}$ from a universal family, and observe whether $m - \lfloor \log_2 h_j(i) \rfloor = j$, which happens with probability $1/2^j$. An independent 1-sparse recovery is then computed for each $\boldsymbol{a}^{(j)}$. The variants differ only in the number of functions used. Variant (a) uses a single hash function for every $\boldsymbol{a}^{(j)}$ (Algorithm 1), while Variant (b) uses a different function for each subvector (Algorithm 2). While Variant (a) is more useful in practice, the error analysis for Variant (b) is more straightforward. We provide empirical evidence that the error in either variant converges quickly as a function of n.

Algorithm 1. Variant (a)	**Algorithm 2.** Variant (b)
1: $M[1..m]$: 1-sparse recoveries	1: $M[1..m]$: 1-sparse recoveries
2: **for each** $(u_i, \Delta_i) \in S$ **do**	2: **for each** $(u_i, \Delta_i) \in S$ **do**
3: $k \leftarrow m - \lfloor \log_2 h(u_i) \rfloor$	3: **for** $j \in [1..m]$ **do**
4: $M[k].b_0 \mathrel{+}= \Delta_i$	4: $k \leftarrow m - \lfloor \log_2 h_j(u_i) \rfloor$
5: $M[k].b_1 \mathrel{+}= \Delta_i u_i$	5: **if** $k = j$ **then**
6: $M[k].b_2 \mathrel{+}= \Delta_i M[k].z^{u_i} \mod p$	6: $M[k].b_0 \mathrel{+}= \Delta_i$
7: **for** $j \in [1..m]$ **do**	7: $M[k].b_1 \mathrel{+}= \Delta_i u_i$
8: $v \leftarrow M[j].b_0 M[j].z^{M[j].b_1/M[j].b_0} \mod p$	8: $M[k].b_2 \mathrel{+}= \Delta_i M[k].z^{u_i} \mod p$
9: **if** $M[j].b_2 = v$ **then**	9: **for** $j \in [1..m]$ **do**
10: **return** $M[j].b_1/M[j].b_0$	10: $v \leftarrow M[j].b_0 M[j].z^{M[j].b_1/M[j].b_0} \mod p$
11: **report** FAILURE	11: **if** $M[j].b_2 = v$ **then**
	12: **return** $M[j].b_1/M[j].b_0$
	13: **report** FAILURE

Each variant either succeeds in returning a single nonzero coordinate of $\boldsymbol{a}$ or reports a failure. The probability of failure is given by the joint probability of failure of all m 1-sparse recoveries. In Variant (b), these are independent events. The probability that a single recovery $M[j]$ fails is the complement of the probability that $\boldsymbol{a}^{(j)}$ is 1-sparse, that is, assuming $\boldsymbol{a}$ has $r \gg 1$ nonzero coordinates:

$$\Pr[\text{FAILURE}] = \prod_{j=1}^{m} \left(1 - r2^{-j}(1 - 2^{-j})^{r-1}\right) \approx \prod_{j=1}^{m} \left(1 - r2^{-j}e^{-r2^{-j}}\right).$$

Theorem 2. *If* $5 \leq \log_2 r \leq m - 5$, *then* $\Pr[\text{FAILURE}] \leq 0.31$ *for Variant (b).*

Proof (sketch). It is easy to see that the lowest probabilities of failure concentrate around j such that $2^j \leq r < 2^{j+1}$. Letting $q = r/2^{\lfloor \log_2 r \rfloor}$, it holds that

$$\Pr[\text{FAILURE}] \leq \prod_{k=-5}^{5} \left(1 - q2^k e^{-q2^k}\right).$$

Note that $1 \leq q < 2$. In this interval, all factors $1 - q2^k e^{-q2^k}$ are either monotonically increasing or decreasing. Analyzing their global maxima, we arrive at a maximum product of approximately 0.3071, therefore $\Pr[\text{FAILURE}] \leq 0.31$. □

This result shows that, as n grows, choosing $m = 5 + \lceil \log_2 n \rceil$ is enough to ensure a constant upper bound on the probability of failure. Furthermore, to ensure a success probability of at least $1 - \delta$, it is sufficient to run $\lceil \log_{0.31} \delta \rceil$ instances of the sketch.

In order to assess the algorithm's behavior in a real implementation, an experiment was set up. Both variants were implemented and tested with a vector of size $n = 4096$ and increasing values of r. We tested both a correctly sized (i.e., for $m = 17$) and an undersized instance of the ℓ_0-sampling sketch. The empirical cumulative distribution was also recorded. The experiment was run 100 000 times and the mean value for each data point is reported in Fig. 5.

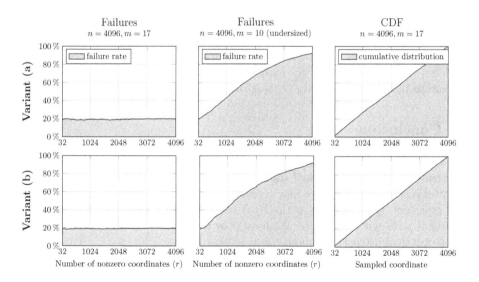

Fig. 5. Failure rate and cumulative distribution of successes.

This experiment suggests that in a correctly sized ℓ_0-sampling sketch, the failure probability stays almost constant and under 20%. There is little difference between Variants (a) and (b). Furthermore, in an undersized setup, the failure rate rapidly reaches critical levels.

3.2   Dynamic Connectivity Using ℓ_0-samplers

It is possible to use ℓ_0-sampling sketches to determine whether a dynamic graph $G = (V, E)$ is connected. One possible randomized algorithm runs in $O(\log n)$ turns and either answers affirmatively with certainty or negatively with a constant probability of error [1].

The algorithm starts with an empty subgraph of G. In each turn, for each connected component $S \subset V$, an edge is drawn (if any) from the cut-set $[S, V \setminus S]$, connecting two components. It is possible to prove that this procedure finishes in at most $\lceil \log_2 n \rceil$ turns, yielding a spanning tree of G if it is connected.

The ℓ_0-sampling sketches are used to represent each vertex set's adjacency, in the form of a modified incidence vector, where each edge is represented twice, one for each ordering of its ends. More formally, given an ordering $u_1 w_1, \ldots, u_m w_m$ of the edges of E, we define a vector $\boldsymbol{a}^v = (a_{u_1 w_1}^v, a_{w_1 u_1}^v, \ldots, a_{u_m w_m}^v, a_{w_m u_m}^v)$, for each vertex $v \in V$, in a way that $a_{u,w}^v = 1$ if $v = u$; $a_{u,w}^v = -1$, if $v = w$; or $a_{u,w}^v = 0$, otherwise.

This representation has the useful property that, for each set of vertices $S = \{v_1, v_2, \ldots, v_q\}$, the nonzero coordinates of $\boldsymbol{a}^S = \sum_{i=1}^q \boldsymbol{a}^{v_i}$ represents the edges across the cut $[S, V \setminus S]$. Therefore, considering that the ℓ_0-sampling representation of any vector $\boldsymbol{a}$ is a linear transformation of that vector, this implies that a set of ℓ_0-sampling sketches can be used to sample edges in any cut-set of a graph.

It is important to note that an ℓ_0-sampling sketch cannot be reused to sample another edge with the same failure probability. Nevertheless, a different sampling sketch can be used in each turn of the algorithm. Keeping $\lceil \log_2 n \rceil$ ℓ_0-sampling sketches (one for each turn) for each vertex allows performing the connectivity algorithm just described using $O(n \log^3 n)$ bits.

4   Conclusion

In this paper we explored the use of sketching data structures for massive graph problems. We have established the concept of probabilistic implicit graph representations, introducing two new representations. One, based on Bloom filters, can represent sparse graphs with $O(m)$ bits; another, based on MinHash, can represent trees with $O(n)$ bits. We have provided empirical evidence confirming the theoretical predictions about these representations.

We have also described a variant of the ℓ_0-sampling sketch and proved its failure probability to be bounded by a constant value, provided a certain structure-size condition is met. A simple dynamic graph connectivity algorithm using this sketch was explained. Research is ongoing on the proof of exact probabilities of failure for both algorithm variants. Future research may also include novel graph algorithms that use ℓ_0-sampling as a primitive.

Acknowledgements. The authors acknowledge partial financial support from CNPq, CAPES, and a FAPERJ BBP grant.

References

1. Ahn, K.J., Guha, S., McGregor, A.: Analyzing graph structure via linear measurements. In: Proceedings of SODA 2012, pp. 459–467 (2012)
2. Bloom, B.H.: Space/time trade-offs in hash coding with allowable errors. Commun. ACM **13**(7), 422–426 (1970)
3. Broder, A.Z.: On the resemblance and containment of documents. In: Proceedings of SEQUENCES 1997, pp. 21–29 (1997)
4. Cormode, G., Firmani, D.: A unifying framework for ℓ_0-sampling algorithms. Distrib. Parallel Databases **32**(3), 315–335 (2014)
5. Cormode, G., Muthukrishnan, S., Rozenbaum, I.: Summarizing and mining inverse distributions on data streams via dynamic inverse sampling. In: Proceedings of VLDB 2005, pp. 25–36 (2005)
6. Eppstein, D., Galil, Z., Italiano, G.F.: Dynamic graph algorithms (chap. 8). In: Atallah, M.J. (ed.) Algorithms and Theory of Computation Handbook. CRC Press, Boca Raton (1999)
7. Flajolet, P., Fusy, É., Gandouet, O., Meunier, F.: HyperLogLog: the analysis of a near-optimal cardinality estimation algorithm. In: Proceedings of AofA 2007, pp. 127–146 (2007)
8. Jowhari, H., Sağlam, M., Tardos, G.: Tight bounds for L_p samplers, finding duplicates in streams, and related problems. In: Proceedings of PODS 2011, pp. 49–58 (2011)
9. Kannan, S., Naor, M., Rudich, S.: Implicit representation of graphs. SIAM J. Discret. Math. **5**(4), 596–603 (1992)
10. Li, P., König, A.C.: b-Bit minwise hashing. In: Proceedings of WWW 2010, pp. 671–680 (2010)
11. Lopes, J.P.A.: Probabilistic data structures applied to implicit graph representation. Master's thesis, State University of Rio de Janeiro (2017, in Portuguese)
12. Lopes, J.P.A., Oliveira, F.S., Pinto, P.E.D.: Estimating the intersection cardinality of sets using MinHash and HyperLogLog. In: Proceedings of CNMAC 2016, pp. 010077- 1–2 (2017, in Portuguese)
13. McGregor, A.: Graph stream algorithms: a survey. ACM SIGMOD Rec. **43**(1), 9–20 (2014)
14. Monemizadeh, M., Woodruff, D.P.: 1-pass relative-error L_p-sampling with applications. In: Proceedings of SODA 2010, pp. 1143–1160 (2010)
15. Muller, J.H.: Local structure in graph classes. Ph.D. thesis, Georgia Institute of Technology (1988)
16. Spinrad, J.P.: Efficient Graph Representations. American Mathematical Society, Providence (2003)

Managing Structurally Heterogeneous Databases in Software Product Lines

Parisa Ataei[(⊠)], Arash Termehchy, and Eric Walkingshaw

Oregon State University, Corvallis, OR 97331, USA
{ataeip,termehca,walkiner}@oregonstate.edu

Abstract. Data variations are prevalent while developing software product lines (SPLs). A SPL enables a software vendor to quickly produce different variants of their software tailored to variations in their clients' business requirements, conventions, desired feature sets, and deployment environments. In database-backed software, the database of each variant may have a different schema and content, giving rise to numerous data variants. Users often need to query and/or analyze all variants in a SPL simultaneously. For example, a software vendor wants to perform common tests or inquiries over all variants. Unfortunately, there is no systematic approach to managing and querying data variations and users have to use their intuition to perform such tasks, often resorting to repeating a task for each variant. We introduce *VDBMS* (Variational Database Management System), a system that provides a compact, expressive, and structured representation of variation in relational databases. In contrast to data integration systems that provide a unified representation for all data sources, VDBMS makes variations explicit in both the schema and query. Although variations can make VDBMS queries more complex than plain queries, a strong static type system ensures that all variants of the query are consistent with the corresponding variants of the database. Additionally, *variational queries* make it possible to compactly represent and efficiently run queries over a huge range of data variations in a single query. This directly supports many tasks that would otherwise be intractable in highly variational database-backed SPLs.

Keywords: Variational databases · Variational queries · VSQL ·
Variational relational algebra · Software product lines ·
Heterogeneous databases

1 Introduction

Data variation is ubiquitous when developing software. Each domain contains numerous databases which differ in terms of schema, data representation, and/or content. In fact, even a single software vendor or project may need to maintain many different data representations of the same concepts. One way this arises is in the context of a *software product line* (SPL), which is a single software project

© Springer Nature Switzerland AG 2019
V. Gadepally et al. (Eds.): Poly 2018/DMAH 2018, LNCS 11470, pp. 68–77, 2019.
https://doi.org/10.1007/978-3-030-14177-6_6

that can be used to generate many different program variants [1]. For instance, software vendors often customize their software and create distinct variants for each client based on the client's geographical settings, business requirements, and the capabilities it wants. Most open source projects have hundreds or thousands of static configuration options, yielding a staggering number of variants [8].

Table 1. A subset of features in an email system SPL and the relations associated with them. If a feature is enabled, the schema of the email database includes the corresponding relation. The first two relations are included in all variants of the SPL. The three different *employee* relations, associated with different countries' naming conventions, are mutually exclusive.

Feature	Associated relation
-	$message(ID, sender, date, subject, body)$
-	$recepientInfo\ (rid, ID, rtype)$
Encryption	$encryption(ID, isEncrypted, encryptionKey)$
Signature	$signature(ID, signed, signKey)$
Verification	$verification(ID, isVerified)$
US	$person(ID, firstName, middleName, lastName)$
France	$person(ID, firstName, lastName)$
Iceland	$person(ID, firstName, fatherName, gender)$

Different variants of a SPL require different data representations. Consider a vendor that develops an email messaging system for customers around the globe. Each country may have a different standard of naming people, for example, in contrast to the US, there is no notion of a *middle name* in France, and in Iceland, a person's last name is determined by their gender and their father's name. Hence, this vendor may have to create a distinct relation schema for the relation *person* according to the country of the customer as shown in Table 1. A common intent in this email system is to retrieve a person's *ID* by their full name. To express this intent, a developer of the system has to write a distinct SQL query for each naming convention in their code. This problem grows multiplicatively when different variations interact, for example, a query to retrieve full names combined with an optional privacy feature, may require two distinct queries for each naming convention. Thus, a developer may end up writing many SQL queries to express the same intent across many software variants.

The database community has long recognized that users must modify their queries to preserve their semantic and syntactic correctness over various schemas and has proposed (declarative) schema mappings to solve this problem [3,5]. For example, in the context of schema evolution, one first defines or discovers the mapping between the original and new schemas. Given this schema mapping, one can safely and automatically translate the queries written over the original schema to the new one. Of course, the new schema must contain the information the query needs. However, the variations in a SPL do *not* enjoy this property.

For instance, if one knows the mapping between the schema for the client in the US and the one in France, they cannot automatically translate the query written for the France-based client to the one for the US-based client as the schema mapping does not imply the need to use the attribute middle name to preserve the intent behind the query. In fact, if one follows the mapping between the schemas, the query written for the US-based client will not use the attribute *middle name*!

In Sect. 2, we describe how such variation is managed in real-world SPLs and why current approaches are unsatisfactory to developers.

As a solution, we propose *VDBMS* (Variational Database Management System), a system that manages structurally heterogeneous databases in similar context and allows users to query multiple variants simultaneously without losing data provenance. In Sect. 3, we describe the core concepts of VDBMS, and describe the architecture of the VDBMS system in Sect. 4.

2 Motivating Example

One way of defining a SPL is to identify and model the *features* that give rise to different variants of the software [1]. For our purposes, a feature is a name that corresponds to some potentially optional unit of functionality, and a *feature model* describes the relationship between features. In the example illustrated in Table 1, *US*, *France*, and *Iceland* are features corresponding to different naming conventions and are mutually exclusive according to the feature model (not shown in the table). Other features in the email system include *Encryption*, *Signature*, and *Verification*. If, say, the *Encryption* feature is enabled, then the corresponding software variants will encrypt and decrypt emails. Features can be combined in different ways and extend or modify a shared code base that implements the basic requirements of the system shared across all variants, such as sending and receiving messages in an email system. By organizing the variability of a SPL around features, a vendor or project can share significant costs and effort in developing and maintaining many software variants [1].

Generating, managing, and maintaining separate schemas for each variant in a SPL is not simply tedious, but often impossible since the number of variants grows exponentially with the number of independent features. From our conversation with SPL experts, the dominant workaround is to create a global schema that contains all relations and attributes used across all variants of the software, then write queries over this global schema. However, such a schema may not be meaningful. For instance, in our email system example, the global schema must contain all attributes required to store various naming conventions for the relation *person*, which will not have any instance in the real world. Also, numerous tuples in the database will contain null values, e.g. middle names for all people in France. If the database is deployed and resides on the client's location, the client has a large schema but uses only a small subset of it. Developers must write distinct SQL queries for different software variants to express an intent that is shared among all variants. It may also be error-prone to write a query directly over such a global schema, as the query has access to many attributes and relations that do not make sense in its variants.

A cleaner approach is to define a view over the global schema for each variant and write queries for each variant against its view. However, developers then have to generate and maintain numerous view definitions and must still write many SQL queries to express the same intent. The developer must manually generate and manage the mappings between views and the global schema for each client. As a result, while querying database variants, they face similar problems to ones mentioned for schema mapping methods in Sect. 1. Moreover, update queries after deployment must deal with the problems of view-updating since the base tables of the products are defined as views. This approach works for a SPL with a small number of clients/variants. However, it doesn't scale to open-source SPLs where the selection of an individual variant is up to the end-user, and the space of potential variants is massive.

VDBMS introduces a novel abstraction called a *variational schema*, a compact representation of all schemas used by the software variants of a SPL, where the presence of relations and attributes in the schema is defined in terms of the features of the SPL. It also provides a novel *variational query* language that enables SPL programmers to refer to features explicitly. Instead of writing separate queries for each variant of a SPL, programmers can express an intent over all possible schema variants of a SPL in a single query. By making variation explicit in schema and queries, VDBMS simplifies the task of testing and maintaining database-related functionality across software variants. Finally, it provides opportunities for sharing query processing across multiple schema variants.

3   Variational Database Framework

A *variational database* (VDB) is conceptually a set of relational database variants that may each have a different schema. It is conceptually useful in any context where one wants to work on some/all of these variants simultaneously.

3.1   Variational Schema

Similar to relational databases, we need to *compactly* express the schema of a VDB. We assume that different variants of a SPL can either include or exclude a relation, and if they include a relation they can either include or exclude an attribute of that relation. A *variational schema* (v-schema) concisely encodes the plain relational database schemas for all of the software variants in a SPL [2]. The representation of v-schemas is based on the formula choice calculus [4,7].

Conceptually, a variational schema is just a relational schema with embedded *choices* that locally capture the differences among variants. A choice $F\langle x, y\rangle$ consists of a *feature expression* F and two alternatives x and y. A feature expression is a propositional formula over the *features* of the SPL, where each feature can either be enabled (*true*) or disabled (*false*). For a particular set of enabled features, the choice $F\langle x, y \rangle$ can be replaced by x if F evaluates to true, or y otherwise. Each software variant of the SPL corresponds to a set of enabled features (its *configuration*); the plain schema for that variant can be obtained by simply eliminating each of the choices in the v-schema as described above.

A v-schema allows for the embedding of choices within the sets of attribute names, forming *variational relation schemas*. We illustrate this in Example 1.

Example 1. Assume our schema contains the relation *person* and our SPL contains the country-specific features. Then $A = US\langle l_1 \cup \{middleName\}, France\langle l_1, l_2 \rangle \rangle$ encodes the set of attribute names for the *person* relation shown in Table 1, where $l_1 = \{ID, firstName, lastName\}, l_2 = \{ID, firstName, fatherName, gender\}$. Note that l_2 contains the attributes for the *Iceland* feature, which are included when neither *US* nor *France* are enabled. The entire v-schema can be represented as $S = (US \vee France \vee Iceland)\langle person(A), \varnothing \rangle$, where $person(A)$ is a variational relation schema (v-relation schema) and $\varnothing$ indicates a non-existing schema.

A *v-relation* is a set of tuples that conform to the same v-relation schema, where each tuple has a feature expression that indicates the software variants that include the tuple (its *presence condition*). A set of v-relations form a VDB.

Within a SPL, not all configurations yield valid software variants. For example, any valid configuration of our email system contains *exactly one* of the features *US*, *France*, and *Iceland*. In practice, the set of valid configurations of a SPL is described by a *feature model* [1]. Here, we consider a feature model to be a feature expression that is satisfied iff the configuration is valid. For example, the corresponding fragment of our email system feature model is:
$(US \wedge \neg France \wedge \neg Iceland) \vee (\neg US \wedge France \wedge \neg Iceland) \vee (\neg US \wedge \neg France \wedge Iceland)$

The feature model is an input to VDBMS and is implicitly applied globally. For example, given the feature model above, the nested choice $US\langle x, France\langle y, z \rangle \rangle$ will resolve to x for the US, y for France, and z for Iceland. Although for simplicity we use propositional formulas for feature expressions and feature models, our model can be easily generalized to other encodings, such as first-order logic.

3.2   Variational SQL

To query a VDB, we introduce the notion of a *variational query* (v-query), which returns a v-relation. We define *variational SQL* (VSQL) as an extension of SQL with a new function CHOICE(f, e_1, e_2), where f is a feature expression and e_1 and e_2 may be VSQL queries, attribute sets used in a SELECT clause, relations (or joins of some relations) used in a FROM clause, or conditions in a WHERE clause. With VSQL, the SPL developer can use the CHOICE function to indicate different attributes, conditions, and relations to use for different variants of the database. This enables expressing a single intent across a potentially huge number of configurations in a single v-query.

In our examples, we use *variational relational algebra* (VRA) rather than VSQL, for brevity. VRA is relational algebra extended by the choice notation introduced in Sect. 3.1. However, we expect end-users to prefer the VSQL notation. Example 2 illustrates different ways of writing a v-query in VRA.

Example 2. Consider again the schema sketched in Table 1 and defined in Example 1. Suppose a developer would like to express the intent of querying a last name by projecting the last name attribute for US and France, and the father's name and gender in Iceland. They can do this with the following query: $Q_1 = \pi_{(France \lor US)\langle\{lastName\},\{fatherName,gender\}\rangle} person$. The output of this query is a v-relation that has the *lastName* attribute for both US and France variants and the *fatherName* and *gender* attributes for the Iceland variant of the data. The user may also submit the following query with nested choice expression to articulate the same intent: $Q_1' = \pi_{France\langle\{lastName\},(US\langle\{lastName\},\{fatherName,gender\}\rangle)\rangle} person$. Without choices and a VDB, expressing this query requires executing two different plain queries against three different databases.

Since VSQL is a strict superset of SQL, a developer may still write queries in plain SQL when the intent is expressed the same way across all variants. That is, VSQL does not impose additional complexity when it is not needed. Additionally, we employ type inference and a strong static type system that enables omitting choices in many cases where the variation in the v-query is completely determined by the corresponding variation in the v-schema. For example, we can express query Q_1 in Example 2 more simply as $\pi_{lastName,fatherName,gender} person$. This will project the *lastName* attribute for the US and France, and the *fatherName* and *gender* attributes for Iceland, and the inferred type of this query will track which attributes and tuples are present in which variants.

The type system also supports usability by ruling out invalid v-queries. For example, a query that contains the condition *lastName = fatherName* would be invalid since there is no configuration of the database that includes both the *lastName* and *fatherName* attributes of the *person* relation.

Type inference enables omitting the "boring" choices that would only be needed to ensure consistency between the v-query and the v-schema, which in turn ensures that each variant of the v-query is structurally consistent with its corresponding variant of the VDB. This frees choices to be reserved for the more interesting cases where a v-query must describe *unsystematic* or *non-structurally determined* differences amongst its variants. This is illustrated in Example 3.

Example 3. Suppose we want to read the body of all emails. Our query must take into account whether an email is encrypted or not. This is illustrated by the following query with a choice over the feature *Encryption*, where Δ is a user-defined function that takes attributes *encryptionKey* and *body* and decodes the body according to the key.

$$Encryption\langle \pi_{\Delta(body,encryptionKey)}(\sigma_{isEncrypted=\textbf{true}} message \bowtie_{ID=ID} encryption)$$
$$\cup\ \pi_{body}(\sigma_{isEncrypted=\textbf{false}} message \bowtie_{ID=ID} encryption), \pi_{body} message\rangle$$

Note that variation in this query is not determined by the v-schema since each alternative of the choice not only queries different attributes and relations, but must also perform different functionality (namely, decoding the email body).

4   VDBMS Architecture

Figure 1 shows the architecture of VDBMS. V-schema and v-query are supported by the VDBMS abstraction layer to enable the SPL developer to interact with the VDB. The SPL developer can include v-queries in the SPL codebase or input them to VDBMS directly. In this section, we briefly report our ongoing effort of implementing VDBMS using an existing RDBMS.

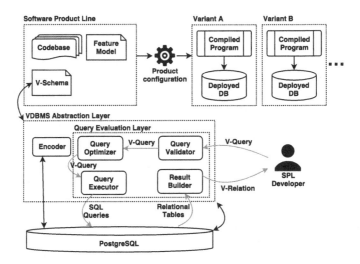

Fig. 1. Overview of VDBMS. The v-schema captures variation in database layouts and is accessible from all modules within the VDBMS layer.

4.1   Encoding the Variational Database

We implement VDBMS on top of PostgreSQL. All variants of a v-relation are encoded as a single relational table in PostgreSQL. This table contains the union of all attributes contained in all variants of the relation schema. We encode both the v-schema and the feature model as additional tables in PostgreSQL. The v-schema associates with each attribute a feature expression, called the *presence condition*, indicating in which variants the attribute is included.

A key aspect of a VDB is that it conceptually represents many different variant databases, and often it is important to both keep these databases distinct, and to keep track of which results come from which databases. One scenario where this is especially important is when features correspond to different clients, in which case we want to ensure that data associated with different clients do not mix. Therefore, our system must not only manage structural differences between variants, but also track which *data* is associated with which variants. We do this by attaching a presence condition to each tuple that indicates the variants in which the tuple is present. The presence condition is represented as a feature expression that VDBMS maintains and updates throughout the execution of a v-query. The key property enforced by maintaining presence conditions on tuples is *variation preservation*, which states that running a v-query on a v-database yields a v-relation that is equivalent to running each variant of the v-query on the corresponding variant of the v-database.

4.2 Optimizing and Evaluating Variational Query

The evaluation of a v-query proceeds in several steps. First, the *query validator* applies the rules of the type system to check whether the query is consistent with the variational schema. For example, the query $\pi_{(France\langle middleName, \varnothing\rangle)} person$ is invalid since it projects the *middleName* attribute when the *France* feature is enabled, but this attribute is present only when the *US* feature is enabled.

The *query optimizer* translates the v-query into a tree whose internal nodes are either relational operators or choices, and whose leaves are v-relations. The optimizer then applies equivalence laws from relational algebra and the choice calculus to achieve better performance.

Conceptually, the *query executor* executes an optimized variational query by translating it into a sequence of relational query operations interspersed by operations that enforce the variation-preservation property (Sect. 4.1). In practice, this is achieved efficiently by embedding user-defined functions in queries that can be executed entirely with the PostgreSQL DBMS. During the execution of a variational query, tuples can be filtered out of intermediate results not only by the selection predicate, but also because the tuples are not present in the variations that are applicable to that part of the query. Additionally, the presence conditions of tuples will be refined as they are processed by the query.

Finally, VDBMS must return a v-relation to the user. The *result builder* module collects the results, including the presence conditions of the relation, attributes, and tuples, and assembles them into a v-relation to return. Note that the query executor and result builder modules can work in a pipeline since the tuples' presence conditions are independent from one another.

5   Related Work

OrpheusDB supports *database versioning* [6]. Both OrpheusDB and VDBMS provide access to some versions or variants of a database at a time. However, unlike database versioning, which manages heterogeneity of content only, VDBMS also supports heterogeneous structure, that is, different schemas for different variants. Both database version and VDBMS support data sharing among versions/variants. In VDBMS, this is supported by presence conditions on tuples that are consistent with many different configurations. For example, a tuple with presence condition *US* ∨ *France* is included in all variants with either the *US* or *France* feature enabled (regardless of the configuration of other features).

Multi-tenant databases [9] take an architectural approach towards sharing resources among various organization that use different applications and hence different databases without any limitation on database variations. They do so by storing data ownership and the database schema in relational tables. However, VDBMS is only used for databases in similar contexts since it adds a level of abstraction to both the schema and content of the database. As a result, it allows for as much sharing as possible among database variants while multi-tenant databases do not allow for any sharing since the variations can be completely different. Interestingly, they both secure client's information, VDBMS does so by providing the *variation-preservation* property and multi-tenant databases do so by tagging the *client ID* to data.

6 Conclusion and Future Work

While developing SPLs, developers must deal with many variants of a database corresponding to different configurations of the software. Maintaining each database and its corresponding set of queries manually doesn't scale to highly configurable SPLs. Alternative solutions, such as including all of the information for all variants in a single schema, are error-prone and don't address the problem of unsystematic variation, that is, when different configurations of the software may require different queries to express the same intent, which are not determined by differences in structure alone. We introduced a conceptual framework for VDBMS, including v-schemas, which compactly represents the schema associated with each configuration of an SPL, and variational queries, which enable users to express both systematic and unsystematic variations of a single intent across all variants of the database. We have also introduced the VDBMS architecture, including how it integrates with the SPL and how it is realized in the underlying DBMS, PostgreSQL. VDBMS enforces a variation-preservation property that ensures that queries and data associated with different configurations remain distinct and consistent.

We plan to extend VDBMS to allow for disciplined overriding of the variation-preservation property, to enable combining results from many different variants in a single v-query. We also plan to explore further optimizations to the system to improve performance, and how to extend VDBMS to support other use cases besides SPL development.

References

1. Apel, S., Batory, D., Kästner, C., Saake, G.: Feature-Oriented Software Product Lines. Springer, Heidelberg (2016). https://doi.org/10.1007/978-3-642-37521-7
2. Ataei, P., Termehchy, A., Walkingshaw, E.: Variational databases. In: International Symposium on Database Programming Languages (DBPL), pp. 11:1–11:4 (2017)

3. Doan, A., Halevy, A., Ives, Z.: Principles of Data Integration. Morgan Kaufmann, San Francisco (2012)
4. Erwig, M., Walkingshaw, E.: The choice calculus: a representation for software variation. ACM Trans. Softw. Eng. Methodol. (TOSEM) **21**(1), 6:1–6:27 (2011)
5. Fagin, R., Kolaitis, P.G., Miller, R.J., Popa, L.: Data exchange: semantics and query answering. In: International Conference on Database Theory (ICDT) (2003)
6. Huang, S., Xu, L., Liu, J., Elmore, A.J., Parameswaran, A.: OrpheusDB: bolt-on versioning for relational databases. Proc. VLDB Endow. **10**(10), 1130–1141 (2017)
7. Hubbard, S., Walkingshaw, E.: Formula choice calculus. In: International Workshop on Feature-Oriented Software Development (FOSD), pp. 49–57 (2016)
8. Liebig, J., Apel, S., Lengauer, C., Kästner, C., Schulze, M.: An analysis of the variability in forty preprocessor-based software product lines. In: ACM/IEEE International Conference on Software Engineering, pp. 105–114 (2010)
9. Weissman, C.D., Bobrowski, S.: The design of the force.com multitenant internet application development platform. In: Proceedings of the 2009 ACM SIGMOD, SIGMOD 2009, pp. 889–896 (2009). https://doi.org/10.1145/1559845.1559942

PDSPTF: Polystore Database System for Scalability and Access to PTF Time-Domain Astronomy Data Archives

Shashank Shrestha[1][(✉)], Manoj Poudel[1], Yilang Wu[1], Wanming Chu[1], Subhash Bhalla[1], Thomas Kupfer[2], and Shrinivas Kulkarni[2]

[1] University of Aizu, Aizu-Wakamatsu, Japan
{d8201104,m5212201,y-wu,w-chu,bhalla}@u-aizu.ac.jp
[2] California Institute of Technology, Pasadena, CA 91125, USA
tkupfer@caltech.edu, srk@astro.caltech.edu

Abstract. Recent developments in time-domain astronomy use a large amount of data for gaining domain-specific information. The ever increasing data size and different data models require the development of new ideas to manage such data. The data type varies from the images of astronomical bodies, unstructured texts and structured (relations and key-values). There are many astronomical data repositories that manage such kind of data. Palomar Transient Factory (PTF) is one such data repository which has large amount of data with different varieties. Managing such variety of data in a single database can have many performance, growth and scalability issues. In this paper, we propose a prototype system for demonstrating the advantages of using Polystore Database System with a scientific workflow based query system.

Keywords: Query management · Polystore databases · Astronomical data · Workflow management · Federation of information

1 Introduction

PTF (Palomar Transient Factory) is a collection of telescopes in San Diego, USA monitoring the Northern Sky for any changes in the astronomical bodies [1]. The study of changes in astronomical bodies with respect to time is called "Time-domain astronomy". Any changes in astronomical bodies is recorded and indexed in their database in real-time. PTF deals with two kinds of data processing (real-time and archival). Like many other astronomical data repositories, PTF contains high-resolution images, key-values, relations and unstructured text files.

The archival data for PTF is available publicly through IRSA (NASA/IPAC Infrared Science Archive) [2]. The IRSA/IPAC has developed an image archive, a high-quality photometry pipeline and a searchable database (relational) of observed astronomical sources [3].

There have been three data releases so far between the years 2009–2016. All those data releases have highly calibrated epochal images and photometric catalogs which have the information of the imagery data.

© Springer Nature Switzerland AG 2019
V. Gadepally et al. (Eds.): Poly 2018/DMAH 2018, LNCS 11470, pp. 78–92, 2019.
https://doi.org/10.1007/978-3-030-14177-6_7

1.1   PTF Data Processing

Palomar observatory is located in Mount Palomar in San Diego, California, USA which routinely monitors the night sky through their telescopes. The images are the raw data which flows through multiple pipelines, creating a variety of science products. These pipelines process the data in real time. PTF uses EXTASCID (EXTensible system for Analyzing SCIentific Data) built around massively parallel GLADE (Generalized Linear Aggregate Distributed Engine) architecture for data aggregation and comparison of new raw images with old ones [4]. Any changes in the images get indexed in their archives or else is rejected and removed. The comparison and removal of images is known as image subtraction.

A Photometric pipeline is used for frame processing where astrometric calibration is done at the individual CCD (Charge-coupled Device)-images level against combined Sloan Digital Sky Survey (SDSS) [5] and UCAC4 catalog [6]. Outputs are calibrated single-CCD FITS (Flexible Image Transport System) images and source catalogs in FITS binary table format [7]. Once the individual CCD images are accumulated, the images are sent to the "reference image" pipeline. This pipeline combines the best image data for a given CCD, field and filter. Reference images products are images, coverage maps and catalogs. After the end of each night, all detected sources from photo-metric pipeline are matched with reference image catalog where gain-correction factors are computed. This pipeline improves the overall relative calibration of images for brighter sources [8]. This pipeline is the Lightcurve pipeline and a new database containing these images and catalogs were published in December 2016. Finally, the raw images pass through a real-time pipeline. In this pipeline, image – differencing is used against the reference-image library to extract transient candidates. The new raw images (candidates) are scored using machine learning. The candidates are scored with the features used by the real-or-bogus classifier during image subtraction. Images with higher scores are then indexed and stored in the archives [4, 9].

1.2   State of Data Access in PTF

PTF alongside its real-time system also maintains an archive for images. The images with the accompanying catalogs are curated and distributed by IPAC/IRSA [2]. By the year 2016, around 4.1 million epochal images with catalogs have already been released. IRSA/IPAC also provides download platform for this data through their own web based systems [10].

The web based system provided by IPAC/IRSA provides public data access to different data available in PTF. Camera images, processed images, reference images, different catalogs and calibration files can be accessed through their web system. For example, a user needs to find images from a particular night in a particular field and from a certain camera. This query has 3 objects to search Nights, Fields and CCD cameras. These kinds of queries need multi-object system searches. However, the system only allows users to simply search for astronomical bodies by name or IDs. Thus, the user can only search for the information from a single object at any time. The users have to write complex programs and compose SQL manually to perform a multi-object search.

1.3 Downloading the PTF Data

All the image data have been released in Flexible Image Transport System (FITS) format [11] which have epochal (single exposure) images and photometric catalogs. The images are taken with 12 CCD cameras which have different filters where quality of the images differs. The photometric catalogs include the information about images which have key-values and header information for the images. Those key-values can be transformed into relations and stored in relational database management systems (RDBMS).

For the purpose of study, we have created a local repository. The header information and key-and-value for the tables are downloaded from the Public Astronomical Catalogs and Data Resources provided by IPAC. The download process is implemented in a Python script named Astropy [12] which dynamically generates SQL which then downloads the optimized catalog data. The downloaded header files and the catalogs are then stored in a PostgreSQL relational database, in the local LINUX server with 16 GB memory and 5 TB disk size. Python script includes a JSON file used for data formatting (assign key-and-values to the relations). As the data size is very large, the Python script only downloads the header information of the FITS file required for the proposed web based system and research activities (Fig. 1).

The downloaded raw data is subsequently restructured in the local Postgres server with header information, key-value of the data in relational form. The attributes of the relations are then defined and stored [13]. The refined data then gives a detailed view about the data in a relational form (Appendix 1). The following entities (objects of interests) are included in the catalog database.

- **Nights.** Contains the dates of observation for each particular image (DBNID).
- **Fields.** Contains the exact X (OBJRAD) and Y (OBJDECD) coordinate of the images in a particular time (DBFIELD). Also includes the information for galaxies.
- **Raw Images/Exposures.** Relation table to map a particular image time and (X, Y) coordinate location for each observation, (DBEXPID). Additionally, it has more detail about the processed images and CCD details such as observation type, image type, exposure time, processed image IDs, CCD IDs etc.
- **Filters.** Contains the filter name and type of filter used in the image, (DBFID).
- **Procimages.** Contains FITS header files of processed images (DBPID) for each observation. Additionally, it has unique serial numbers required to map the primary keys of each table and exposures ID (DBEXPID) required to map Raw Images/Exposures table to show the image.
- **CCD.** Contains the camera details per CCD (CCDID) and the names of the CCD (CCDNAME).
- **Host Galaxy.** Contains information for the host galaxies (DBHOST) and the names of the galaxies (HOST_NAME).
- **Instrument Telemetry.** Contains information for the measurements and other communication details of the instruments used for capturing images of the astronomical bodies.
- **Host Fields.** Contains information of the host galaxies (DBHOST) as well as the information for the coordinates of the images in a particular time (DBFIELD).

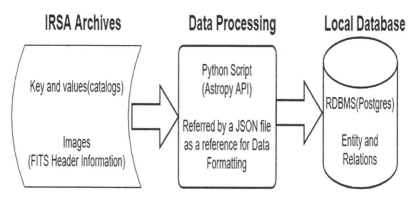

Fig. 1. Importing FITS header files to local PostgresDB

2   System Overview and Use of Polystore Databases

PTF data has different types of data (images, texts, relations). In this study, we propose an architecture to manage different data models through polystore databases. Key-values and the header information for the images downloaded from IPAC/IRSA are stored in PostgreSQL. The images are stored in NED/IPAC Extragalactic Database [14] which is an online astronomical database. The header files have HTML tags and predefined URLs to connect to the NED/IPAC remote database for image retrieval.

2.1   Existing IPAC Sources

Current solutions for domain-specific search in astronomical domain requires user to write complex programs or create complex queries themselves in order to gain information. Writing complex queries and complex programs require time and effort depending on the skill of the user. The users make different queries to gain access to the information (mainly epochal images of Northern sky) provided by the data. The query can be simple or complex regarding the information that a user needs. Thus, the proposed query system eliminates the need of complex programming for information retrieval and provides query language support for the users to communicate with the data via the Internet.

2.2   Proposed System

By the use of workflow method, the users have easily accessible query language and can interact with the data. Workflow of the system is based on the steps a user may take during finding information about the astronomical bodies. As PTF deals with "Time-domain Astronomy" which is the study of how astronomical bodies change with time, the main concern of the astronomical domain experts is to find particular images of astronomical bodies in a certain place at a certain time. So, most of the queries are about finding images related to time and space. Other general queries can be about finding images with certain cameras or filters or finding images from an entire galaxy. A sample of queries for the PTF data can be found in Appendix 2.

The system maintains a web-based GUI with an image visualizer where simple and complex queries can be executed. It supports complex query manipulation where SQL is generated dynamically as per user interaction with the GUI. The query generated is then transformed into predefined URL requests to get the images from the IPAC/IRSA web system which is managed by the image database at IPAC/IRSA server. The query formulation, query transformation and visualization of information are performed in a sequence of stages as follows (Fig. 2).

- **Query Formulation:** The underlying relations and data sources can be formulated in web based GUI for workflow query management named Datawnt0. The system allows the users to compose queries by selecting the objects and relating it to other objects through logical (and/or) operators. Each time an object is selected and the input is filled, the system generates an SQL. After relating the result of the first object to other object and continuing the same process; the system generates a new SQL by appending the resulting SQL with the new one. The system uses join operation between the objects. After the queries are formulated, they are stored and sent to the Postgres database. Simultaneously, image SQLs are also formulated which are used for the next process of query transformation.
- **Query Transformation:** The formulated queries after being sent to the Postgres database are processed. The image SQLs are formed by joining the resulting SQL of the formulated queries with ProcImages table and the Raw Images table which have information about the header files of images. In this stage, the Image SQLs are matched with the header files of the URL links for the images and then transformed into server requests to retrieve the images and information of the images from the NED/IPAC image database.
- **Visualization:** Retrieved images and the information are then visualized in the FITS image viewer which is an API to connect with the NED/IPAC image database and view FITS image files. The resulting query answers are visualized as images and tables which can be downloaded.

The current system consists of multiple components to support workflow based query language. It supports image viewing, download of images and tables, query formulation and manipulation for end users. It shares common characteristics with Polystore databases. The connection between two database engines with the flow of queries and transforming it to the local dialect of each engines matches the Polystore terminology. The federation of information from relational data source and images with a query language and transformation of queries into server requests can be compared with the 'islands of information' which was defined in the research [15]. The visualizer in the system also uses an API for viewing images and connecting to the image database which acts as a middleware.

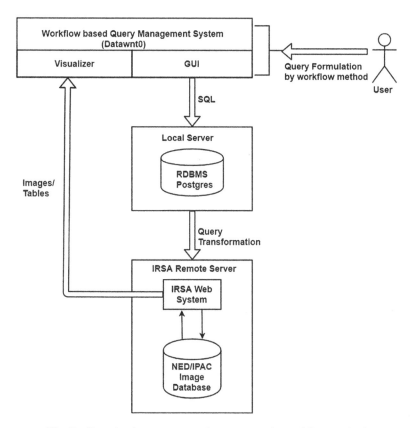

Fig. 2. Querying heterogeneous data sources via workflow method

3   Workflow Based Query Management System

Astronomical domain experts need query tools to access various information from multiple astronomical bodies. Images and information of the images are the major searches. The user may have different queries according to different scenarios. The users may want to query a single object or multiple objects to gain information. The user may also want to choose some logical operators (and, or) between multiple objects to enhance the query. The system maintains a GUI for Information Requirements Elicitation (IRE). The user interaction with the system generates SQL. Two SQLs are generated for each task performed. One SQL is generated to retrieve the information of images in a tabular form which is stored in the local database. The other SQL is generated to connect to the NED/IPAC image database to get the queried images. The system supports querying for 8 object parametric combinations. The system provides simple relate and join operation between those objects (Fig. 3). The system uses SQL for handling structured data in the relational database. Composing SQL manually for single object can be simple but as the number of objects are increased, the difficulty in composing SQL can be much complex [16, 17].

Relate Matrix	Nights	Fields	Filters	Exposures/Raw Images	CCD	Host Galaxy	Host Fields	Instruments
Nights				✓				
Fields				✓			✓	
Filters				✓				
Exposures/Raw Images	✓	✓	✓		✓			✓
CCD				✓				
Host Galaxy							✓	
Host Fields		✓				✓		
Instruments				✓				

Fig. 3. Relate matrix of the objects in the system

3.1   Query Language Interface

The proposed system supports formulation of queries from an interactive GUI (Fig. 4) where the users can select the object and input the IDs and object names predefined in the system [18]. The user can relate multiple objects as per the requirement of the query. Each time a user selects an object while querying, a query is generated. Adding those queries together while relating multiple objects transforms the initial query into more complex one. The process of appending queries in multiple steps has been termed multi-stage querying [17]. The query is then stored in the server which on clicking the results button gives the table with information as a result. Clicking on the contents of the table it connects to the FITS image viewer and visualize the images.

Example 1: Let us consider a query where a user wants to find an image of a certain astronomical object at a certain place. The user has DBFIELD ID as 100001.

Process: First the user selects the object 'Fields'. Enters 100001 as Field ID in the query system (Fig. 5), then clicks on search button and get the results.

SQL for Example 1: Select distinct on (A."DBFIELD") A.*
from "_FIELDS" A
where A."DBFIELD"='100001';

At the local catalog database, SQL for connecting to the image database is also formulated which subsequently sends server request to the IPAC/IRSA image server which uses the URLs to select and send the images.

Image SQL for Example 1: Select A.*,B.* from "_RAWIMAGES" A, "_PROCIMAGES" B, (select distinct on (A."DBFIELD") A.*
from "_FIELDS" A
where A."DBFIELD"='100001') C
where A."DBFIELD" = C."DBFIELD" and A."UNIQUE_SERIAL_NUMBER"=
B."UNIQUE_SERIAL_NUMBER" offset 0 limit 10;

Example 1 is a single-object search where only one object 'Fields' was queried to get the information.

Example 2: Let us consider a query where a user wants to find an image from a certain place with a certain camera. The user has Field ID as 100001 and Camera (CCD) ID as 5.
Process: First the user selects the object 'Fields'. Enters 100001 as Field ID in the query system. Then, the user clicks on search button and then related button and relate to 'Raw Images'. The user again clicks on search button and then related button and then relate to 'CCD' where the user can enter 5 as the CCD ID, search and get the results.

SQL for Example 2: Select distinct on (A."CCDID") A.* from "_CCD" A,
(select distinct on (A."DBRID") A.*
from "_RAWIMAGES" A, (select distinct on (A."DBFIELD") A.* from "_FIELDS" A
where A."DBFIELD"='100001') B
where A."DBFIELD"=B."DBFIELD") B
where A."CCDID"='5' and A."CCDID"=B."CCDID" ;
Image SQL for Example 2: Select A.*,B.* from "_RAWIMAGES" A, "_PROCIMAGES" B, (select distinct on (A."CCDID") A.* from "_CCD" A, (select distinct on (A."DBRID") A.*
from "_RAWIMAGES" A, (select distinct on (A."DBFIELD") A.* from "_FIELDS" A
where A."DBFIELD"='100001') B
where A."DBFIELD"=B."DBFIELD") B
where A."CCDID"='5' and A."CCDID"=B."CCDID") C
where A."CCDID" = C."CCDID" and A."UNIQUE_SERIAL_NUMBER"=
B."UNIQUE_SERIAL_NUMBER" offset 0 limit 10;

Example 2 is a multi-object search where three objects, 'Fields', 'Raw Images' and 'CCD' were queried to get the information. The information was retrieved using simple relate and join operation between those objects (Fig. 4).

The system supports querying for multiple objects using the workflow method as query is generated through user interaction in the GUI. The results are visualized in the form of tables and images (Fig. 6). When an object is queried, the system generates two SQLs one for the GUI and one for the FITS image viewer (visualizer). The image SQL is used to connect to the remote image database which is transformed into server URL requests to fetch the images and display it in the visualizer.

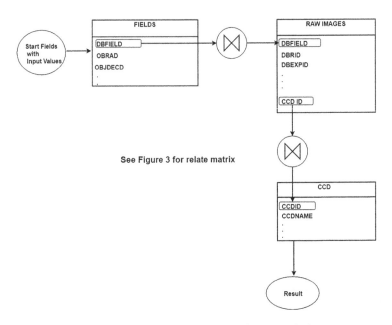

Fig. 4. Relate and join operation for Example 2

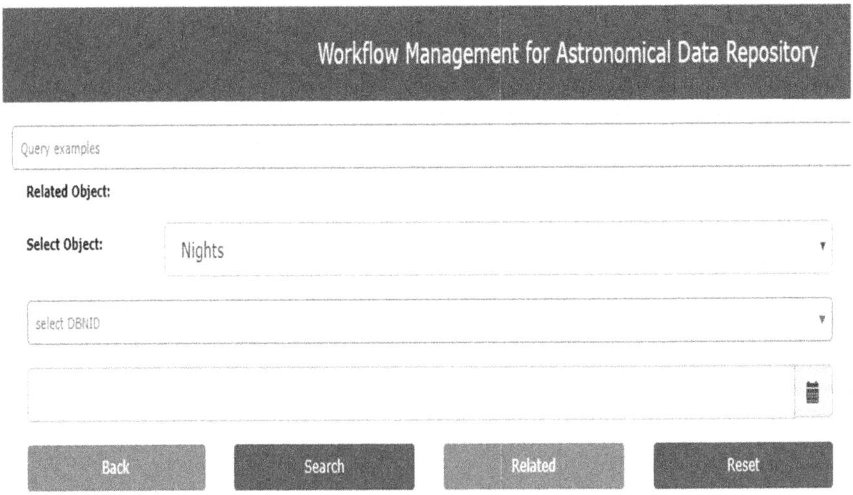

Workflow Management for Astronomical Data Repository

Query examples

Related Object:

Select Object: Nights   ▾

select DBNID   ▾

[📱]

[Back]   [Search]   [Related]   [Reset]

Fig. 5. GUI for Datawnt0 workflow management system

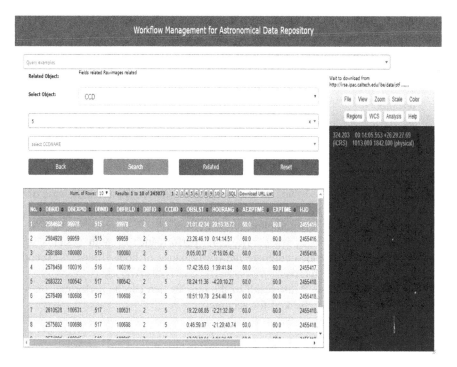

Fig. 6. Results table and visualizer (FITS image viewer)

4 Performance Enhancement Through PDSPTF

We present and compare the performance of Datawnt0 workflow based query management system and the IPAC web based system for accessing PTF data. The comparison is based on the usability, accuracy and the range of queries that can be performed on these systems for requirements elicitation. The Datawnt0 presents a simple set theoretic query language that can be easily mastered by skilled users of Astronomy data resources.

4.1 Experiment

For the experiment, we select 25 queries (Appendix 2) and invite 30 students as participants. The range of queries are divided into 3 categories. The query where only a single object is used, the query where multiple objects are used and query to search entire set of fields and galaxies. The participants are at different levels of skill on the basis of experience on working with query systems. The participants are divided into two groups with matching level of ability. One group (G1) is given an explanation on how to use both systems and brief background on the data. The other group (G2) is just given list of queries and links to the systems. The experiment follows with three hypotheses.

Hypothesis 1: Datawnt0 workflow query system is easier to understand and use.
Hypothesis 2: Datawnt0 workflow query system can perform more range of queries.
Hypothesis 3: Datawnt0 workflow based query system results are accurate and corresponds to the results of IPAC web based system.

4.2   Methods

The participants are given a list of 25 queries with the ER model of the database. They are also given paper and pencil to map their workflow in order to gain the intended information. The participants have to use both systems to get the result to see the usability, performance and correctness. There is no time limit to perform the task.

To examine Hypothesis 1, we take feedbacks from the groups about the ease of use and understandability of the systems through a questionnaire. We also consider the time taken for completing the complete set of queries.

To examine Hypothesis 2, we compare the performance of both systems while executing the queries. We also compare the performance of both groups in executing the different categories of queries.

To examine Hypothesis 3, the result of the queries that can be performed on both systems are compared and checked for accuracy.

4.3   Findings

As a result, we found that G1 performed all the queries faster with minimal use of paper and pencil. G2, on the other hand, performed all the queries taking more time and also showed the tendency to use paper and pencil to formulate the queries. We also found that more range of queries could be performed in Datawnt0 compared to IPAC web based system. Out of 25 queries, the participants in average could perform 22 queries in the Datawnt0 system in comparison to 11 queries in IPAC web based system (Fig. 7). The IPAC web based system could not perform most queries that required participants to use multiple objects. The experiment also found that Datawnt0 system perform most of the queries performed by IPAC web based system.

25 out of 30 participants stated that Datawnt0 was easier to understand and use. The results from both systems were also compared and returned same number of rows which means Datawnt0 system is accurate and corresponds with the source of PTF data (IPAC web system). Table 1 represents the range of queries supported by IPAC and Datawnt0 systems. IPAC only supports manual multi-object search where complex programming is required.

Table 1. Range of queries that can be performed

IPAC	Both systems	Datawnt0
Manual multi-object search	Single object search	Multi-object search
	Search entire fields and galaxies	

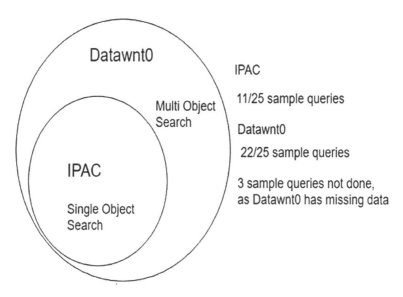

Fig. 7. Comparing the amount of queries the systems can perform

5 Summary and Conclusions

The astronomical domain has seen an exponential growth of data in recent years. The astronomical data provided by PTF is very large and has different varieties of data. It requires specific reorganizing of its catalog part and processing to import most recent data and images from the IPAC/IRSA database and store it in the local relational database. By use of polystore system, we have demonstrated how heterogeneous data can be managed and queried across multiple database engines. The proposal considers growth of data and scalability problems.

Analyzing the current scenario, there is a lack of proper query tools for supporting domain-specific language. Therefore, this study presents a workflow based query man-agreement system (Datawnt0) using the polystore database approach. We compared data access for PTF data with Datawnt0 and web based system of IPAC. As a result of an experiment, we found that by the use of workflow method, querying is easier and more understandable. Datawnt0 also supports multi-object search where users from astronomical domain do not have to write complex programs. Range of queries that can be performed is also higher in Datawnt0 because of multi-object search support.

Astronomical data archives in PTF is updated frequently. New database for Lightcurve data has been introduced. PTF collaboration with IPAC are planning to release new astronomical data soon as ZTF (Zwicky Transient Facility) [19]. So, to update our local database on a regular basis would provide a major challenge. In view of growth and scalability of the current system, we plan to include lightcurve data and all the new releases. We hope the scalability and growth of the system can be met with polystore database systems approach.

Appendix

Appendix 1: ER Model of the Database with Relations and Attributes

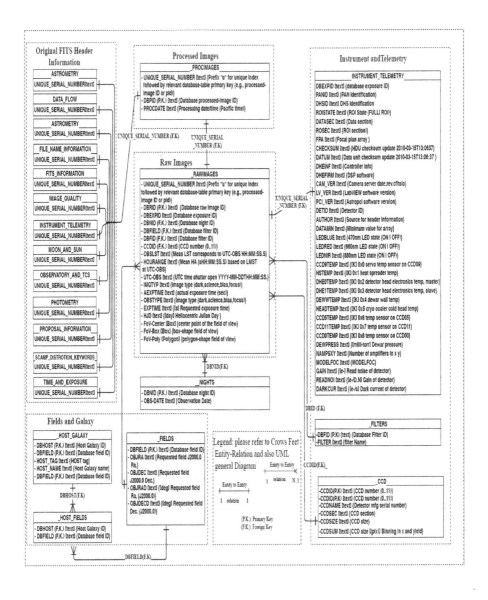

Appendix 2: List of Queries

1. Find all the images from the Host Galaxy 'm81'
2. Find all images where Field ID = '100043'
3. Find all images from Host Galaxy 'm44' where CCD ID = '2'
4. Find all images from Fields where Fields ID = '100045' and CCD ID = '5'
5. Find all images where Filter ID = '11' and Filter name = 'Ha656'
6. Find all images for the Asteroid name '20 massalia'.
7. Find all the images where Nights ID = '1001' from 2009-01-01 to 2010-03-03
8. Find all images where Field ID = '100001' and Night ID = '1014'
9. Find all images where Field ID = '100003' with Filter = 'R'
10. Find images with coordinates 12.3.634, −12.29167
11. Find all images where Field ID = '10027', Filter ID = '1' and CCDID = '7'
12. Find all images from Host Galaxy where CCD ID = '8'
13. Find all images from Nights where date is 2010-03-06 2010-03-05 with CCDID = '10'
14. Find all images from Host Galaxy where Field ID = '22683' and CCD ID = '9'
15. Find all images of CCD ID = '2' with CCD name 'w91c2'
16. Find all images of Galaxy = 'm81' with data product 'level 1'
17. Find all images of raw images with ID = '1772174'
18. Find all images of raw images with Field ID = '148577' and CCDID = '2'
19. Find all images from Night ID = '1000' with date 2011-06-06 2011-12-06 with CCD ID = '10'
20. Find all images from Filter with Field ID = 12234' and CCD ID = '2'.
21. Find all images where Filter ID = '1' and Filter name = 'g'.
22. Find all images by field position where OBJRAD = '127.41573' and OBJDECD = '32.625'.
23. Find all images from Nights from observation date (OBS-DATE) between 2009-01-01 to '2009-12-31'.
24. Find all images where Field ID = '110003' and galaxy name = 'M44'.
25. Find all images where Filter ID = '2'.

References

1. Palomar Transient Factory, July 2018. www.ptf.caltech.edu/iptf
2. NASA/IPAC Infrared Science Archive, July 2018. http://irsa.ipac.caltech.edu/ibe/index.html
3. Law, N.M., et al.: The Palomar Transient Factory: system overview, performance, and first results. Publ. Astron. Soc. Pac. **121**(886), 1395 (2009)
4. Rusu, F., Nugent, P., Wu, K.: Implementing the Palomar Transient Factory real-time detection pipeline in GLADE: results and observations. In: Madaan, A., Kikuchi, S., Bhalla, S. (eds.) DNIS 2014. LNCS, vol. 8381, pp. 53–66. Springer, Cham (2014). https://doi.org/10.1007/978-3-319-05693-7_4
5. Sloan Digital Sky Survey (SDSS), July 2018. www.sdss3.org
6. UCAC4 catalog, July 2018. http://cdsarc.u-strasbg.fr/viz-bin/Cat?I/322A

7. Information about FITS image, July 2018. https://fits.gsfc.nasa.gov/iaufwg/iaufwg.html

8. Lightcurve Database, July 2018. https://www.ptf.caltech.edu/page/lcgui

9. Cheng, Y., Qin, C., Rusu, F.: GLADE: big data analytics made easy. In: Proceedings of the 2012 ACM SIGMOD International Conference on Management of Data. ACM (2012)

10. General Information on IRSA/IPAC web systems. http://irsa.ipac.caltech.edu/applications/ptf/

11. Pence, W.D., et al.: Definition of the flexible image transport system (FITS), version 3.0. Astron. Astrophys. **524**, A42 (2010)

12. Ginsburg, A., Robitaille, T., Parikh, M.: Astroquery v0. 1 (2013)

13. Wu, Y., et al.: Query languages for domain specific information from PTF astronomical catalogs and data resources. In: BASE 2015 (2015). http://yilang.me/activity/BASE/2015/

14. NED/IPAC website, July 2018. https://ned.ipac.caltech.edu/

15. Gadepally, V., et al.: The BigDAWG polystore system and architecture. In: 2016 IEEE High Performance Extreme Computing Conference (HPEC). IEEE (2016)

16. Shrestha, S., et al.: Workflow based query management system for astronomical data repository. In: SoMeT, pp. 719–730 (2017)

17. Madaan, A., Bhalla, S.: Domain specific multistage query language for medical document repositories. Proc. VLDB Endow. **6**(12), 1410–1415 (2013)

18. Datawnt0 workflow based query system, July 2018. http://datawnt0.u-aizu.ac.jp/demo/dbv4-20180320/astrodemo-newdbv4/

19. Zwicky Transient Facility (ZTF), July 2018. http://www.ztf.caltech.edu/

Demonstration: API Federation in the BigDAWG Polystore

Matthew J. Mucklo[(✉)] [iD]

Massachusetts Institute of Technology, Cambridge, MA 02139, USA
mmucklo@mit.edu

Abstract. The BigDAWG polystore has been a successful demonstration of the principle that "one size does not fit all" in the world of database management. BigDAWG binds together multiple diverse sets of datastores to form a cohesive unit that allows users to focus their data analysis using the most appropriate store for data and the result set without the time consuming and cumbersome Extract-Transform-Load (ETL) pipelines and their associated setup processes. In this article, we introduce a new BigDAWG Island that can be used to pull data from API-based data sources to enrich the access to remote data and enhance BigDAWG's capabilities.

Keywords: Polystore · API · Federation · BigDAWG

1 Introduction

This paper introduces a system of federating data fed through APIs within a polystore. The polystore chosen for demonstration purposes is known as Big-DAWG - developed as a joint project across multiple universities, as well as with various other participants, and supported via the Intel Science and Technology Center for Big Data [4]. The notion of BigDAWG, of course, is to execute against the vision of "one size does not fit all" [3] by binding together disparate data storage systems from RDBMSes to text and stream stores to form a single cohesive system that excels at managing and processing data in the format that best suits both the data being processed and the desired result.

With the ever increasing number of systems offering API access over standard internet protocols such as HTTP and HTTPS, there's become an opportunity to offer greater integration with existing external data sources to enhance the ability to correlate data from not only within the polystore, but also without. Previously this would had to be accomplished via a standard ETL (extract-transform-load) against a third-party API into one of the RDBMS or other types of stores that the polystore supports. By allowing the polystore to directly access these systems without an ETL step, this enhancement to BigDAWG enables easier access to existing data available via these APIs. In addition it makes near realtime data access possible as well.

© Springer Nature Switzerland AG 2019
V. Gadepally et al. (Eds.): Poly 2018/DMAH 2018, LNCS 11470, pp. 93–103, 2019.
https://doi.org/10.1007/978-3-030-14177-6_8

One of the other considerations that came up when crafting the BigDAWG API integration was the ability to support multiple different types of APIs and various API authentication schemes. While only support for JSON over REST or a REST-like approach has been implemented so far, the ability exists to extend to the up-and-coming GraphQL format or even legacy protocols such as SOAP. Also the authentication features support both OAuth, Basic Authentication, Bearer Tokens, as well as url-based tokens with flexible parameters so that diverse APIs should be able to be connected to the system without a problem. These parameters were determined by taking a survey of a number of public APIs including some very well known ones, as well as those that were very domain-specific.

2   Island Architecture

The Island architecture of BigDAWG was used in order to implement this new feature [9]. As explained in previous papers [4] and online documentation [1], BigDAWG organizes its stores around the concepts of *Islands*. For example, there's a *Relational Island* which talks to RDBMSes such as Postgres, MySQL and Vertica, a *Text Island* which talks to the text key-value store Accumulo, an *Array-based Island* for talking to SciDB, as well as several others. The idea behind the Island concept is that each of these *Islands* represents a different data-model and language that would be hard to conform to anything else without loss of features or functionality. Largely the *Islands* expose much of the syntax of the underlying stores (SQL for the Relational Island, Array-based for SciDB, etc.).

Although discussion was made around making the API connection part of an existing *Island*, after studying the parameters needed and carefully considering the different types of APIs, it was decided that it would be most appropriate to create an entirely new *Island* to support the API queries. Presently, therefore a new *API Island* has been developed, and an initial proof-of-concept handler has been developed for that Island for REST-based APIs.

Underneath the hood, the REST API queries are made using the standard Java URLConnection libraries that ship with the JDK, however the methods for API authentication are abstracted in into their own separate classes. For example, there's a separate class for handling the OAuth2 authentication steps, which involves an initial query to fetch the appropriate authorization token, which is then cached in memory in BigDAWG for a configurable amount of time.

3   Cast

In addition a *cast* functionality is exposed via the BigDAWG architecture. *Casting* is a core feature of BigDAWG that enables the migration of data between various datastores [3,5]. For example, data may come into BigDAWG stuffed into standard SQL tables, but that doesn't limit it's processing to RDBMS-based queries. If, for instance, there was a large text field in one of the tables that contained doctors notes on patients, it might be better to *cast* that data over to a text store such as Accumulo, and using the Graphulo [2] extensions, one can then more easily do things such as calculate the Non-Negative Matrix Factorization on the data set [8].

By allowing data from an API to be cast into another data store, some of the basic limitations that APIs have are overcome. These limitations are typically greatly-constrained filtering, sorting, and aggregation abilities. However, these sort of querying operations are typically very easy for relational database systems of today's age to perform. By simply casting responses from the *API Island* into the *Relational Island* one can take full advantage of the capabilities of a well-established RDBMS such as Postgres.

The *cast* intelligently breaks the data into rows using the *result key* provided. Then it further breaks each row into columns using the headings provided in the response, even comparing each row's headers to previous row's headers in case the data is sparse (as possible in JSON) to make sure the full complement of headers is obtained. Finally as JSON data can be hierarchical, it also exposes the ability to further query nested objects using the PostgreSQL JSON query operators (See 1).

Further one can take advantage of the capabilities of the other stores to do additional processing on the data, by simply casting the data to a supported *Island*.

This capability works well with the philosophy of the polystore in that the different components of the system can be utilized for their strengths. For example, the collective amount of effort to write native support for supporting SQL-like queries against a public API could take months if not years of effort and culminate in the attempt to write an RDBMS on top of an API. Although though this may be a valiant effort (and even one considered at the start of this endeavor), it brings a certain amount of re-invent-the-wheel-ism to the approach. Contrastingly, with BigDAWG, one already has a state-of-the-art RDBMs system at hand. Depending on the data needs, it's a much easier effort to just allow the polystore to migrate the data to such a store and run a SQL query against a system that's designed for such uses.

```
bdrel(select text from bdcast( bdapi({ 'name' : 'twitter', '
    endpoint' : 'tweets', 'query' : { 'q': '#mit' } }), tab3,
    '(metadata json, text text)', relational)  where metadata
    ->> 'iso_language_code' = 'en')
```

Fig. 1. An example API query through BigDAWG cast to the Relational Island for processing

Another problem with a typical *raw* API response revolves around the fact that they don't usually allow for projections, such as using SELECT to return only the columns needed. While GraphQL [6] has provided a way to overcome that limitation, it is still new and not fully adopted across the industry, with the majority of APIs fully embracing REST at this point.

Consequently our query mechanism for APIs revolves around simply calling the API and passing the relevant parameters to it in order to gather a full JSON response. The *cast* ability of BigDAWG is what is fully relied in order to do relevant querying or composing of the data with other sources.

4   Design

One of the design considerations made with the BigDAWG API was to keep the interface simple and easy to understand. A similar format to the BigDAWG Accumulo interface was chosen - a pseudo-json like query definition language, but details abstracted away so that things such as the actual URL of the endpoint doesn't have to be entered on every query (see Fig. 2).

```
bdapi({ 'name' : 'twitter', 'endpoint' : 'tweets', 'query' : {
    'q': '#mit' } })
```

Fig. 2. API query: simple example

It was decided to support both parameterized and raw queries, where the parameterized version is generally turned into a URL-encoded query string that is passed to the endpoint, but could also become a JSON string depending on configuration parameters setup for the endpoint itself.

Configuration details for each endpoint are stored in the BigDAWG catalog. It was the vision of this project to also provide an easy to use Administrative interface for adding and managing these API stores. To this end, the BigDAWG admin-ui has been enhanced (see Fig. 3).

To smoothly Add, Edit, and Delete APIs, the existing administrative interface now has a new API page. In this page there are two tabs, one for showing the List of APIs, and one for adding or editing them.

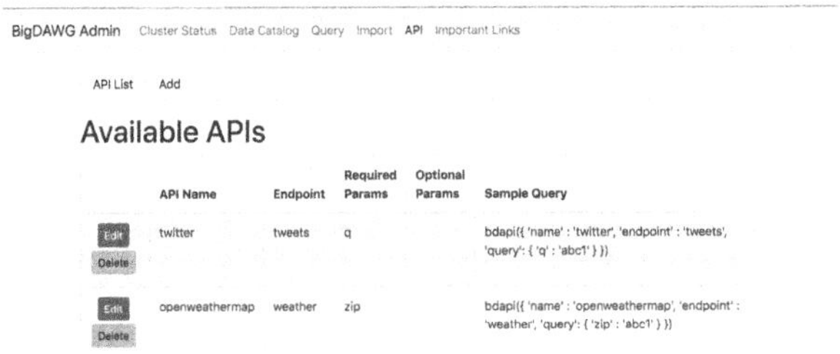

Fig. 3. BigDAWG List APIs

Also as detailed later, some new functionality has been added in addition to the API page, such as the ability to query, export to CSV, and import from CSV all from the same interface.

The idea with all of the administrative enhancements is to abstract away the details of managing the APIs into something easier to use. After spending time working with various APIs, it's amazing even among REST implementations the diversity of different manners of connecting to them. While the concept of REST is generally implemented as some form of JSON over HTTP (which albeit is not necessarily "true REST" [7]), and there is general agreement about using HTTP verbs to access Resources, the actual details of the means of access, from query parameters to authentication have significant variances (Fig. 4).

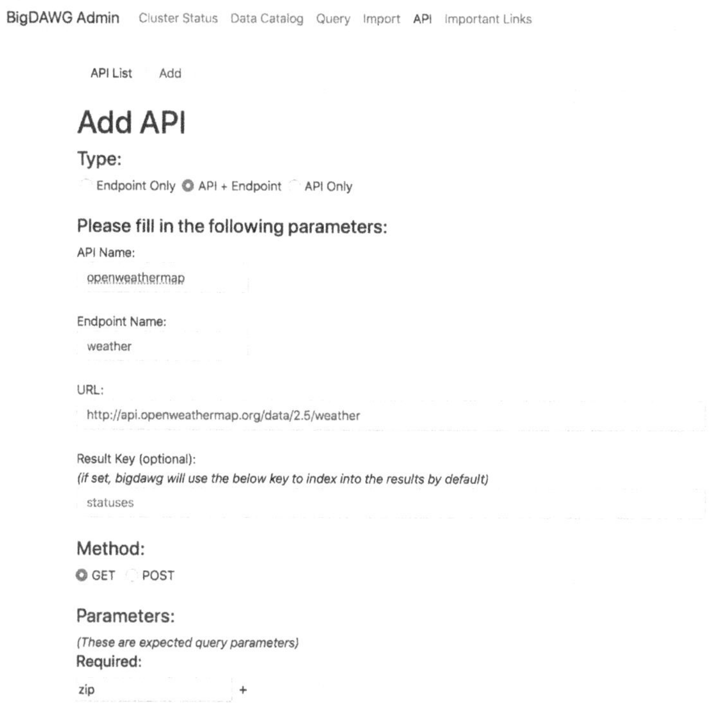

BigDAWG Admin   Cluster Status   Data Catalog   Query   Import   **API**   Important Links

API List   Add

Add API

Type:
   Endpoint Only ◉ API + Endpoint ⃝ API Only

Please fill in the following parameters:

API Name:
   openweathermap

Endpoint Name:
   weather

URL:
   http://api.openweathermap.org/data/2.5/weather

Result Key (optional):
(if set, bigdawg will use the below key to index into the results by default)
   statuses

Method:
◉ GET ⃝ POST

Parameters:
(These are expected query parameters)
Required:
   zip   +

Fig. 4. BigDAWG Add API administrative interface

Result Key. In order to support the ability to *cast* data into other formats, one additional parameter was necessary. When JSON-based results come back, typically they come back in object form, with a key, or series of keys that gives access into the actual array of entities. For instance, the twitter 7-day tweets API returns tweets under a key called "statuses" (see Fig. 5).

```
{
    "statuses": [
        { ... "text": "the text of the tweet", ... },
        { ... "text": "etc.", ... }
        ...
    ]
}
```

Fig. 5. Sample Twitter tweets.json API Response format

In order to extract these results into actual rows, one additional parameter that is the "key" into the results must be stored. Otherwise BigDAWG doesn't know how to properly index into the results. Presently this "result_key" is stored in the BigDAWG objects table in the catalog. For instance, the key stored in the case of a response like Fig. 5 would be "statuses".

5   Output

The raw output from a bdapi query is simply a list of entries sent back from the API endpoint. Using the "result_key" of "statuses" mentioned above, we're able to index into into the Twitter object that is returned in a typical tweets api response, and output a list of tweet objects similar to what is seen in Fig. 6.

```
{"metadata":{"result_type":"recent","iso_language_code":"ta"},"inreplyto...
{"metadata":{"result_type":"recent","iso_language_code":"es"},"inreplyto...
{"metadata":{"result_type":"recent","iso_language_code":"en"},"inreplyto...
...
```

Fig. 6. Sample (truncated) raw output from Twitter API indexed by the "statuses" key

The *cast* functionality of BigDAWG can then be used to further trim the results and manipulate them in the appropriate store. For example say one wanted to filter the results that came back by "iso_language_code" - one could do that by simply casting into the Relational Island and appending a where clause at the end of the query. An example of this sort of BigDAWG query can be seen in Fig. 7.

```
bdrel(select full_text from bdcast( bdapi({ 'name' : 'twitter
    ', 'endpoint' : 'tweets', 'query' : { 'q': '#mit', '
    tweet_mode': 'extended' } }), tab3, '(metadata json,
    full_text text)', relational) where metadata ->> '
    iso_language_code' = 'en')
```

Fig. 7. Casting the same query into the relational store and filtering by language code

The resulting output of such a query from Fig. 7 would look like the example in Fig. 8.

```
full_text
RT @southcinetalkie: Is #SureshChandra gave money to #MIT...
RT @MiriKrupkin: Selective hydrogel cake! Made from gummy...
RT @tn_ajith: This week #Kungumam Magazine about our #Thala...
Meet Mareena Robinson Snowden, the first black woman to...
...
```

Fig. 8. Sample (truncated) output from the bdcast in Fig. 7

5.1 Column Auto-Detection

When the data is *cast* into the relational store, the columns are chosen based on the key/value pairs in the JSON response object. This particular response has both a metadata column, and a full_text column which is utilized during the subsequent relational query. In fact the system detects that the metadata column contains a further JSON object, allowing us to index deeper into the object using a Postgres-style JSON query syntax (see Fig. 9).

```
where metadata ->> 'iso_language_code' = 'en'
```

Fig. 9. Highlight of the where clause illustrating the Postgres-style JSON query syntax

6 Future Work

Presently the data that comes back is either fed directly back to the requesting client, or stored in a temporary table for the duration of any *cast* operations. It would be perhaps a nice enhancement to add the ability to support the *caching* of data retrieved from APIs for a longer period of time. This would allow both offline or air-gapped processing, as well as the ability to store lengthy or historic result sets that perhaps take a significant amount of time to load over standard internet access.

Secondly while out of the box a number of query and authentication schemes are supported, it is by no means comprehensive as alluded elsewhere. Future work might be to enhance this effort with support for GraphQL, and other types of APIs (such as those that perhaps do a significant amount of asynchronous processing before allowing access to a result of a query).

Though the first implementation has been for REST base queries, the implementation should be generic enough to allow new *shims* (as they are called) to be added to the *API Island* in BigDAWG in order to support other types of API query languages.

7   Additional Administrative Enhancements

7.1   Import by CSV

During the course of this project, the BigDAWG administrative interface was also extended to enable importing of data via CSV.

One can upload a CSV file to the page, and choose an existing (see Fig. 10) or a new (see Fig. 11) table into which to insert the data. It will optionally check the headers of the CSV if they exist and compare them against those of the underlying table, or in the case of a new table use them as the basis of the "CREATE" statement.

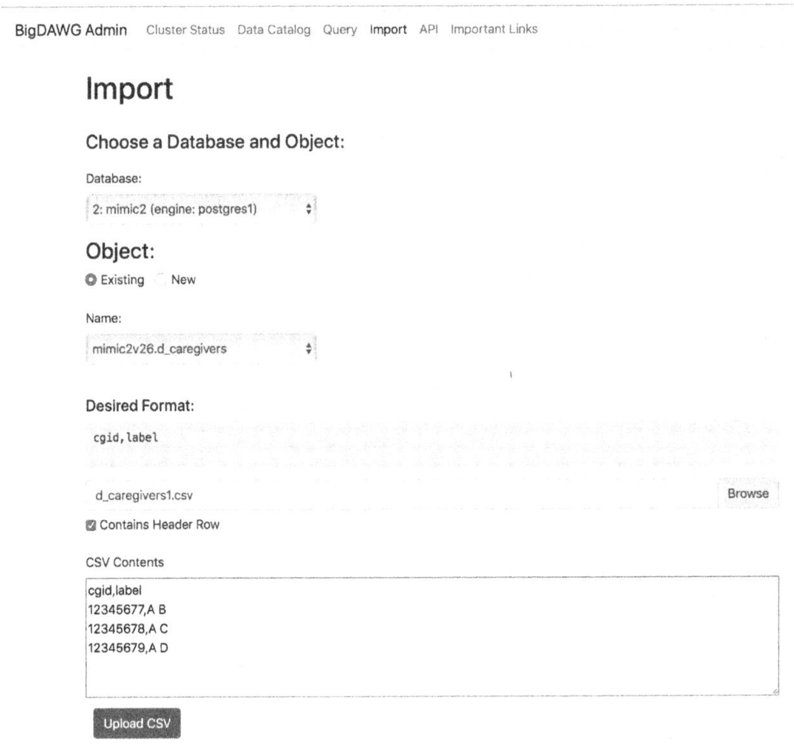

Fig. 10. BigDAWG import into existing interface

Further it allows one to specify column types for both the table definition, and the BigDAWG schema definition if appropriate.

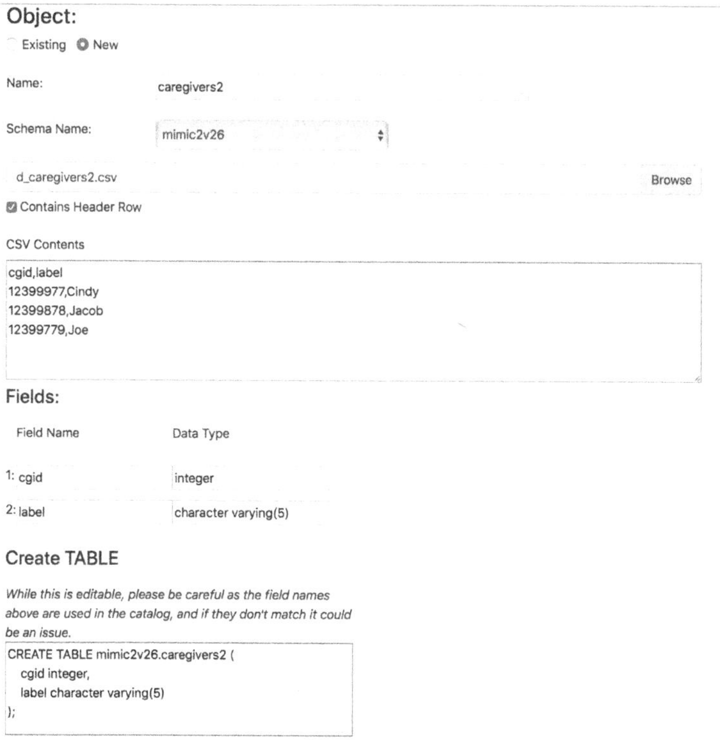

Object:

Existing ⦿ New

Name: caregivers2

Schema Name: mimic2v26   ⇕

d_caregivers2.csv   Browse
☑ Contains Header Row

CSV Contents

```
cgid,label
12399977,Cindy
12399878,Jacob
12399779,Joe
```

Fields:

Field Name   Data Type

1: cgid   integer

2: label   character varying(5)

Create TABLE

While this is editable, please be careful as the field names above are used in the catalog, and if they don't match it could be an issue.

```
CREATE TABLE mimic2v26.caregivers2 (
   cgid integer,
   label character varying(5)
);
```

Fig. 11. BigDAWG import into new interface

7.2 Query Page

One other thing that was done is to create a web-based query page that allows one to execute BigDAWG queries from within the browser, returning a formatted result (see Fig. 12).

Futher one can the export the results into a CSV if desired directly from the administrative interface. The hope is that this should make BigDAWG easier for researchers to work with in the future.

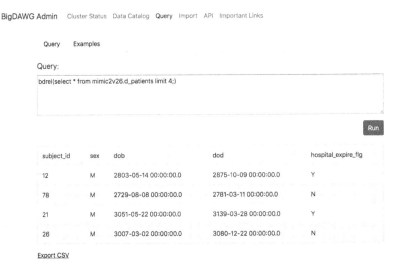

Fig. 12. BigDAWG new query page

8 Conclusion

Through this paper it's hoped to have given a brief overview of the BigDAWG subsystem for allowing a polystore to communicate to publicly available APIs without need of heavy customization (i.e. writing code). It's also hoped that some new additions to the BigDAWG administrative interface were adequately demonstrated that should make working with BigDAWG and APIs easier in the future.

Acknowledgments. The author would like to give special thanks to the following people for their contributions to the guidance of this project: Dr. Vijay Gadepally of MIT's Lincoln Labs for his continual oversight, wisdom, and attentiveness to having me see this through, Professor Samuel Madden for his oversight of the project and overall guidance and advising, plus Professor Michael Stonebraker for his initial guidance as well, all three of which have been influential contributors to BigDAWG in the past as well. The author thanks God for all the wonderful help and guidance that has been given and that he's received over the course of this project, he couldn't have done it without.

References

1. BigDAWG Polystore. http://bigdawg.mit.edu
2. Graphulo: Accumulo library of matrix math primitives and graph algorithms. http://graphulo.mit.edu/, https://github.com/Accla/graphulo
3. Gupta, A.M., Vijay Gadepally, M.S.: Cross-engine query execution in federated database systems. In: IEEE High Performance Extreme Computing (2016)

4. Duggan, J., et al.: The BigDAWG polystore system. ACM SIGMOD Rec. **44**, 11–16 (2015)
5. Dziedzic, A., Elmore, A.J., Stonebraker, M.: Data transformation and migration in polystores. In: IEEE High Performance Extreme Computing (2016)
6. Facebook Inc.: GraphQL — A query language for your API. https://graphql.org
7. Fowler, M.: Richardson maturity model - steps toward the glory of REST (2010). https://martinfowler.com/articles/richardsonMaturityModel.html
8. Gadepally, V.: BigDAWG polystore applied to MIMIC II medical dataset. https://www.youtube.com/watch?time_continue=299&v=1GjA2mJFBb0
9. Gadepally, V., et al.: The BigDAWG polystore system and architecture. In: IEEE High Performance Extreme Computing (2016)

DMAH 2018

Augmented Therapy with Online
Support Groups

Behrooz Omidvar-Tehrani[✉]

University of Grenoble Alpes, Grenoble, France
behrooz.omidvar-tehrani@univ-grenoble-alpes.fr

Abstract. Support groups are often formed in hospitals and clinics to enable group therapy. A support group consists of patients suffering from a same disease. Manual formation of support groups has three drawbacks. First, it is "local", i.e., a support group for a specific type of cancer in a local hospital may contain patients with different symptoms and treatments. Discussions in such heterogeneous groups are not necessarily useful for their members. Second, support groups are often "static" and do not meet emerging needs of patients. Third, there may not be enough motivation in patients to join such groups. In this paper, we use the social Web to envision a framework for the automatic formation of dynamic support groups. Our framework consists of several components to build support groups, motivate patients to join, and keep them engaged in those groups.

1   Introduction

Most medical operations consist of two different stages: *treatment* and *outcome*. The former begins as soon as a patient is detected with a disease and spans over the whole period of medical tests, check-ups and hospitalizations. The outcome, however, captures the final status of the patient after the treatment period, e.g., "survived" or "dead". Medical research has a focus on the outcome by investigating various directions from epidemiology to molecular bioscience. However, there has been less attention to psychological factors of patients during the treatment stage [1,2]. Patients often suffer from extreme depression or fear of the dire and unknown world of their disease.

Without loss of generality, we focus on "cancer" as an explicit use case. A cancer treatment is typically a 4 to 6-month period depending on the type and gravity. Beside physical burdens in this period (e.g., going through a tunnel for positron emission tomography, losing hair due to Chemotherapy, constant feeling of nausea, etc.), the patient should resist a high mental pressure as well. This pressure often leads to depression and treatment deprivation, as the patient feels that he/she is approaching death [3].

If patients keep an optimistic and positive mood during the treatment process, this will reduce tension, anxiety, tiredness and depression [4,5]. It has been frequently shown in the literature that *group therapy* has direct impact on the

© Springer Nature Switzerland AG 2019
V. Gadepally et al. (Eds.): Poly 2018/DMAH 2018, LNCS 11470, pp. 107–114, 2019.
https://doi.org/10.1007/978-3-030-14177-6_9

treatment process, by letting the patient know how similar cases are going [6–9]. Formation of support groups is a common practice in hospitals and clinics to enable group therapy [10,11]. A support group consists of patients suffering from a same disease and a moderator (i.e., a medical doctor) to lead discussions between the group members. However, there exists three main drawbacks for this implementation of group therapy, i.e., "locality", "staticity", and "reluctance".

Locality. A support group for patients suffering from a specific type of cancer may contain patients with totally different symptoms and treatments. This is because there exists vast amount of sub-categories in cancers (e.g., see [12] for the case of breast cancer). However, a hospital has only access to local patients. In case a world-wide audience is available, more specific and homogeneous groups can be tailored whose members can be cherry-picked to derive more insightful discussions.

Staticity. Support groups are often static, i.e., they are built only based on pre-defined statistics in a medial unit. For instance, University Hospital of Cleveland lists 15 different static support groups for patients suffering from Alzheimer, Breast cancer, weight loss, etc.[1] As these groups do not regularly evolve over time, they do not meet emerging needs of patients.

Reluctance. Patients with cancer may not necessarily feel motivated for any social involvement including support groups [13]. There should be visible motivations and explicit benefits in the support group to capture patients' verve.

We believe that the social Web provides an infrastructure for methods which can address the aforementioned deficiencies. Users express their likes and dislikes and share their experiences in different platforms of the social Web [14]. This opportunity can be investigated for the development of tools which enable the automatic formation of dynamic support groups in a global spectrum.

Beyond general-use social networks such as Twitter and Facebook, there are many instances of patient-oriented networks where patients can share experiences with their peers. Examples are PATIENTSLIKEME for connecting patients together suffering from any disease, WHATNEXT and CAREACROSS for patients with cancer, BEN'S FRIENDS for patients with rare diseases or chronic illnesses, and MyGlu for patients with type-1 diabetes. Although these networks overcome the challenge of locality, still groups should be created manually (i.e., the challenge of staticity) and patients should seek and join those groups all by themselves (i.e., the challenge of reluctance).

In this paper, we propose a framework on top of the data collected from the online activities of patients in the social Web, in order to automatically build dynamic groups, recommend them to patients to join, and keep them engaged. Section 2 details the components of our proposed framework.

---

[1] http://www.uhhospitals.org/health-and-wellness/support-groups.

Table 1. Patient demographics.

Attributes → Examples ↓	Gender	Age category	Occupation	Location	Life status
p_1	Female	Young	Student	Paris	Alive
p_2	Male	Old	Teacher	Rio	Dead

Table 2. Patient activities.

Attributes → Examples ↓	Patient	Activity	Time
a_1	p_1	Posted a comment about "anemia"	May 22, 2018
a_2	p_2	Is diagnosed with "lymphoma" cancer	June 12, 2018

2   System Overview

We propose a framework which exploits the social Web in order to automatically construct and recommend support groups to patients. This augments the human-oriented quality of the treatment stage.

We follow our discussion with an example to motivate our approach using a real-world scenario. Consider Julia who is suffering from kidney cancer and her blood pressure is often running high at night. But she is not able or doesn't feel motivated to seek the causality and solution. In case a group of patients is already formed whose members are all suffering from the same cancer (with same symptoms), she could see the profiles of other people like her, and see where she falls relative to the "norm".

Terabytes of online activities are available in the social Web. Beyond activities, each user is also associated to a set of demographics (e.g., age, gender, birth location and occupation). We rely on this data to automatically build support groups for patients with similar profiles. A support group G consists of n patients $G = \{p_1, p_2 \ldots p_n\}$ with at least one common demographic or activity. For instance, the set of all female patients forms a group G_1. Also, the set of all patients suffering from kidney cancer forms another group G_2. Obviously, groups may overlap: a female patient suffering from kidney cancer is a member of both G_1 and G_2. In order to tackle the aforementioned challenges (i.e., locality, staticity, and reluctance), our framework contains five following components (**C1** to **C5**), from preparing data for dynamic group formation, to engaging patients in groups.

C1: Data Preparation. Our first necessary step is to prepare data for a fruitful group formation. Our data comes from various sources: social networks, local resources such as cancer research centers (e.g., Cancer Data Warehouse, abbr., CDW) and existing support groups. Hence there should be "data integration" and "data cleaning" steps right after collecting the data from the resources. Tasks include anonymizing data of real patients to protect their privacy and conform with GDPR [15], matching schemata to a unified schema, and prune incorrect and unnecessary data.

In [16], we consider a gold-standard data structure for the collected data, shown in Tables 1 and 2. Patient demographics (Table 1) are obtained either in an admission process prior to a hospitalization, or in an online registration in a health-oriented social network. We assume that demographics do not change in time. Patient activities (Table 2) reflect either health-care interactions (e.g., diagnoses, compliances, marker reads) or what patients do online. We call the online activities of patients, "discussions".

C2: Group Formation. Once the data is ready-to-use, we discover interesting support groups in a dynamic fashion. Any subset of patients with at least one common demographic or activity can form a group. However, a set of "interesting support groups" should adhere to the following desiderata [17].

- *Coverage.* Together, the set of support groups should cover most patients in the data. While ideally we would like each and every patient to belong to at least one support group, that is not always feasible due to other desiderata associated with the set of groups. Given a set of support groups $\mathcal{G} = \{G_1, G_2, \dots\}$ and the set of patients $\mathcal{P}$, we define coverage as in Eq. 1.

$$coverage(\mathcal{G}, \mathcal{P}) = |\cup_{G \in \mathcal{G}} (p \in \mathcal{P}, p \in G)|/|\mathcal{P}| \qquad (1)$$

- *Diversity.* Support groups need to be different from each other in order to provide complementary information. The diversity of a set of support groups $\mathcal{G}$ is computed as follows.

$$diversity(\mathcal{G}, \mathcal{P}) = 1/(1 + \Sigma_{G,G' \in \mathcal{G}} |p \in \mathcal{P}, p \in G \wedge p \in G'|) \qquad (2)$$

- *Cardinality.* The number of returned support groups should not be too high in order to prevent information overload. Also each single support group should contain a minimum number of patients to be meaningful.

We employ the group set discovery approach that we proposed in [17] which returns a group set $\mathcal{G}$ where $diversity(\mathcal{G}, \mathcal{P})$ and $coverage(\mathcal{G}, \mathcal{P})$ are maximized simultaneously. The size of the set $\mathcal{G}$ is bounded to an input parameter k, where k is often considered to be a small value [18]. Each support group is also verified to contain more users than a given frequency threshold.

C3: Group Recommendation. Once the set of all groups is mined, we recommend a limited set of groups to each patient. We employ a group navigation approach that we proposed in [19] to iteratively refine the recommendation list based on patient's feedback (likes and dislikes about recommended groups). At each iteration, the patient receives k different support groups, each described by common demographics and activities of its members. The patient picks one group out of k. In the next iteration, the system will immediately return k other groups which are highly relevant to the selected group. The patient may join a group and stop the navigation at any time. The goal is to motivate the patient by showing the most relevant set of groups which is in line with patient's preferences.

C4: Discussion Recommendation. A patient may join one or several groups. Then she needs to reach useful discussions in each group. An example of a discussion in support groups is shown in Table 2 where patient p_1, a young female student in Paris, posts a comment about "anemia" on May 22, 2018. A valid assumption is that the patient may not be interested to skim over all previous discussions. Hence, we employ a recommendation approach which discovers discussions which are more suited for the patient by considering her profile. Given the preferences of the patient, collaborative filtering [20,21] is the best fit for recommending discussions.

In order to quantify the recommendation value of a discussion a for a patient p_1, we need to know either the similarity of p_1's discussions and a (item-item collaborative filtering), or the similarity of p_1 and another patient p_2 who liked a (user-user collaborative filtering). The similarity between two patients p_1 and p_2 is computed using $cosine(\overrightarrow{p_1}, \overrightarrow{p_2})$ where $\overrightarrow{p}$ is a vector which concatenates p's demographics and p's activities. The similarity between a patient p and a discussion a is computed using the cosine between TF-IDF vectors of p's discussions and the discussion a.

C5: Engagement. The other need in our approach is to keep patients engaged in joined groups, as their motivations may quickly drop [22]. This is only possible if patients take an active role in the group through personalization [23]. For this aim, we employ a question-answering system [24] which discovers the best set of proactive questions (in form of questions like *"did you know"* or *"do you think"*) to engage patients in group discussions. We are inspired from related work on routing "right questions" to "right users" [25,26] to outguess patients' interest and keep them motivated.

We also build a *time decay* model which determines the domain of engaging questions [27,28]. At early stages, the system *explores* different domains of discussions to capture patient's reaction. At later stages, the system *exploits* previously well-adopted domains to reduce the risk of losing the patient.

3   Use Case

We provide an example which describes one real-world use case of our approach and shows the functionality of each component in practice (Fig. 1). Our data preparation component (i.e., component **C1**) collects data from the PATIENTS-LIKEME network to obtain all users who talked about "cancer" and its relevant terms, at least once. We obtain around 3000 patients. Our group formation component (i.e., component **C2**) constructs various dynamic groups. Julia (suffering from kidney cancer) has already subscribed to our framework via her hospital. Our system then recommends her (i.e., component **C3**) to join three following groups: *"genetic-based cancers"*, *"patients with Renal cell carcinoma"*, *"patients concerned with blood pressure"*. Julia decides to join the second and third group.

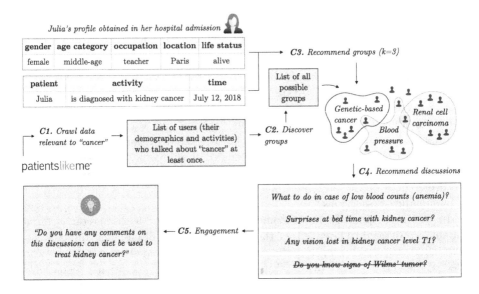

Fig. 1. Components of our framework for automatic construction and recommendation of dynamic support groups.

There exist one million discussions in the selected groups. Each discussion in a support group is posted by one of the members of that group. Our discussion recommendation component (**C4**) selects three following discussions for Julia: *"what to do in case of low blood counts (anemia)?"*, *"surprises at bed time with kidney cancer"* and *"any vision lost in kidney cancer level T1?"*. Note that an example discussion *"do you know signs of Wilms' tumor?"* does not show up for Julia, because she has already shown interest in the second group (i.e., patients suffering from Renal cell carcinoma) which potentially means that her cancer type is RCC and not Wilms tumor.

Julia delves into the second discussion where she finds some common experiences about her problem of having high blood pressure at night. She reads the discussion posted by a group member and understands that her problem is common among others as well. A week later, our engagement component (**C5**) will send a notification to Julia and asks her the following question: *"do you have any comments on this discussion: can diet be used to treat kidney cancer?"*. The system picks this specific discussion for her because Julia has already investigated other discussions about diet.

4   Conclusion

Group therapy can increase the quality of the treatment phase by making patients more social and knowledgeable about their disease. The availability of social data enables our approach to go beyond local and manual discussions and provide global insights. This paper discusses our proposed framework for automatic construction and recommendation of dynamic support groups as a means for group therapy. Our immediate future direction is to run an extensive user study to evaluate the usability and adaptability of the system in practice.

Acknowledgment. The author would like to thank Sihem Amer-Yahia for her valuable comments about this paper. This work is partially supported by CDP LIFE project under grant C7H-ID16-PR4-LIFELIG and COFECUB-CAPES 2018 project under grant 40022TB.

References

1. Parush, A., Parush, D., Ilan, R.: Human factors in healthcare: a field guide to continuous improvement. Synth. Lect. Assistive, Rehabilitative, Health-Preserving Technol. **6**(1), i202 (2017)
2. Conti, C.M., Maccauro, G., Fulcheri, M.: Psychological stress and cancer (2011)
3. Cancer Center: Cancer-related depression: what is it and what can you do about it? (2017). https://www.cancercenter.com/discussions/blog/cancer-related-depression-what-is-it-and-what-can-you-do-about-it/
4. The American Cancer Society: Attitudes and cancer (2014). http://www.cancer.org
5. The American Cancer Society: Anxiety, fear, and depression: having cancer affects your emotional health (2016). http://www.cancer.org
6. Cain, E.N., Kohorn, E.I., Quinlan, D.M., Latimer, K., Schwartz, P.E.: Psychosocial benefits of a cancer support group. Cancer **57**, 183–189 (1986)
7. Klemm, P., Reppert, K., Visich, L.: A nontraditional cancer support group. The internet. Comput. Nurs. **16**(1), 31–36 (1998)
8. Høybye, M.T., Johansen, C., Tjørnhøj-Thomsen, T.: Online interaction. Effects of storytelling in an internet breast cancer support group. Psycho-Oncology **14**(3), 211–220 (2005)
9. Orenstein, B.W.: Benefits of group therapy in mental health treatment (2014). http://www.everydayhealth.com/news/benefits-group-therapy-mental-health-treatment/
10. Ussher, J., Kirsten, L., Butow, P., Sandoval, M.: What do cancer support groups provide which other supportive relationships do not? The experience of peer support groups for people with cancer. Soc. Sci. Med. **62**(10), 2565–2576 (2006)
11. BCancer.Net Editorial Board: Support groups (2016). http://www.cancer.net/coping-with-cancer/finding-support-and-information/support-groups
12. Yersal, O., Barutca, S.: Biological subtypes of breast cancer: prognostic and therapeutic implications. World J. Clin. Oncol. **5**(3), 412 (2014)
13. Aabom, B., Pfeiffer, P.E.R.: Why are some patients in treatment for advanced cancer reluctant to consult their GP? Scand. J. Prim. Health Care **27**(1), 58–62 (2009)
14. Swan, M.: Crowdsourced health research studies: an important emerging complement to clinical trials in the public health research ecosystem. J. Med. Internet Res. **14**(2), e46 (2012)
15. Irwin, L.: The GDPR: what exactly is personal data? (2018). https://www.itgovernance.eu/blog/en/the-gdpr-what-exactly-is-personal-data
16. Omidvar-Tehrani, B., Amer-Yahia, D., Lakshmanan, L.: Cohort representation and exploration. In: 2017 IEEE International Conference on Data Science and Advanced Analytics (DSAA). IEEE (2018)

17. Omidvar-Tehrani, B., Amer-Yahia, S., Dutot, P.-F., Trystram, D.: Multi-objective group discovery on the social web. In: Frasconi, P., Landwehr, N., Manco, G., Vreeken, J. (eds.) ECML PKDD 2016. LNCS (LNAI), vol. 9851, pp. 296–312. Springer, Cham (2016). https://doi.org/10.1007/978-3-319-46128-1_19

18. Miller, G.: Human memory and the storage of information. IRE Trans. Inf. Theory **2**(3), 129–137 (1956)

19. Omidvar-Tehrani, B., Amer-Yahia, S., Termier, A.: Interactive user group analysis. In: Proceedings of the 24th ACM International on Conference on Information and Knowledge Management, pp. 403–412. ACM (2015)

20. Sarwar, B., Karypis, G., Konstan, J., Riedl, J.: Item-based collaborative filtering recommendation algorithms. In: Proceedings of the 10th International Conference on World Wide Web, pp. 285–295. ACM (2001)

21. Adomavicius, G., Tuzhilin, A.: Toward the next generation of recommender systems: a survey of the state-of-the-art and possible extensions. IEEE Trans. Knowl. Data Eng. **6**, 734–749 (2005)

22. Heldman, A.B., Schindelar, J., Weaver, J.B.: Social media engagement and public health communication: implications for public health organizations being truly "social". Public Health Rev. **35**(1), 13 (2013)

23. Mobasher, B., Cooley, R., Srivastava, J.: Automatic personalization based on web usage mining. Commun. ACM **43**, 142–151 (2000)

24. Sun, H., Ma, H., He, X., Yih, W., Su, Y., Yan, C.: Table cell search for question answering. In: Proceedings of the 25th International Conference on World Wide Web, pp. 771–782. International World Wide Web Conferences Steering Committee (2016)

25. Dror, G., Koren, Y., Maarek, Y., Szpektor, I.: I want to answer; who has a question?: Yahoo! answers recommender system. In: Proceedings of the 17th ACM SIGKDD International Conference on Knowledge Discovery and Data Mining, pp. 1109–1117. ACM (2011)

26. Geiger, D., Schader, M.: Personalized task recommendation in crowdsourcing information systems-current state of the art. Decis. Support Syst. **65**, 3–16 (2014)

27. Koren, Y.: Collaborative filtering with temporal dynamics. In: Proceedings of the 15th ACM SIGKDD International Conference on Knowledge Discovery and Data Mining, pp. 447–456. ACM (2009)

28. Zhou, S., Valentine, M., Bernstein, M.S.: In search of the dream team: temporally constrained multi-armed bandits for identifying effective team structures. In: Proceedings of the 2018 CHI Conference on Human Factors in Computing Systems, p. 108. ACM (2018)

RHCS - A Clinical Recommendation System for Geriatric Patients

Saliha Irem Besik[1,2(✉)] and Ferda Nur Alpaslan[2]

[1] Department of Computer Science,
Humboldt-Universität zu Berlin, Berlin, Germany
besiksal@informatik.hu-berlin.de
[2] Department of Computer Engineering,
Middle East Technical University, Ankara, Turkey
alpaslan@ceng.metu.edu.tr

Abstract. Medication errors caused by the mistakes of healthcare professionals are still one of the leading causes of death. The problem is even more serious with the elderly people suffering from multiple health problems at the same time. Clinical recommendation systems can be used to prevent such medication errors. In this paper, we present our clinical recommendation system (*RHCS*) which generates drug recommendations to assist healthcare professionals in making decisions on treatment process of geriatric patients. Geriatric patients refer to elderly patients aged 65 years or over. One of the distinctive points of our study lies in the methodology used, which is empowering collaborative filtering recommendation approach with historical data of geriatric patients. Its ontology-based approach and compatibility with clinical classification systems also make this study prominent. We evaluated *RHCS* with different types of evaluation metrics, and the results show that it is promising.

Keywords: Recommendation systems · Collaborative filtering · Ontology · Data mining · Similarity measures

1 Introduction

The healthcare of geriatric patients is a complex and error-prone process. Geriatric patients are highly vulnerable to chronic diseases and they tend to take several different drugs at the same time [1]. Therefore, healthcare professionals should put a special effort in order to avoid the risk of making medication errors. In this regard, clinical recommendation systems are important by aiding healthcare professionals during clinical decision-making.

Our proposed system *RHCS* generates drug recommendations as Anatomical Therapeutic Chemical (ATC) Classification System codes. ATC classification mechanism is an international standard to classify drugs according to their active ingredients. We follow this standard because recommending drug names is not

© Springer Nature Switzerland AG 2019
V. Gadepally et al. (Eds.): Poly 2018/DMAH 2018, LNCS 11470, pp. 115–132, 2019.
https://doi.org/10.1007/978-3-030-14177-6_10

a proper way to recommend drugs. Different drugs might have similar active ingredients and therefore they have similar treatment effects on diseases. *RHCS* is compatible with ICD-10 coding mechanism which is an international classification system for diagnoses. We use ICD-10 diagnoses codes to define diagnoses because working with textual diagnosis data is both error-prone and costly. We also use a clinical ontology, SNOMED CT, in order to examine the relationships between different diagnoses.

RHCS uses a collaborative filtering recommendation approach which is empowered by historical data of patients. So, it generates recommendations by considering both medical records of different similar patients and historical medical records of the patients themselves. Although *RHCS* is specialized for geriatric patients, our methodology can be adapted to different age groups.

We evaluated *RHCS* through both offline experiments with historical patient data taken by Ankara Numune Hospital and user studies conducted with medical doctors. Offline experiment results are evaluated by three well-known types of metrics which are precision, recall, and f-measure.

The remainder of this paper is organized as follows: Sect. 2 gives some background information about clinical classification systems and clinical ontology used in *RHCS*. Section 3 explains *RHCS* in detail which includes information on how to prepare data, how to define similarity and how to implement recommendation system. Section 4 evaluates RHCS with different evaluation metrics and shows the results. Section 5 discusses the related work on clinical recommendation systems. Finally, Sect. 6 concludes with a summary and future research work based on *RHCS*.

2   Background and Terminology

RHCS follows two international clinical classification standards which are ATC and ICD-10 and it works integrated with a clinical ontology (SNOMED CT). In this section, we give some background information about these classification mechanisms and SNOMED CT as a clinical ontology.

2.1   ATC Classification System

ATC classification system is used for classifying drugs according to their active ingredients. ATC classification system is controlled by the World Health Organization Collaborating Centre for Drug Statistics Methodology (WHOCC). The significant principals for ATC classification can be listed as follows:

- In ATC system, drugs are classified in groups at five different levels. As an example, the ATC code of *metformin* "*A10BA02*" which is at 5th level. 1st level is "*A*", 2nd level is "*A10*", 3rd level is "*A10B*", 4th level is "*A10BA*" and finally 5th level is "*A10BA02*".
- In order to treat a certain disease, health professionals can use different drugs with same or similar active ingredients. Different drugs with same ingredients

have similar effects on treatment. Drugs having ATC codes same until 3rd level can be considered as similar. For instance, *lidocaine* with ATC code *"N01BB02"* and *prilocaine* with ATC code *"N01BB04"* can be considered as similar.

2.2 ICD-10 Classification System

The International Classification of Diseases (ICD) is a standard classification system developed by World Health Organization (WHO). It is "the standard diagnostic tool for epidemiology, health management and clinical purposes" [2]. The diagnoses and their correlated ICD-10 codes can be accessed online on WHO website. For instance; the ICD-10 code of the diagnosis "Hypertensive heart disease with (congestive) heart failure" is *"I11.0"*.

2.3 SNOMED CT as Clinical Ontology

Ontology is an agreed-upon vocabulary compromising set of semantically related "concepts" in order to exchange information in a domain. SNOMED CT is a clinical healthcare terminology file that includes three main types of components which are concepts, descriptions, and relationships [3].

- Concepts are unique clinical definitions which are organized into hierarchies. Related concepts range from general to specific within a hierarchy.
- Descriptions are textual explanations of concepts in order to make concepts human readable.
- Relationships are links between related concepts.

Within SNOMED CT Release, there are mapping files to other code systems and classifications including ICD-10. ICD-10 mapping file consists of SNOMED CT concept ids and textual SNOMED CT descriptions; and their correlated ICD-10 codes and textual ICD-10 descriptions. For instance, diagnosis *"Pneumonia in mycosis"* is coded as *"J17.2"* in ICD-10 classification. The corresponding SNOMED CT concept is —*Pneumonia in aspergillosis (disorder)*— and the corresponding concept id is *"111900000"*.

3 Methodology

Figure 1 illustrates the conceptual diagram of our research. There are two major modules which are "Electronic Health Record Module" and "Main Module". Electronic Health Record Module prepares clinical data for reliable analysis. Main Module is used to generate recommendation list. It generates top-K treatment plans as ATC codes. "K" is the size of the recommendation list. We will explain how to determine "K" in Sect. 4. This decision is made empirically after some logical statements.

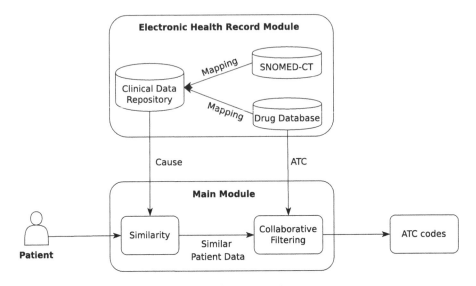

Fig. 1. System architecture for RHCS.

3.1   Data Preparation

We used only real data in order to have a platform being suitable for real-life scenarios. Our main database, "Clinical Data Repository" (CDR), is a patient database of Ankara Numune Hospital which includes the data of inmate patients who are older than 65 (geriatrics). CDR includes medical data of patients which are complaints, laboratory procedures, diagnosis, and drugs used for treatment. We also used two explicit knowledge sources which are a drug database used for classifying drugs and a clinical ontology (SNOMED CT) to understand the relationships between diagnoses.

Preparing Complaints Data: CDR includes textual complaints data which have misspellings and noise. We corrected them manually and grouped the similar complaints into one. We created separate fields for each complaint. We filled them with "1" if a patient has that complaint, and "0" otherwise.

Preparing Diagnoses Data: Ignoring the tuple with missing prominent features is a common way to get rid of incomplete data. In our case, information related to diagnoses are indispensable. Therefore, we simply eliminated the tuples with missing diagnosis codes. After data cleaning, we integrated SNOMED CT ontology to determine the relationships between diagnoses. CDR includes ICD-10 codes to define diagnoses, we converted those ICD-10 diagnoses codes into SNOMED CT concept-ids by using SNOMED CT ontology. We created separate fields for each diagnosis. We filled them with "1" if a patient has that diagnosis, and "0" otherwise.

Preparing Laboratory Data: We worked with medical domain experts to determine diseases which are detected by laboratory procedures. For instance, for blood glucose test, we have two related diseases, which are *hyperglycemia* (high blood sugar) and *hypoglycemia* (low blood sugar). We used test results of patients and reference range values to determine whether patients have that diseases. For instance, for glucose laboratory reference ranges in healthy adults is 65–110 mg/dL. A patient whose blood glucose test result is lower than 65 can be diagnosed as *hypoglycemia*. We created separate fields for each laboratory procedure related disease. We filled them with "1" if a patient has that disease, and "0" otherwise.

Preparing Drugs Data: CDR includes barcodes to identify the drugs. We eliminated the tuples with missing drug barcodes. We then converted these drug barcodes into ATC codes through a drug database.

Transformation Phase: When we used collaborative filtering algorithm [16] with data from our CDR, *RHCS* generated recommendations based on only a few similar patients. It was because geriatric patients, in general, use lots of drugs and it restricts *RHCS* to generate diverse drug recommendations and so decrease the success of the system. Hence, we needed to transform our data into a more convenient format.

After data cleaning and data integration phases, we had almost prepared (clean, meaningful and structured) data. For each patient, we had information about complaints, diagnoses, laboratory procedures and the active ingredients of the drugs used. However, we were not able to comprehend the direct reason behind the usage of these drugs. The reason could be based on a diagnosis or a complaint or the result of a laboratory procedure. In order to determine the exact reasons for use of drugs, we worked with medical domain experts and we used different clinical guidelines and books [4–7]. By referring these guidelines and books, we manually determined the causes (complaints or diagnoses or laboratory procedures) which can be correlated to each drug.

Table 1 is an illustrative example for patient data before transformation phase. In this example, a patient with complaints (Hypertension, Asthenia, Fever, Cough, Nasal Obstruction) is diagnosed with Acute Sinusitis. S/he has two laboratory results which are outside of reference range (Hyperglycaemia and Albumin deficiency). S/he uses drugs listed as ATC codes which are given in alphabetical order.

In transformation phase, we manually determined correlation between *causes* and *ATC codes*. Table 2 illustrates the patient data used in Table 1 after transformation phase. In this example; complaints, diagnosis and laboratory procedures are all considered as *causes*. As it is shown in the example, some causes might not have a corresponding ATC code and some others might have more than one. There might be some overlapping conditions as well, for instance *"R05C"* and *"R05D"* ATC codes can be used for both "Cough" and "Acute Sinusitis".

Table 1. An example of patient data before transformation phase.

Complaints	Diagnosis	Lab	ATC-Codes
Hypertension, Asthenia, Fever, Cough, Nasal Obstruction	Acute Sinusitis	Hyperglycaemia, Albumin deficiency	A10A, B05A, C09C, J01C, J01E, J01F, M01A, N02B, R01A, R05C, R05D

We defined a frequency measure named as "priority score" (Eq. 1) to determine how frequent to use a certain ATC code to treat an illness based on a
certain cause. As it is shown in Table 2, "Acute Sinusitis" can be treated with
7 different ATC codes. For each of these ATC codes, priority scores were calculated. For instance, $priority - score_{AcuteSinusitis,J01C}$ is 70%. It means within
all patients diagnosed as "Acute Sinusitis", 70% of them use drugs with *"J01C"*
ATC code.

$$priority - score_{d,ATC} = \frac{\# \ of \ patients \ with \ d \ using \ ATC}{\# \ of \ patients \ with \ d} \qquad (1)$$

In the priority-score calculation, there is an exceptional case; when some ATC
codes can be used for more than one cause. In such cases, we first determined
main cause regarding that ATC code usage. We used the same formula (Eq. 1) to
calculate the priority score of that main cause; however for the other additional
causes we used Eq. 2 where c is main cause to use *ATC*. For instance; as it is
shown in Table 2, *"R05C"* ATC code can be used for both "Cough" complaint

Table 2. An example of patient data after transformation phase.

Cause	ATC	Priority (%)
Acute Sinusitis	J01C	70
	J01E	30
	J01F	10
	M01A	20
	R01A	60
	R05C	60
	R05D	40
Albumin deficiency	B05A	90
Fever	N02B	90
Nasal Obstruction	R01A	95
Hyperglycaemia	A10A	30
Hypertension	C09C	20
Cough	R05C	70
	R05D	70

and "Acute Sinusitis" diagnosis. But, the main cause to use *"R05C"* is based on "Cough" complaint. Hence, $priority - score_{Cough,R05C}$ is calculated as in Eq. 1. However, for "Acute Sinusitis" diagnosis, $priority - score_{AcuteSinusitis,R05C}$ is calculated with Eq. 2 where c; main cause; is "Cough".

$$priority - score_{d,ATC} = \frac{\# \text{ of patients with } d \text{ not having } c \text{ who use } ATC}{\# \text{ of patients with } d \text{ not having } c}$$
(2)

3.2 Similarity Measures

After transformation phase, we had several different causes of different illnesses and corresponding treatment plans as ATC codes. We considered these entries as "patient entries" since these cause-ATC mappings belong to patients. We represented each of these patient entries as a vector. We used Algorithm 1 to define the vectorial representation of patient entries in CDR.

Algorithm 1. Pseudo code for the algorithm to define a vectorial representation for patient entries in the database.

$P \leftarrow$ patient vector space

$v(pM) \leftarrow$ vectorial representation of patient-entryM

$v(pM) \in P$

$diagnosis_{iM} \leftarrow$ "1" if the patient-entryM is related to diagnosisi and "0" otherwise.

$complaint_{iM} \leftarrow$ "1" if the patient-entryM is related to complainti and "0" otherwise.

$lab_{iM} \leftarrow$ "1" if the patient-entryM is related to labi and "0" otherwise.

$diagnosis_{iM} \in 0, 1$, where $0 < i < D, D \leftarrow$ number of diagnoses

$complaint_{iM} \in 0, 1$, where $0 < i < C, C \leftarrow$ number of complaints

$lab_{iM} \in 0, 1$, where $0 < i < L, L \leftarrow$ number of laboratory procedures

$v(pM) = \{diagnosis_{1M}, ..., diagnosis_{D-1M}, complaint_{1M}, ..., complaint_{C-1M}, lab1M, ... , labL - 1M\}$

Assume we have a target patient ($Patient_N$) and we would like to find similar patient entries to generate a recommendation list accordingly. For this purpose, we also represented target patient ($Patient_N$) as a vector by using Algorithm 2.

We basically defined similarity as "closeness". When two patient vectors are close to each other, then these patients can be considered as similar. Distance and/or similarity functions provide a way to measure how close two elements are, where elements do not have to be numbers but can also be different arbitrary objects. A typical distance for real number vectors is the absolute difference. In our case, patient vectors have non-numeric attribute values thus instead of using absolute difference metric, we used a different metric. In order to calculate the distance between patient entry $Patient_M$ and target patient ($Patient_N$), we generated a specialized weighted Hamming distance measure as given in Eq. 3.

Algorithm 2. Pseudo code for the algorithm to define target patient vector.

$v(pN) \leftarrow$ vectorial representation of target patient PatientN

$diagnosis_{iN} \leftarrow$ "1" if PatientN has the diagnosisi and "0" otherwise.

$complaint_{iN} \leftarrow$ "1" if PatientN has the complainti and "0" otherwise.

$lab_{iN} \leftarrow$ "1" if PatientN has the laboratory procedure labi and "0" otherwise.

$diagnosis_{iN} \in 0, 1$, where $0 < i < D, D \leftarrow$ number of diagnoses

$complaint_{iN} \in 0, 1$, where $0 < i < C, C \leftarrow$ number of complaints

$lab_{iN} \in 0, 1$, where $0 < i < L, L \leftarrow$ number of laboratory procedures

$v(pN) = \{diagnosis_{1N}, ..., diagnosis_{D-1N}, complaint_{1N}, ..., complaint_{C-1N}, lab1N, ..., labL - 1N\}$

$$d-Weighted\ Hamming_{M,N} = \sum_{i=0}^{D-1} (w_i \times \phi_{M_i N_i}) + \sum_{i=D}^{D+C+L-1} w_i \times (N_i \otimes M_i) \quad (3)$$

where M_i is the value for i^{th} attribute for PatientM, N_i is the value for i^{th} attribute for PatientN and w_i is the weight for i^{th} attribute. $\otimes$ is used as bit-wise XOR operator, which results in 1 if the two bits are different, and 0 if they are the same. $\phi_{M_i N_i}$ is a distance value used to determine the distance between diagnosis codes M_i and N_i. $\phi_{M_i N_i}$ is "1" if the diagnosis codes are the same. $\phi_{M_i N_i}$ is "0.5" if the diagnosis codes are related to each other. We used SNOMED CT ontology to decide whether diagnosis codes are related to each other or not. Diagnosis codes are all SNOMED CT concept identifiers (IDs). The ' "Relationship" table in SNOMED CT stores the related concepts. We mapped the relational data of the "Relationship" table into a graph database. Through the graph database we determined the direct relationships between parent and child nodes and neighborhood relationships with distant nodes. If there is no relation between two diagnosis codes, we stated that they are different and the value of $\phi_{M_i N_i}$ is "0".

The similarity, $sim_{WeightedHamming}$, between target patient (PatientN), $v(pN)$ and the patient entry in database (PatientM), $v(pM)$, is calculated by the formula given in Eq. 4.

$$sim - Weighted\ Hamming_{M,N} = \frac{1}{d - Weighted\ Hamming_{M,N}} \quad (4)$$

,

We measured similarity according to three major attributes which are diagnosis, complaints and laboratory procedures. We determined whether these attributes are equally important or not. In Eq. 3, w_i is used as the weight for i^{th} attribute of target patient. We considered weight as importance of the attribute. We used a metric related to frequency score to determine the weights of each attribute. This metric is named as "priority score" and the formula is given in Eqs. 1 and 2. We calculated "priority score" for each cause. Weights w_i are equal to this priority score.

3.3   Implementation

RHCS system takes target patient data as input and generates a treatment plan list as ATC codes accordingly. We used an algorithm based on user-based collaborative-filtering recommendation technique [16]. The general algorithm used for this approach can be summarized into these following steps:

1. Group patient entries into three (diagnosis or complaint or laboratory procedure) according to their attributes.
2. For each patient, measure similarity with the target patient.
3. Until we have "K" patient entries,
   (a) For each group, select patient entries with the highest similarity scores.
4. If size of selected patient entries bigger than "K", remove patient entries with minimum similarity scores until we have "K" patient entries.
5. Generate a recommendation list consisting of ATC codes of the selected patient entries.

We used Algorithm 3 to generate the recommendation list R_N for PatientN (target patient). We categorized patient entries into three according to their types. We had set of diagnosis related patient entries (P_d), set of complaint related patient entries (P_c) and set of laboratory related patient entries (P_l). For each group, we tried to find total K nearest neighbor patient entries which have highest similarity measures $s_{u,N}$. The value $s_{u,N}$ is a similarity measure between the patient Patientu and the target patient PatientN. K is a predefined number which was determined according to the results we get after evaluations.

4   Results and Evaluation

We evaluated *RHCS* by offline experiments and a user study.

4.1   Evaluation Results of Offline Experiments

We used patient data in CDR (pre-collected data) as test users (target patients). Table 3 shows numeric information about Offline Experiments.

Table 3. The numeric information about offline experiments.

Number of patients before data preprocessing	2866
Number of patients used after data preprocessing	2453
Number of patients tested	2453
Number of all ATC codes recommended	14817
Average number of ATC codes used per patient	≈6.04

For each of the test patients, we aimed to generate top-K recommendation plans. K is the number of ATC codes generated, we determined K empirically.

Algorithm 3. Pseudo code for the User-based Collaborative Filtering algorithm used in RHCS to generate top-K recommendation list for PatientN.

$P \leftarrow$ set of all patient entries.

$T \leftarrow$ set of all treatment plans for each patient entry.

$Patient_N \leftarrow$ target patient data.

$P_d \leftarrow$ set of all patient entries whose causes are diagnoses.

$P_c \leftarrow$ set of all patient entries whose causes are complaints.

$P_l \leftarrow$ set of all patient entries whose causes are laboratory procedures.

$P = \{Patient_1, Patient_2, ..., Patient_M\}$

$T = \{T_1, T_2, ..., T_M\}$ where T_M is the treatment applied for $Patient_M$.

$M \in \mathbb{R}_{>0}$ where M is the size of P.

$S_{1,N} \leftarrow$ similarity measure between $Patient_1$ and target patient $Patient_N$.

for i=1 **to** M+1 **do**

    calculate similarity scores $S_{i,N}$

end for

$K \in \mathbb{R}_{>0}$ where K, a predefined number, is the size for recommendation.

$S_{selectedK}$ set of selected K similarity scores.

$temp = 1$

repeat

    find patient entry $temp_d$ in P_d with maximum similarity score

    if $temp_d > 0$ **then**

        add $temp_d$ to $S_{selectedK}$

        add 1 to $temp$

    end if

    find patient entry $temp_c$ in P_c with maximum similarity score

    if $temp_c > 0$ **then**

        add $temp_c$ to $S_{selectedK}$

        add 1 to $temp$

    end if

    find patient entry $temp_l$ in P_l with maximum similarity score

    if $temp_l > 0$ **then**

        add $temp_l$ to $S_{selectedK}$

        add 1 to $temp$

    end if

until $temp = K$

$size \leftarrow$ size of set $S_{selectedK}$.

for i=0 **to** K-$size$ **do**

    find minimum similarity score min in $S_{selectedK}$

    remove min from $S_{selectedK}$

end for

Assume $S_{selectedK} = \{S_{1,N}, S_{2,N}, ..., S_{K,N}\}$

$R_N = \{T_1, T_2, ..., T_K\}$ recommendation list for $Patient_N$.

The average number of ATC codes used per patient is measured as 6 approximately. As a logical interpretation, we picked two close numbers to this average number 6 as K which are 5 and 10. Hence, we evaluated *RHCS* both for K = 5 and K = 10 by using three evaluation metrics which are precision, recall, and f-measure.

Precision, recall, and f-measure accuracy metrics are generally used to evaluate recommendation systems which focus on top-N recommendation problem [8]. The relevant and irrelevant recommendations generated by a recommender system can be displayed in a two-by-two *confusion matrix* as shown in Table 4.

Table 4. Confusion matrix.

		Recommended	
		Relevant	Irrelevant
Autual	Relevant	True Positive (tp)	False Negative (fn)
	Irrelevant	False Positive (fp)	True Negative (tn)

Precision (Eq. 5) is to measure that within all recommendations how many is relevant.

$$precision = \frac{True\ positives}{True\ positives + False\ positives} \tag{5}$$

Recall (Eq. 6) is to measure that within all recommendable or relevant items how many is recommended.

$$recall = \frac{True\ positives}{True\ positives + False\ negatives} \tag{6}$$

F-measure also known as balanced F-score or F1 score (Eq. 7) is the harmonic mean of precision and recall.

$$f\text{-}measure = \frac{2 \times precision \times recall}{precision + recall} \tag{7}$$

The evaluation results are illustrated in Table 5.

Table 5. The evaluation results of offline experiments.

	TP	FP	TN	FN	Precision (%)	Recall (%)	F-measure (%)
K = 5	11438	827	447973	3379	93.257236	77.1951137	84.4693893
K = 10	14804	9726	439074	13	60.3505911	99.9122629	75.2484306

In our CDR, the number of ATC codes used per patient is varied from 3 to 10. As a more detailed evaluation, we also looked through the evaluation results for patients grouped by number of ATC codes per them.

Figure 2 is the precision vs. number of ATC codes used per patient graph. For both K = 5 and K = 10, the precision values getting higher with the number of ATC codes per patient is increased; as it is expected. When we generate a recommendation list with the size of 5, we can get 60% as the maximum precision value for a patient who uses 3 ATC codes. However, for a patient who uses more than 5 ATC codes, the precision value can reach 100%. Precision scores we get for K = 5 are greater than the scores for K = 10. This is also an expected situation as K (number of recommendations) is denominator to measure precision, and higher denominator results in a lower ratio. Precision for K = 5 is approximately 93.26% and precision for K = 10 is approximately 60.35%.

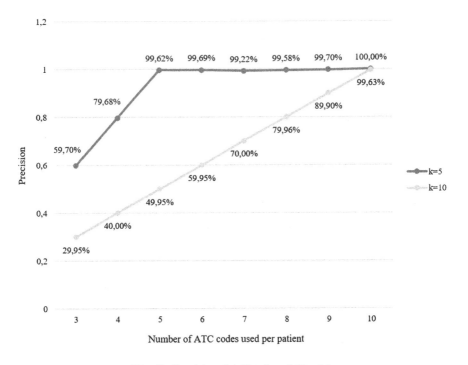

Fig. 2. Precision for K = 5 and K = 10.

Figure 3 is the recall vs. number of ATC codes used per patient graph. For K = 5, patients who use 5 or more ATC codes have lower recall values than those using 3 or 4 ATC codes. This is because the number of ATC codes per patient is denominator to measure recall. When we generate a recommendation list with the size of 5, we can get 50% as the maximum recall value for a patient who uses 10 ATC codes. However, for a patient who uses 5 or less ATC codes, this value can reach 100%. For K = 10, the numbers of ATC codes used per patient do not affect recall values too much since there is no patient who uses more than 10 ATC codes. In general, recall scores we get for K = 10 are greater than the scores for K = 5. In order to have higher recall values, we have to increase nominator part which is the number of truly recommended ATC codes (*true-positive*). For K = 10, we have a higher chance to have more truly recommended ATC codes. Hence, it is expected to have higher recall scores for K = 10. Recall for K = 5 is approximately 77.2% and recall for K = 10 is approximately 99.9%.

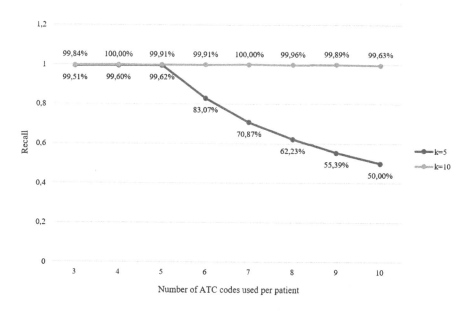

Fig. 3. Recall for K = 5 and K = 10.

Figure 4 is the f-measure vs. number of ATC codes used per patient graph. F-measure is a measure to make use of both precision and recall evaluation metrics and so it is difficult to find a direct correlation between f-measure values and number of ATC codes used per patient. The f-measure values for overall system RHCS are illustrated in Table 5. F-measure for K = 5 is approximately 84.47% and f-measure for K = 10 is approximately 75.25%.

4.2   Evaluation Results of User Study

The user study is conducted with real system users (medical doctors) that perform some predetermined tasks. We provided a user study set with 8 different patients and 13 different medical doctors. We asked doctors to evaluate recommendation lists generated for these 8 patients.

In offline experiments, we showed that the number of ATC codes per patient might affect the evaluation results. Therefore, selecting random patients without considering the number of ATC codes used for them might result in biased evaluation results. In order to build a more reliable experiment set, we randomly selected one patient from each of 8 different groups classified by the number of ATC codes (from 3 to 10).

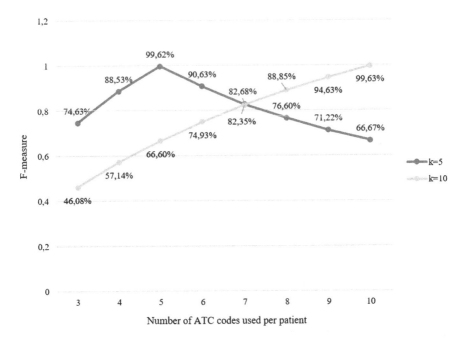

Fig. 4. F-measure for K = 5 and K = 10.

Doctors evaluated ATC codes generated for these 8 patients one by one picking scores between "1" to "5". "1" means not-related and "5" means very related. This scoring mechanism enables doctors to scale relatedness of ATC codes.

We generated a formula (Eq. 8) to evaluate online experiment. Our aim is to measure the relevancy of generated ATC codes for a given patient. "1" is 0% relevant and 2 means 25% relevant, 3 means 50%, 4 means 75% and 5 means 100% relevant. For each doctor and patient pair a relevancy score is calculated by the Eq. 8 where # of 5 $scores_{doctor,patient}$ is the number of "5" scores given by *doctor* to generated ATC codes for *patient* and K is the number of ATC codes generated which are 5 and 10 respectively.

$$
\begin{aligned}
r_{doctor,patient,K}(\%) = \frac{1}{K} * (\#\ &of\ 5\ scores_{doctor,patient} * 100 \\
+\ \#\ &of\ 4\ scores_{doctor,patient} * 75 \\
+\ \#\ &of\ 3\ scores_{doctor,patient} * 50 \\
+\ \#\ &of\ 2\ scores_{doctor,patient} * 25 \\
+\ \#\ &of\ 1\ scores_{doctor,patient} * 0)
\end{aligned}
\tag{8}
$$

The success of *RHCS* according to a doctor is determined by Eq. 9 which is the mean of relevancy scores related to that doctor. Table 6 illustrates the relevancy score of *RHCS* according to different doctors participated in user study when K is equal to 5 and 10.

$$relevancy - score_{Di,K}\ (\%) = \frac{\sum_{j=1}^{8} r_{Di,Pj,K}}{8} \tag{9}$$

Table 6. Relevancy scores for each doctor calculated for K = 5 and K = 10.

Doctor	Relevancy score for K = 5	Relevancy score for K = 10
D1	100	100
D2	98.125	97.5
D3	100	98.4375
D4	100	98.4375
D5	100	100
D6	100	97.5
D7	100	100
D8	97.5	95.625
D9	99.375	99.6875
D10	98.125	96.875
D11	100	100
D12	100	98.4375
D13	98.125	98.4375

In order to evaluate the overall relevancy of *RHCS*, we use Eq. 10 which is the mean of relevancy scores measured by each doctor.

$$relevancy - score_K\ (\%) = \frac{\sum_{i=1}^{13} relevancy - score_{Di,K}}{13} \tag{10}$$

Table 7 shows the relevancy score we calculated for K = 5 and K = 10. These values are too close to each other, so it is not obvious that K = 5 is superior than K = 10 in terms of relevancy score.

Table 7. Relevancy score for overall system RHCS for K = 5 and K = 10.

	Relevancy score
K = 5	99.32692308
K = 10	98.60576923

4.3   Overall Analysis

We can summarize our findings and remarks as follows:

– In offline experiments, we assumed that only ATC codes used for patients are recommendable. If generated ATC codes were not used by patients, we classified them as falsely recommended (FP). However, this assumption is not totally accurate. ATC codes generated by RHCS can be relevant in spite of not using in our CDR. Hence, our precision percentages measured on offline experiment set might be under presented, and so it may be misleading.

- User study has some drawbacks. The first problem is that it is not an objective method since the success is related to personal decisions of doctors. Second drawback is that we can evaluate the relevance, however, we cannot learn whether there is a missing ATC code in recommendation list or not. So we cannot evaluate system by a metric like recall. Lastly, the number of patient data used for online evaluation is limited and this might affect the evaluation results.
- Determining which K is more preferable depends on our aim. If we want to have a greater precision value than K should be selected as 5. If recall value is more important for us than K should be 10. We prefer K as 10 and there are three main reasons behind this preference:
  - Because one of our motivation points is guiding health professionals in terms of reminding ATC codes, recall is an important metric for us.
  - Precision measured on offline experiment set can be misleading.
  - According to user study results, it is not worth to consider the difference between scores for K = 5 and 10; both are acceptable.
- For K=10 on offline experiment set; precision is approximately 60.35%, recall is approximately 99.91% and f-measure is approximately 75.25%. For K = 10 on online experiment set; the relevancy score is approximately 98.6%.

5   Related Work

In this section, some prominent related studies will be explained. Shimadaa et. al. develop a clinical decision support system in order to recommend drugs for patients who have infectious diseases. They aim to help health professionals particularly doctors to select first-line drugs appropriate for the risk level of an infection drug [9]. Meisamshabanpoor and Mahdavi study medical decisions for disease recognition, treatment, and time of period needed for recovery. Their proposed system use classification techniques and collaborative filtering recommendation approach [10]. Duan, Street and Lu generate a nursing care plan recommender system to provide a ranked list of nursing plans based on historical data. This ranked list is updated as new items are entered. They use association-rule measures (*support* and *confidence*). They also propose a novel approach named as "information value" that expects which selections may improve the future rankings [11]. Hoens, Blanton and Chawla have a research on generating a reliable medical recommender system considering privacy. In their article, they explain a physician recommending system. Patients can rate physicians based on their satisfactions and the system considers these ratings to generate a recommendation. Two important features of their research are secure processing architecture and anonymous contributions architecture. Secure processing architecture provides patients to contribute encrypted ratings and the recommendations are generated over encrypted data. Anonymous contributions architecture provides patient to submit their ratings anonymously. In order to have a more reliable system, dishonest users and physicians cannot tamper with ratings. They evaluate their recommendation system in terms of reliability of recommendations and system performance [12]. Rodríguez et al. propose a medical recommendation system SemMed to assist health professionals by recommending possible drugs or medications by using Semantic Web Technologies. They use an ontology in OWL format with three main related classes which are diseases, allergies and medicines. The system generate drug recommendations by using information within this ontology [13]. Lim, Husain and Zakaria generate personalized wellness treatment recommendations using an Artificial Intelligence technique, hybrid case-based reasoning. They propose an online consultation form to users. Users state their wellness concerns on consultation form and the system tries to find similar cases by case-based reasoning. If there is no suitable similar cases, the system provides recommendations by rule-based reasoning [14]. Su and Chiang introduce their system "IAServ" as a personalized health-care service implemented as a web service and deployed in a cloud computing setting. IAServ cannot be directly classified as a medical recommendation system, rather it is a clinical decision support system. IAServ generates personalized care plan by using the patient's ontological profile and formulated rules [15]. Our proposed system *RHCS* is different from others since it provides a distinct similarity approach and recommendation algorithm which give promising evaluation results. Its compatibility with classification standards and ontology usage also make the research prominent.

6   Conclusion and Future Work

In this paper, we introduced our clinical recommendation system *RHCS*. Deciding proper drugs for the treatment of geriatric patients is a difficult task since such patients likely require lots of drugs during their treatment process. For this reason, *RHCS* generates drug recommendations as ATC codes to assist health professionals. ATC is an international standard to classify drugs according to their active ingredients. The system works with a clinical ontology named SNOMED CT in order to determine relationships between different diagnoses. It is also compatible with ICD-10 coding mechanism which is an international classification system for diagnoses. *RHCS* uses an algorithm based on user-based collaborative filtering recommendation approach. We evaluated *RHCS* with both offline experiments and a user study. For offline experiments, we used three evaluation metrics which are precision, recall, and f-measure and the results were all higher than 60%. We conducted a user study with 13 medical doctors and evaluated user study through a relevancy score which we generated. We measured this relevancy score as approximately 98% and it shows an evidence that according to 13 medical doctors, *RHCS* generates relevant recommendations.

As a future work, we are planning to use *RHCS* as part of a patient based home health care service. *RHCS* can also be adapted to work with instantaneous data measurements through different biomedical sensors and medical devices like electrocardiography (ECG), digital scales, glucometers and so on.

References

1. Hale, W.E., Marks, R.G., Stewart, R.B.: Drug use in a geriatric population. J. Am. Geriatr. Soc. **27**(8), 374–377 (1979)
2. International Classification of Diseases (ICD). http://www.who.int/classifications/icd/en/. Accessed 2 May 2018
3. SNOMED CT Starter Guide. Technical report, IHTSDO (2014)
4. Chisholm-Burns, M.A., Wells, B.G., Schwinghammer, T.L.: Pharmacotherapy Principles and Practice. McGraw-Hill, New York (2016)
5. McPhee, S.J., Papadakis, M.A., Tierney, L.M. (eds.): Current Medical Diagnosis & Treatment 2010. McGraw-Hill Medical, New York (2010)
6. Ferri, F.F.: Ferri's Clinical Advisor: Instant Diagnosis and Treatment, 2006. W.B. Saunders Company, Philadelphia (2003)
7. Sinclair, A.J., Morley, J.E., Vellas, B. (eds.): Pathy's Principles and Practice of Geriatric Medicine. Wiley, Hoboken (2012)
8. Sarwar, B., Karypis, G., Konstan, J., Riedl, J.: Item-based collaborative filtering recommendation algorithms. In: Proceedings of the 10th International Conference on World Wide Web, pp. 285–295. ACM (2001)
9. Shimada, K., et al.: Drug-recommendation system for patients with infectious diseases. In: AMIA Annual Symposium Proceedings, vol. 2005, pp. 1112. American Medical Informatics Association (2005)
10. Shabanpoor, M., Mahdavi, M.: Implementation of a recommender system on medical recognition and treatment. Int. J. e-Educ. e-Bus. e-Manag. e-Learn. **2**(4), 315 (2012)
11. Duan, L., Street, W., Lu, D.: A nursing care plan recommender system using a data mining approach. In: 3rd INFORMS Workshop on Data Mining and Health Informatics, Washington DC (2008)
12. Hoens, T.R., Blanton, M., Steele, A., Chawla, N.V.: Reliable medical recommendation systems with patient privacy. ACM Trans. Intell. Syst. Technol. (TIST) **4**(4), 67 (2013)
13. Rodríguez, A., et al.: SemMed: applying semantic web to medical recommendation systems. In: First International Conference on Intensive Applications and Services, INTENSIVE 2009, pp. 47–52. IEEE (2009)
14. Lim, T.P., Husain, W., Zakaria, N.: Recommender system for personalised wellness therapy. Int. J. Adv. Comput. Sci. Appl. **4**(9), 54–60 (2013)
15. Su, C.J., Chiang, C.Y.: IAServ: an intelligent home care web services platform in a cloud for aging-in-place. Int. J. Environ. Res. Publ. Health **10**(11), 6106–6130 (2013)
16. Hiralall, M., Kowalczyk, W.: Recommender systems for e-shops. Business Mathematics and Informatics Paper. Vrije Universiteit, Amsterdam (2011)

Implementation of a Medical Coding Support System by Combining Approaches: NLP and Machine Learning

Idir Amine Amarouche[1(✉)], Dehbia Ahmed Zaid[1(✉)], and Tayeb Kenaza[2(✉)]

[1] Department of Medical and Hospital Informatics, Central Hospital of Army,
Ain Naadja, 16005 Algiers, Algeria
`i.a.amarouche@gmail.com,ahmed_zaid_dehbia@hotmail.fr`
[2] Ecole Militaire Polytechnique, BP 17, 16046 Bordj El Bahri, Algiers, Algeria
`ken.tayeb@gmail.com`

Abstract. Diagnosis-Related Groups (DRG) billing for hospital stays is based on the collection of coded and standardized information constituting the Hospital Discharge Abstract (HDA). The HDA describes the pathological state of the patient and the care provided during his stay. This work aims to design and implement a coding support system for diagnoses and acts expressed in ICD-10 (ICD-10: International Classification of Disease, 10th version) and GNPA (GNPA: General Nomenclature of Professional Acts), respectively. The proposed solution takes a medical report as input and provides a list of recommended diagnoses and acts. It is based on the combination of two approaches, namely, NLP (NLP: Natural Language Processing) and machine learning. Firstly, the medical reports are pre-processed, via the NLP algorithms, in order to better understand the extent of the codes concerned. Secondly, the use of machine learning approaches offers the means of making the choice of codes as relevant as possible. The experiments carried out showed very satisfactory results, which are confirmed by hospital practitioners.

Keywords: Medical coding support ·
Natural language processing (NLP) · Machine learning · ICD-10 ·
GNPA

1 Introduction

Hospital Information Systems (HIS) are distinguished by their ability to record, process, share and communicate medical and hospital information. The automatic processing of this information, mainly providing support for quality care, also aims at ensuring optimal management of hospital resources [1].

Hospitals use Information System as a support to improve both the quality of healthcare services and the cost control. For instance, at the patient discharge, the Hospital Information System (HIS) provides functionalities that allow the production of Hospital Discharge Abstract (HDA). The HDA summarizes the

V. Gadepally et al. (Eds.): Poly 2018/DMAH 2018, LNCS 11470, pp. 133–147, 2019.
https://doi.org/10.1007/978-3-030-14177-6_11

medico-administrative information produced or captured during a hospital stay and used for billing. Precisely, the HDA contains identification and medical data (e.g. main diagnosis, associated (s) diagnosis (s) and performed acts) expressed in international, or local purpose, and standardized terminologies. Generally, the coding of diagnoses and acts is done manually by hospital practitioners (doctors, coding technicians, etc.) and is therefore subject to errors. According to [2], the coding constitutes the basis of the valuation of the inpatient stay, and therefore, any error related to its results leads to an erroneous coverage (at most or at least) of the costs incurred by the hospital.

The International Statistical Classification of Diseases and Related Health Problems in its tenth version (ICD-10)[1] and the General Nomenclature of Professional Acts (GNPA)[2] are the two terminologies used, in our context, to document the medical records in terms of diagnoses and acts performed respectively. For this purpose, it is relevant to provide practitioners with a support in the form of an assistant that will recommend the most appropriate codes, among nearly 40,000 diagnostic listed in the ICD-10 and 10,000 acts of the GNPA. This is made effective, mainly, through information contained in unstructured medical reports, such as, Operating Report (OR), Hospitalization Report (HR), etc.

1.1 Challenges

The HIS provides practitioners with required tools to document patient records with diagnoses and acts. However, the functionalities provided by these tools are based mainly on a manual exploration of terminologies. Given the considerable number of codes provided by these terminologies, the coding operation is perceived by practitioners as long and tedious. This weighs negatively on the activity of hospital departments and can lead to the erroneous billing of hospital stays. In addition, the challenges of medical coding are not only financial. Coded diagnoses and acts can be used for epidemiological studies. Similarly, reliable statistics are essential for optimal management of hospital resources. As a result, the medical coding challenges raises the need to develop a solution that provides assistance to practitioners during the medical codes selection. This solution must use the patient medical record that includes unstructured data (reports, clinical notes, etc.). The use of unstructured data is largely due to their richness in terms of information and are mainly the support whereby healthcare practitioners express their activities mostly. As a result, the following challenges arise:

– Need to achieve a solution to provide medical coding assistance from unstructured textual data (medical reports, observations, clinical notes, etc.).
– The solution to be proposed must cover all diagnoses treated and performed acts in the hospital that is the subject of our study.

---

[1] http://www.atih.sante.fr/cim-10-fr-2017-usage-pmsi.
[2] https://www.ameli.fr/medecin/exercice-liberal/facturation-remuneration/nomencla tures-codage/ngap.

1.2 Contributions

In view of the challenges mentioned above, the realization of an automated solution for medical coding support is of interest. This paper proposes a solution to assist practitioners in the choice of diagnoses and acts by using textual data from the patient's medical record (Hospitalization Report, Operating Report). This solution is based essentially on the combination of two approaches, namely: the NLP and the multi-class classification by machine learning. Thus, the main contributions are as follows:

- The realization of a workflow (pipeline) ensuring the preprocessing of the medical reports by exploiting the techniques of NLP. This is dictated by the unstructured aspect of these reports.
- The use of machine learning techniques and algorithms to realize prediction models of the diagnoses and acts. This is the naive Bayes and the Support Vector Machines (SVM) algorithms. We choose these two algorithms for the prediction models they generate, that have proved their worth in the classification of medical documents according to [5,7,11].

The rest of this paper is structured as follows: Sect. 2 provides a concise description of the theoretical background inherent to the problematic. Section 3 presents the proposed architecture. Sections 4 and 5 present respectively the experiments conducted and the evaluation results of the proposed solution. The sixth section concludes with a review of our contributions and the resulting perspectives.

2 Background

This section describes the medical coding support system, declines the flow of related tasks or the general pipeline and details the different phases for its realization.

2.1 Medical Coding Support System

The automatic processing of medical information is based on the collection of clinical data relating to hospital stays of patients. As a result, considerable efforts have been made to construct the terminological resources used to express these data in coded form, similar to ICD-10 and GNPA [3]. However, despite the increasing use of these terminologies, natural language remains the privileged vector of information and medical knowledge. From hospital reports to diagnostic and therapeutic protocols, the text is omnipresent. A medical coding support system is a system that analyzes medical documents and produces the appropriate codes according to the sentences and terms mentioned on these documents [4].

2.2 Pipeline of Medical Coding Support System

Figure 1 illustrates the sequence of steps commonly used for the realization of a medical coding support system [4]. In the first step, known as preprocessing, the contents of the reports are structured in sections. For each section, the text is subdivided into sentences (sentence splitting) and words (tokenization). At the "word" level, additional normalizations can be applied to obtain the lexical root of the term, referred to as stemming. This includes correcting misspellings and replacing abbreviations with their complete forms and eliminating stop words. Secondly, the treatment step requires as input the result of the preprocessing step. It can be done according to three types of approaches, namely, a classification approach based on machine learning, a rule-based approach or a hybrid approach combining the first two. An evaluation step of the coding support system succeeds immediately the processing phase.

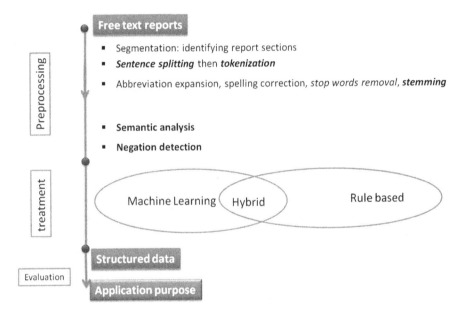

Fig. 1. Pipeline of medical coding support system [4].

Several previous studies, namely [4–6] have used NLP techniques associated with automatic classification approaches to extract coded clinical information from unstructured medical reports expressed in English.

2.3 Automatic Classification of Textual Medical Reports

The classification consists of assigning instances of a given domain described by a set of discrete or continuous value attributes to a set of classes, which can be considered as values of a selected discrete target attribute [7]. The process of classifying texts is based on a learning set $D = \{d_1,...,d_n\}$ composed of documents labeled with classes $\{C_1,...,C_k\}$ [8]. In the case of medical coding assistance, these classes may correspond to diagnosis codes expressed according to ICD-10. This enables to create a classification model based on a corpus of labeled documents able to assign the correct class (es) to any new document d [9]. This corpus is partitioned into two sets: one for learning and another for testing. As illustrated in Fig. 2, the classification process consists first in training the model with the learning set. Once learned, its effectiveness will be tested with the test set. It should be noted that before beginning the construction of the classification model, it is important to make the textual documents understandable by the learning algorithms [5]. This occurs at the step designated by "Document Representation" illustrated in Fig. 2.

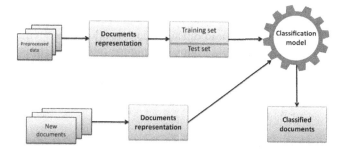

Fig. 2. Process of automatic classification of documents

Representation of Textual Documents. The representation by bag of words is often preferred. It consists to describe the content of a text by means of descriptors (words or groups of words) [5]. The idea is to transform the different documents of a corpus into vectors where each element of a text vector represents textual units or simply words [9]. The set of these words will be referred to as "vocabulary". In the vector model, the components of a vector are determined according to the occurrences of words in the text. These words are selected according to their appearance frequency in the documents and according to the number of documents containing these words. Let C be a corpus of textual documents of size n and D_i a document belonging to C. Let m be the number of terms and $T = \{T_1, ..., T_m\}$ be the set of these terms. In the vector representation, the document D_i is represented by a vector V_i. The collection of texts can be represented by a matrix whose columns represent the words and lines represent the documents as illustrated in Fig. 3. The W_{ij} represent the weighting of a term T_j in the document D_i where $0 < j < m$, $0 < i < n$. There are several possibilities for defining the weight of the words w_{ij}. Among others, Boolean weighting, weighting with word frequencies, $TF \times IDF$, etc. [9].

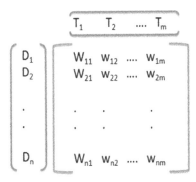

Fig. 3. Documents-terms matrix

Machine Learning. Machine Learning is a computer science and statistics sub-domain that aims to solve problems in different scientific fields. It is deeply related to artificial intelligence and optimization. It allows the creation of mathematical models from data [10]. Many techniques and algorithms inherent in machine learning have been proposed in the literature. We present below two variants of these algorithms namely: Naive Bayes and SVM. The prediction models generated by these algorithms have proved their worth in the classification of documents according to [5,7,11].

- Naive Bayes is a probabilistic algorithm based on Bayes' theorem. The naive aspect is due to the assumption that the variables are independent and fixed at the beginning. In the classification of texts the descriptors are designated by variables [7].
  The hypothesis of independence of the descriptors of the Naive Bayes model, makes it simple and effective. Its training does not require many documents. This classification model has proven itself in the classification of short documents, including emails (Ham/Spam).
- Support Vector Machines (SVM) are methods that come from an accurate and advanced mathematical analysis of the learning problem and based on binary separator in a vector space. The separators are hyperplanes. To choose the best hyperplane, the notion of "margin" is solicited. The margin of a separating hyperplane is the smallest distance that separates it from the nearest points. The SVM algorithm favors the hyperplane which ensures the largest possible margin [7]. SVMs are powerful tools, which often obtain the best classification performance [11].

3   Medical Coding Support System: Proposed Approach

In this section, we describe the different steps that highlight the implementation of our solution which is based on a multi-class classification approach considering our data characteristics. In order to properly describe our solution, we first explain the functionalities for each step constituting the proposed pipeline shown in Fig. 4.

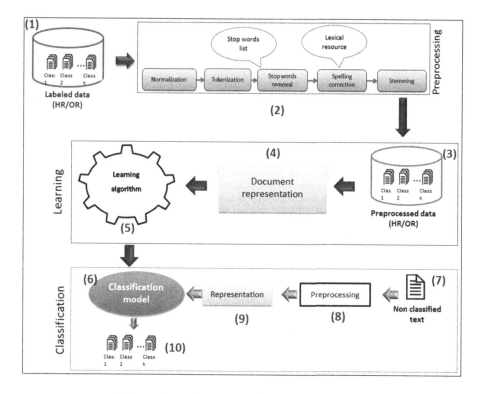

Fig. 4. Overall scheme of the proposed solution

Corpus (1 of Fig. 4). The textual documents we are interested in are HRs for ICD-10 diagnoses coding and ORs for GNPA acts coding. The advantage of using these reports lies in the fact that they are the most requested by medical information doctor to document a clinical case and verify the coding performed by the treating physician. Indeed, the HR is a document that includes a summary of the main elements relating to the patient's stay as well as the elements useful for the continuity of care. The OR is a medical-technical document that accompanies every surgery performed on the patient. It summaries the findings and procedures performed during the surgical procedure.

Preprocessing (2 of Fig. 4). Our medical data source includes HRs and ORs written in French by doctors from different hospital departments (surgery, medical and obstetrics). These reports are characterized by their narrative, unstructured and sometimes ambiguous aspects. That is why, the passage through a preprocessing step, based on NLP techniques is unavoidable (see Sect. 3.1).

Data Representation (4 of Fig. 4*)*. The preprocessed HRs and ORs (3 in Fig. 4) go through a representation step that includes a vocabulary extraction task and another formatting one for these documents based on that vocabulary.

Machine Learning (5 of Fig. 4*)*. Machine learning algorithms have been used to construct a prediction model (6 in Fig. 4) of a collection of codes that best reflect the pathology of the patient and the set of cares provided.

Classification. Any new unclassified document (7 in Fig. 4) needs preprocessing (8 of Fig. 4) and representation (9 of Fig. 4) steps. This document then serves as an input parameter for the classification model (6 in Fig. 4) to produce the appropriate code (s) (10 in Fig. 4) which is a multi-class classification.

3.1   Preprocessing Phase of Medical Reports

The HRs and ORs that are available to us are written in French. The preprocessing phase illustrated in Fig. 4 aims at mitigating anomalies recorded in medical reports. It consists of a series of steps, broken down as follows:

Normalization. It consists mainly of a lowercase text.

Tokenization. It immediately succeeds the normalization step. It allows recognition and separation of lexical entities in the texts "tokens". This separation is preceded by a cleanup task that deletes dates, digits, and special characters, reduces consecutive spaces to one, and removes line breaks.

Elimination of Stop Words. This step directly follows the tokenization. Once the textual documents cut into tokens, some of them appear in all texts of the corpus in the form of articles, prepositions, determinants, adverbs ... etc. The presence of these so-called meaningless words in all the texts renders them non-discriminating, therefore their use for a classification task turns out to be useless, hence the need for their removal.

Automatic Correction of Spelling. HRs and ORs corpus sometimes include spelling mistakes. Thus, the passage through this step is inevitable.

Stemming. In this step, it is a question of managing the different inflections of a word. This step allows considering only the root of the word rather than the entire word without worrying about grammatical analysis.

3.2   Classification Phase by Machine Learning

After the preprocessing of medical reports, we proceed to the treatment phase. In our case, it consists of a multi-class classification by machine learning. This involves designing a prediction model that assigns each HR and each OR to one or more corresponding classes, which are designated by ICD-10 codes and

GNPA codes respectively. At first, the corpus is partitioned into two sets: one for learning and the other for testing, as shown in Fig. 5. The classification process consists, in the first instance, of training the model with the learning set. Once learned, its effectiveness will be tested with the test set.

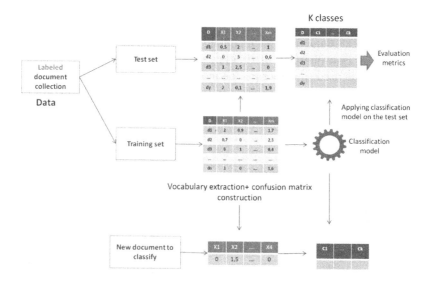

Fig. 5. Classification process for medical reports

Data Description (Documents-Terms Matrix). The implementation of predictive techniques requires the mandatory passage through a phase of representation of the data. The nature of the predictive variable, which is in our case textual document, denotes the peculiarity of operation, which was achieved by using the bag of words representation to bring the description of the text corpus back to a table.

Individuals (documents) - Variables (terms)': this is the documents-terms matrix described in Sect. 2.3. The construction of the documents-terms matrix is done in two steps: the first consists of a descriptor selection operation, designated by generation of the vocabulary representing the corpus and a second step designated by text formatting. In this sense, we have considered "words" as descriptors and the "Term Frequency (TF) x Inverse Document Frequency (IDF)" as a type of text formatting, allowing relativizing the importance of a word in a document (TF) by its importance in the corpus (IDF). $TF \times IDF$ is defined as follows:

$$TF \times IDF(t_k, d_j) = N(t_k, d_j) * log(|Tr|/Tr(t_k)) \tag{1}$$

where:

- $N(t_k, d_j)$: the number of occurrences of the descriptor t_k in the document d_j;
- $|Tr|$: the number of documents in the learning corpus;
- $Tr(t_k)$: the number of documents in the set in which the descriptor t_k appears once at least.

Machine Learning. In the classification of texts by machine learning, it is important not to use the same data for modeling and evaluation of prediction models. In this case, it is a question of dividing data into two parts: a first sample, called learning, is used to elaborate the model; a second one, called test, is used to measure the performance. This task occurs before the construction of the matrix documents terms. Indeed, the texts of the test corpus must intervene neither in the constitution of vocabulary nor in calculation of the weights of the matrix used for learning.

4 Experiments and Results

This section describes the experimental settings including experimental environment, data and coding support system implementation. The experimental results are also presented.

4.1 Experimental Environment

The operating system under which our solution is implemented, tested and installed is the Microsoft Windows 64-bit system with 4 GB RAM, Intel (R) Core (TM) 3.70 GHz processor. In order to implement our solution, we opted for the Python programming language. Indeed, the processing of texts written in natural language requires some basic treatments and tedious to implement, hence the use of services offered by the library "NLTK (Natural Language Tool Kit)". We also exploited the functionality of Python's "scikit-learn" package, which provided the machine learning algorithms used in our case, namely: Bayes' naive algorithm and the SVM algorithm.

4.2 Experimental Approach

After preparing learning and test data, the construction of the document-term matrix was carried out according to the following two criteria:

- The abundance of descriptors in the corpus: it is the maximum number of documents where a descriptor appears. Indeed, the more a descriptor is common in the corpus, the less it will be used as discriminating between classes.
- The size of the vocabulary: it is the number of descriptors to be selected from the corpus.

The challenge is to find the combination of the two parameters above, which will lead to better system accuracy. For this purpose, an experimental study involving our data is required. It consists of varying the variable characterizing the abundance of descriptors in the corpus as well as the size of the vocabulary representing the latter. For each combination of these variables, a prediction model is generated and is evaluated in terms of usual NLP based system performance indicators that are defined in Sect. 4.3 (precision, F-measure, recall rate). Since our goal is to provide practitioners with coding support for medical information, evaluation metrics are calculated so that the correct code appears among the first k propositions of the system (see Sect. 4.4).

4.3   Evaluation Metrics

Evaluation is an important step in the same way as the other phases of the prediction model construction process. There are several indicators that reflect the success or the failure of a prediction model. In our case, we define the evaluation metrics commonly used in the literature for the evaluation of medical coding support systems, in this case:

Precision: The ratio of the number of documents correctly classified in a class to the number of documents to which this class is assigned.

Recall: It is the ratio between the number of documents correctly classified in a class on the number of documents belonging to this class.

F-Measure: It is an indicator that combines recall and precision. It is given by the following formula:

$$F - Measure = \frac{2 * (Precision * Recall)}{(Precision + recall)} \tag{2}$$

4.4   Results

For a corpus composed of 19 605 HRs spread over 225 ICD-10 classes, the following table shows the results obtained in terms of precision, recall and F-measure calculated so that the correct code appears among the first 10 proposals of the system (see Table 1).

Table 1. Evaluation of the coding support system: case of the ICD-10 diagnostics.

Model	Vocabulary size	Documents-termes matrics	Precision	Recall	F-measure
Naif Bayes	2000	(19605,2000)	68%	96%	79.7%
SVM	4000	(19605,4000)	87.4%	96%	91.5%

The plot in the Fig. 6a illustrates the precision values based on the number of ICD-10 diagnoses proposed by our solution.

As for the corpus composed of 8 973 ORs spread over 67 GNPA codes, the results of the evaluation of the system for coding the acts are presented in the

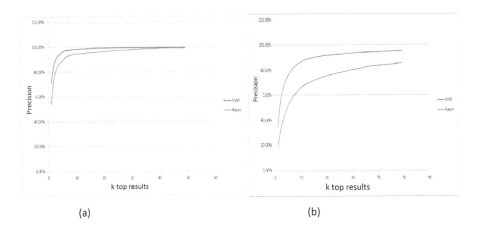

(a)   (b)

Fig. 6. Precision values of the coding support system.

Table 2. Evaluation of the coding support system: case of GNPA acts.

Model	Vocabulary size	Documents-termes matrics	Precision	Recall	F-measure
Naif Bayes	2000	(8973,2000)	95%	86%	90.4%
SVM	6000	(8973,6000)	99%	86%	92%

Table 2. The evaluation metrics are calculated so that the correct code appears among the first 10 propositions of the system.

By varying the number of GNPA acts proposed by our solution, the precision was evaluated as shown in Fig. 6b. In this case, when the number of proposals exceeds 40, the precision reaches a value of 100%. It should be noted that the precision rate, calculated on the system involving ORs, is higher than the precision rate by involving HRs. This difference can be explained by the quality of these documents. Indeed, the ORs are characterized by a direct style, generally in the affirmative form, concise and precise sentences through which the surgeon expresses only the succession of steps constituting the operating protocol. Unlike the HRs in which the attending physician details the hospital stay of the patient by describing his pathology and all the care provided.

Evaluation of the Classification Model. The accuracy of a classification can be evaluated by calculating the confusion matrix [12] shown in Fig. 7.

One of the interests of this matrix is that it quickly shows if the system manages to classify correctly. In this sense, a classification system will be all the better as its confusion matrix approaches a diagonal matrix. In a confusion matrix, each class in the classification model is represented by a column and a row. The line indicates the number of real documents belonging to the class (C) and the column indicates to which number of documents this class (C) is assigned. Note that whatever the class C different from the class $C\prime$, We distinguish four situations:

		Predicted classes	
		C	C′
Actual	C	TP	FN
classes	C′	FP	TN

Fig. 7. Components of a confusion matrix [12].

- *TP* (True positives): The documents belonging to the class C that the classification model has classified to the class C.
- *FP* (False positives): The documents that do not belong to the class C and that the classification model has classified to the class C'.
- *TN* (True negatives): The documents belonging to the class C' that the classification model has classified to the class C'.
- *FN* (False negatives): The documents belonging to the class C that the classification model has classified to the class C'.

Considering the classification models constructed by the SVM learning algorithm for the coding of the ICD-10 HRs and the GNPA coded ORs, we proceeded to their evaluation using their respective confounding matrices. For this purpose, the composition of the test corpus is shown in Table 3.

Table 3. Composition of the test corpus for the construction of the confusion matrix.

Corpus	Number of documents	Number of classes	Number of documents per class
HR	4500	225	20
OR	1340	67	20

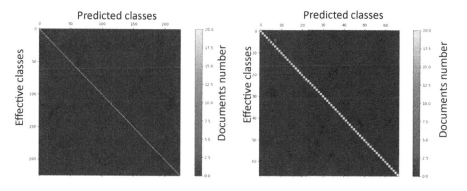

(a) Prediction model confusion matrix for "HR" coding   (b) Prediction Model Confusion Matrix for "OR" Coding
in ICD-10   in GNPA

Fig. 8. Confusion matrices of models of prediction by SVM.

The confusion matrices, calculated for the two corpora (HR and OR) respectively, are refined to approximate a diagonal matrix and is illustrated in Fig. 8.

For a better readability of the contents of the confusion matrices, we presented the results in a tabular form. Since our system returns k codes (ICD-10 or GNPA), we considered two cases as illustrated in Fig. 9, namely: the case where the solution proposes a single code and the case where the solution proposes 10 codes.

(1) Case of the first code proposed by the system (k=1).

Classe CIM-10	FP	FN	VP	VN	Rappel	Précision
K76.8	0	19	1	4480	0.05	1
K40.9	5	13	7	4475	0.35	0.58
K60.1	2	7	13	4478	0.65	0.87
K76.9	4	18	2	4476	0.1	0.33
L05.9	0	0	20	4480	1	1
M16.1	1	20	0	4479	0	0
...	...	...	...	...	...	...

Classe	FP	FN	VP	VN	Rappel	Précision
02.04.05.01.02	2	19	1	1318	0.05	0.33
02.04.05.01.01	0	20	0	1320	0	0
02.04.05.07.09	31	0	20	1289	1	0.39
04.04.03.06.01	1	20	0	1319	0	0
04.05.08.02.02	0	0	20	1320	1	1
07.04.10.02	1	4	16	1319	0.8	0.94

(2) Case of ten codes proposed by the system (k=10).

Classe CIM-10	FP	FN	VP	VN	Rappel	Précision
K76.8	0	6	14	4480	0.7	1
K40.9	0	0	20	4476	1	0.83
K60.1	1	2	18	4479	0.9	0.95
K76.9	7	5	15	4473	0.75	0.68
L05.9	0	0	20	4480	1	1
M16.1	3	2	18	4477	0.9	0.86
...	...	...	...	...	...	...

Classe	FP	FN	VP	VN	Rappel	Précision
02.04.05.01.02	2	1	19	1318	0.95	0.9
02.04.05.01.01	0	0	20	1320	1	1
02.04.05.07.09	29	0	20	1291	1	0.41
04.04.03.06.01	0	0	20	1320	1	1
04.05.08.02.02	0	0	20	1320	1	1
07.04.10.02	1	0	20	1315	1	0.95

(a)   HR Corpus   (a)   OR Corpus

Fig. 9. Preview on some values of the components of confusion matrices.

The evaluation of the classification model of the HRs and the ORs shows the existence of heterogeneity in the precision values of the classes taken individually. We find that the precision of some classes is very low when the system returns only one code. However, when the system returns 10 codes, the accuracy of these classes marks a significant increase, so the doctor will be more likely to find the best code describing the diagnosis and acts performed on a patient.

5   Conclusion

The main purpose of the present paper is to propose a solution that reduces the burden of medical coding on practitioners. Precisely, we have developed a solution that helps hospital practitioners during medical coding. This solution affords a list of relevant diagnosis and acts codes that best match a given clinical situation. Doing so, we reduce the searching time spent by practitioners in the selection of required ICD-10 and GNPA codes. An empirical evaluation of the proposed solution with real clinical data provides preliminary evidence for the effectiveness of our proposal. Future work will focus on the following perspectives:

– Develop a solution to differentiate between different types of diagnosis (main, associated, etc.) based on multi-label classification. This evolution will best help the practitioner when choosing diagnoses codes;

– The performance improvement of the proposed solution, in terms of accuracy, based on the use of structured data in electronic patient records (medications, laboratory results, etc.).

References

1. Scheurwegs, E., et al.: Selecting relevant features from the electronic health record for clinical code prediction. J. Biomed. Inform. **74**, 92–103 (2017)
2. Weathers, A.L.: Use of the electronic health record for coding in outpatient neurology. CONTINUUM: Lifelong Learn. Neurol. **23**(2), e12–e16 (2017). Selected Topics in Outpatient Neurology
3. Duclos, C., et al.: Medical vocabulary, terminological resources and information coding in the health domain. In: Venot, A., Burgun, A., Quantin, C. (eds.) Medical Informatics, e-Health, pp. 11–41. Springer, Heidelberg (2014). https://doi.org/10. 1007/978-2-8178-0478-1_2
4. Pons, E., et al.: Natural language processing in radiology: a systematic review. Radiology **279**(2), 329–343 (2016)
5. Holzinger, A., Schantl, J., Schroettner, M., Seifert, C., Verspoor, K.: Biomedical text mining: state-of-the-art, open problems and future challenges. In: Holzinger, A., Jurisica, I. (eds.) Interactive Knowledge Discovery and Data Mining in Biomedical Informatics. LNCS, vol. 8401, pp. 271–300. Springer, Heidelberg (2014). https://doi.org/10.1007/978-3-662-43968-5_16
6. Doan, S., et al.: Natural language processing in biomedicine: a unified system architecture overview. In: Clinical Bioinformatics, pp. 275–294. Humana Press, New York (2014)
7. Zaki, M.J., Meira Jr., W., Meira, W.: Data Mining and Analysis: Fundamental Concepts and Algorithms. Cambridge University Press, Cambridge (2014)
8. Aggarwal, C.C., Zhai, C.: A survey of text classification algorithms. In: Aggarwal, C., Zhai, C. (eds.) Mining text data, pp. 163–222. Springer, Boston (2012). https:// doi.org/10.1007/978-1-4614-3223-4_6
9. Korde, V., Mahender, C.N.: Text classification and classifiers: a survey. Int. J. Artif. Intell. Appl. **3**(2), 85 (2012)
10. Holzinger, A. (ed.): Machine Learning for Health Informatics: State-of-the-Art and Future Challenges, vol. 9605. Springer, Heidelberg (2016). https://doi.org/ 10.1007/978-3-319-50478-0
11. Wang, Z., Xue, X.: Multi-class support vector machine. In: Ma, Y., Guo, G. (eds.) Support Vector Machines Applications, pp. 23–48. Springer, Cham (2014). https:// doi.org/10.1007/978-3-319-02300-7_2
12. Sokolova, M., Lapalme, G.: A systematic analysis of performance measures for classification tasks. Inf. Process. Manag. **45**(4), 427–437 (2009)

Building a Research-Quality Copy Number Variation Data Repository for Translational Research

Chen Wang$^{(\boxtimes)}$, Raymond M. Moore, Jared M. Evans, Xiaonan Hou,
S. John Weroha, and Guoqian Jiang

Mayo Clinic, 200 First Street SW, Rochester, MN 55905, USA
{wang.chen, moore.raymond, evans.jared, hou.xiaonan,
weroha.saravut, jiang.guoqian}@mayo.edu

Abstract. Copy number variation (CNV) has known associations with population diversities and disease conditions. However, research communities face great challenges in reusing the CNV data due to the heterogeneity of existing CNV data sources. The objective of the study is to design, develop and evaluate a scalable CNV data repository based on a proposed common data schema for facilitating research-quality CNV data integration and reuse. We created a proposal for a CNV common data schema through analyzing multiple existing CNV data sources. We designed a collection of the CNV quality metrics and demonstrated its usefulness using the CNV data from a study of ovarian cancer xenograft models. We implemented a CNV data repository using a MongoDB database backend and established the CNV genomic data services that enable reusing of the curated CNV data and answering CNV-relevant research questions. The critical issues and future plan for the system enhancement and community engagement were discussed.

Keywords: Copy number variation · Standardization ·
Integrated data repository · Quality assurance

1 Introduction

Copy number variation (CNV) is usually defined as genomic regions with a duplication or loss more than 1 kb in size. CNV includes copy number polymorphism (CNP) common in population, rare pathogenic copy number variation (PCNV), and somatic copy number aberration (SCNA). CNVs have been shown to play an important role in regulating gene expression levels [1, 2]. CNVs also have associations with human population diversity, common phenotypes, and human diseases [3–5]. Most of the CNPs are inherited and very few are de-novo events. The category of CNVs with known disease associations can be defined as pathogenic CNV (PCNV). The size of PCNV could be ranging from large as entire chromosome (e.g. chr21 trisomy causing Down-syndrome), a few Mega base-pair regions (e.g. p22.1q deletion, associated with DiGeorge Syndrome), to a single gene (e.g. germline TP53 deletion defined for Li-Syndrome). SCNAs in somatic tissues can be introduced through normal cell division processes, genetic defects of DNA damage repairing, as well as environmental exposures [6].

© Springer Nature Switzerland AG 2019
V. Gadepally et al. (Eds.): Poly 2018/DMAH 2018, LNCS 11470, pp. 148–161, 2019.
https://doi.org/10.1007/978-3-030-14177-6_12

Increasing amounts of CNV data have been produced based on microarray and sequencing techniques [7–10]. At least three public large data sources exist: Database of Genomic Variants (DGV) [11], Exome Aggregation Consortium (ExAC) [12], The Cancer Genome Atlas (TCGA) [3]. However, consistent storage and efficient re-use of CNV data are challenging and the FAIR (findable, accessible, interoperable, reusable) data principles remain unmet [13], due to various and incomparable ways of CNV data generation and lack of quality-ensured data reuse. In particular, we identified three major informatics hurdles for effective and efficient curation of existing large CNV datasets: (1) data standardization issue: lack of common CNV data schema scalable to accommodate different levels and types of CNV data from various data sources. (2) lack of quality assurance: CNV events are estimated based on microarray or sequencing measurements with various levels of noises. (3) data not queryable: lack of genomic service to ease query and facilitate biological hypothesis examination and formulation. Given increasingly generated genomic datasets, future advancements of basic and translational research will be increasingly dependent on well-organized genomic databases with queryable and re-usable genomic services.

The objective of this study is to design, develop and evaluate a genomic service for effectively managing storage and enabling flexible queries of various CNV data sources. We first design a common data schema through a review of existing major CNV data sources. Second, we design and implement a CNV quality assurance module using an internal dataset from an ovarian cancer PDX study. Third, we create a series of extraction, transformation and loading (ETL) scripts for converting various data sources into a centralized MongoDB database according to designed common data schema. Finally, we demonstrate the utility of the CNV genomic services through answering a collection of sample-level queries. In addition, we discuss the lessons learnt from the common schema and future functional requirements for using the genomic service to facilitate integrative biological research with further phenotype incorporation.

2   System Architecture

In this study, we intend to build a CNV data repository and associated genomic services for integrating several representative CNV data sources and an internal CNV PDX dataset. The overall design is presented in Fig. 1. The ultimate goal is to facilitate commonly needed CNV-based research examinations or hypothesis formulations. In particular, we considered three major modules for a CNV data repository.

2.1   A Common Data Schema

Existing CNV data sources are very heterogeneous and direct result comparisons are often impossible. According to analytical convince, CNV call data might be reported based on feature- or segment-level, e.g. ExAC reports on exon feature-level and TCGA reports on gene feature-level. Each individual CNV study may report CNVs at different and incomparable levels due to the lack of a common data schema. For examples, the DGV database collected all the called CNV events at regional levels, with both individual sample- and study-population level; ExAC reported CNV frequency at exon- and gene-level, with only availability of aggregated calls at population level; TCGA reported CNVs in both regional and genomic feature levels (i.e. gene-level), with both segmented CNV and CNV calls; CCLE and PDX studies only report gene-level segmented CNV values. As another example, while DGV has both hg37 and hg38 version of CNV results, TCGA only has hg37 results ready. With all these inconsistent ways of reporting and publishing CNV results, various levels of challenges exist to query CNV results from different studies and make efficient data-reuse. In order to summarize and reuse existing CNV data sets in a comparable way, a common CNV data schema is highly needed.

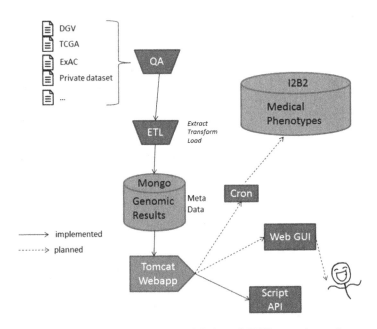

Fig. 1. Function requirements and design of CNV genomic service

2.2   A Quality Assurance Module

Regardless measurement platforms (e.g. aCGH, NGS), CNV events were all computationally inferred based on DNA-level measurements with inherent variability stemming from biological sample extraction, DNA library preparations and platform noises. CNV data without quality assurance may confound or even mislead formulation of particular research questions. CNV measuring and calling steps have been reported sensitive to biochemistry sample processing procedures, individual platforms, as well as original Biospecimen DNA qualities [14, 15]. CNV data without quality examinations could lead to artifacts-associated false discoveries [16, 17]. Therefore, we believe it is critical to include a module dedicated to summarize CNV-specific quality metrics and assure only research-quality results going into the genomic service collections.

2.3   A Data Repository and Service Module

With a well-designed common data schema, we implement a CNV data repository with a series of ETL processes to convert original data sources to standard format of CNV results. For the prototype implementation, we use the MongoDB database as the backend. This is in order to enable gene- or region-level CNV queries, with either sample-level or population-level results return. At gene-level, it is well known that loss or deletion events of tumor suppressor genes, e.g. BRCA1 or TP53, are associated with significantly increased cancer incidences; at region-level, it is also established that many genetic syndromes are associated with Mb-level to chromosome-level specific CNV events.

Besides of above-mentioned three considerations, we will also consider expanding the CNV data repository and services from two aspects: (i) a web user interface and a script API expansion based on Tomcat; (ii) further connections with a medical phenotype database such as the solution enabled by i2b2.

3   System Implementation

3.1   Analyzing Existing CNV Reports and Data Types

CNV event of a genomic region is measured by relative signal differences of genomics features, which could be individual probe-sets for aCGH and SNP microarray, exons for whole-exome sequencing (WXS) data, and genomic bins for whole-genome sequencing (WGS) data. These original CNV signals, often referred as raw CNV data, correspond to hybridization intensity differences in microarray or sequencing coverage differences in NGS platforms. The raw CNV data will be typically normalized to remove technical artifacts correlated with genomic contexts (e.g. GC content), and then segmented to infer regional copy number changes using computational algorithm, leading to a typical regional notation of start, end, and regional average amplitude of segmented CNV data. To determine types of CNV, complex mathematics and probability models are often used to determine whether each segment of CNV is likely to correspond to CNV calls, e.g. duplication, deletion events in DGV. As the consequence of lacking a common schema, each individual CNV study may report CNVs at different and incomparable levels due to several of reasons. For examples, the DGV database collected all the called CNV events at regional levels, with both individual sample- and study-population level; ExAC reported CNV frequency at exon- and gene-level, with only availability of aggregated calls at population level; TCGA reported CNVs in both regional and genomic feature levels (i.e. gene-level), with both segmented CNV and CNV calls; CCLE and PDX studies only report gene-level segmented CNV values. With all these inconsistent ways of reporting and publishing CNV results, various levels of challenges exist to query CNV results from different studies and make efficient data-reuse.

CNV data results could be reported from individual sample, or aggregated as population-level. CNV event of a genomic region is measured by relative signal differences of genomics features, which could be individual probe-sets for aCGH and SNP microarray, exons for WXS, and genomic bins for WGS. CNV data are often expressed as a relative form comparing observed signals versus expect signals, such as Log2Ratio (L2R) transformation: L2R = log2[(observed signal)/(expected signal)]. For two channel aCGH measurement, the observed signal is measured from sample of interest and expected signal coming from control channel; for whole genome sequencing data, the observed signal is the actual observed coverage and expected signal is expected average/median coverage in given sample. L2R = -inf, $-1, 0, 0.58, 1$ correspond to homozygous deletion, loss, normal copy number, one copy gain, and two copies gain, respectively. According to review of existing CNV data sources, we summarized three types of CNV results:

Feature L2R Data. The feature-level CNV data are defined as L2R CNV measurements derived from individual genomic features, which could be microarray probe-sets for SNP microarray and aCGH, or genomic regions either dividing according to genomic coordinates or exon/gene coordinates. At this level, normalization has been done to make different samples in a same study comparable, and further adjustment is often made to remove technical artifacts correlated with genomic contexts (e.g. GC content).

Segment L2R Data. Based on feature-level L2R data, the copy number segmentation algorithm is often applied to smooth adjacent genomic features, to infer candidate CNV events, each of which is defined by genomic start and end positions, as well as an average L2R across multiple features in given segment. Non-CNV segments (i.e. close to diploid state) are also reported at this level, and type of CNV events is not determined.

CNV Call Data. Given multiple evidences, including segment-level L2R and noise level within each CNV region, CNV event might be called as "loss" or "deletion" if the genomic region is determined to be of less than 2 copies; "gain" or "amplification" if more than 2 copies. Copy number neural event such as loss-of-heterozygosity (LOH) might be called as well based on allelic imbalance evidence (Table 1).

Table 1. Overview of representative CNV data sources. DGV: Database of genomic variants; ExAC: Exome Aggregation Consortium; TCGA: The Cancer Genome Atlas; CCLE: Cancer Cell Line Encyclopedia; PCT: Patient derived xenograft clinical trial.

CNV data sources	CNV data type				Report level	
	Feature L2R	Segment L2R	CNV call		Sample	Population
			Exon/gene call	Segment-call		
DGV [11]				x	x	x
ExAC [12]			x			x
TCGA [3]	x	x	x	x	x	
CCLE [18]		x	x		x	
PCT [19]			x		x	

3.2   Designing a CNV Common Data Schema

As reflected from our summary of existing data sources, CNV data types are hetero-geneous and lack standards for harmonizing different CNV data sources. We selectively described a few recommended elements included in the three types of collections for making this genomic service reusable:

Data Collection. Data-collection includes basic CNV data and calling results, containing chromosome coordinates and other details of CNV events. Noticeably, most of the CNV data sources even not contain original CNV dosage (i.e. log2ratio data), making the future reuse of data challenging. In addition, we found none of existing CNV data sources contains confidence measurement of each called CNV region. To address paucity of QC metrics, we made further recommendations to include several additional meta-data:

- *N_feature*: number of CNV features used to derive the given CNV segment;
- *Seg_L2R_Mean*: mean estimate of log2ratio across multiple features in a same segment;
- *Seg_L2R_Std*: standard-deviation estimate of log2ratio across multiple features in a same segment.

Sample Collection. Sample collection contains basic sample-level metadata. Besides of biological sample information such as original tissue type and reported gender, we also recommended to include more details of CNV data-types and sample-level QC metrics:

- *data_type*: type of CNV data, e.g. feature L2R, segment L2R, or CNV call;
- *feature_type*: the type of genomic features used for deriving CNV call, e.g. probe, exon, or genomic bin;
- *N_called_CNV*: number of called CNV events in a given sample;
- *smoothness*: a sample-level QC metric describing the smoothness of feature-level L2R data, defined as $MAD(x\_i - x\_i + 1)$.

Study Collection. Study Collection contains basic study-level metadata, including reference and contact information. Detailed metadata of each study, such as reference literature and web link, are recommended to ensure future access and reproducible research.

3.3   CNV Quality Assurance Module

In practice, it is very difficult to summarize quality metrics without accesses to original data. While it may be infeasible to retrospectively assess and assure quality of existing CNV data sources, we considered a quality assurance (QA) module with required inputs of feature- and segment-L2R data. Specifically, we implemented R scripts to form several CNV and sample-level quality metrics, in order to allow cross-platform based examinations of important sample-level quality metadata. According to several literatures focusing on CNV quality checks [14, 16], we included both CNV- and sample-level metrics applicable to both microarray- and NGS-based CNV calls, such as smoothness and N_called_CNV defined in Sect. 3.2. In addition, we also implemented a function for facilitating visual inspection of CNV QCs, which will be described in more details in results sections.

3.4   ETL Processes and MongoDB Solution for Centralizing Each Individual Data Sources

Several considerations were taken to develop the Extract-Transform-Load process including; minimizing dependencies, modular code design, quality checks and database performance. Python was chosen as a common scripting language that contained a mature database connection library, pymongo. Python is used at various institutions, which we anticipate will lower the barrier to entry for collaborators. These scripts have been released under the MIT open source license. Due to each dataset having varied, individual formatting, we decided rather than pursuing a robust single extraction strategy requiring many iterations, we developed a single script per each new data source. However, this strategy is mitigated by a collection of common, utility functions. These functions include; formatting data types from strings, quality checking assumed data type, and converting keywords. Each python script is a complete ETL operation that follows a modular template. Each script follows these basic steps, check dependencies, gather command line arguments, transform and load sample-meta data, check then transform and load the CNV event data. The data transformations focused around filling out our core schema, then allocating the overflow fields into a nested document, with dynamic fields, retaining the keyword names from their source. An example of this in DVG, is determining the genomic chromosome, start, and end fields, then transforming the string based designation [loss, gain, deletion, duplication] to a standardized CNV call. Those fields along with associated metadata describing type where saved in to the static, common core schema. The remaining fields specific to that data source where just allocated to a nested object referred to as 'features'. Thus both common and specific fields can be queried, but only the common core fields can be leveraged across multiple data types. The effort going forward is to determine which fields in the dynamic schema can be transformed and moved into the common core.

For databasing solution, we used MongoDB storing the CNV data and associated sample and study metadata. As a NoSQL database solution, MongoDB is a free and open-source database program, with features such as cross-platform compatibility and document-oriented flexibilities. MongoDB uses JSON-like documents with schemas, which make it an inherent choice for leveraging a centralized API system. There are a number of solutions that can provide API end points, for purposes we chose another common choice written in Java; SpringMVC served by Tomcat. The coding strategy follows the same path as the scripts, end points are specific to a use case, but there are modular functions to minimize impact when adding another. For example there are end points that return full records based on queries of gene symbols, genomic coordinates or accession numbers. The underlining functions are then reused to provide summarizations of those same records, by bins or field aggregations.

4   Results

In this section, we will summarize two representative aspects of our results, for loading and querying public data sources, and examining QC for an in-house PDX study.

4.1   A Draft Proposal of the CNV Common Data Schema

Through iterative literature and data source reviews, we designed CNV data common schema, shown as Table 2. The common schema was recommend as minimum requirement and additional recommendations were made to fulfil quality assurance and further sample-/study-tracking purposes.

Table 2. CNV data common schema

Attribute name	Brief description	Collections in MongoDB			Availability in representative CNV data sources		
		Data	Sample	Study	DGV	ExAC	TCGA
genome_ver	Reference genome version, e.g. hg37, hg38	m	m	m	✓	✓	✓
study_unique_ID	Unique identifier for a study	m	m	m	✓	✓	✓
data_source_ID	Unique identifier for a CNV data source, e.g. TCGA	m	m	m			
sample_unique_ID	Unique identifier for a CNV sample	m	m		✓	✓	✓
Chr	Chromosome of CNV event, e.g. chr3	m			✓	✓	✓
start	Bp-level start position of CNV, e.g. 1001	m			✓	✓	✓
end	Bp-level end position of CNV, e.g. 8336	m			✓	✓	✓
CNV_call	Called CNV event, e.g. duplication	m			✓	✓	✓
Feature_type	Type of CNV features, e.g. probe, exon	o					
N_feature	Number of features in this segmental CNV	o					
Seg_L2R_Mean	Log2ratio mean in this segmental CNV	o					
Seg_L2R_Std	Log2ratio standard-deviation in this segmental CNV	o					
Seg.pval	Nominal p-value of calling this CNV	o					
Seg.FDR	False-discovery rate of calling this CNV	o					

(*continued*)

Table 2. (*continued*)

Attribute name	Brief description	Data	Sample	Study	DGV	ExAC	TCGA
		Collections in MongoDB			Availability in representative CNV data sources		
bio_sample_type	Type of samples, e.g. normal, disease		m				✓
bio_sample_origin	Type of sample tissue origin, e.g. blood, breast, prostate		m				✓
report_type	Type of CNV reports, e.g. sample-level, population-level		m		✓	✓	✓
data_type	Type of CNV calls e.g. exon-/gene-/segment-CNV calls		m		✓	✓	✓
assay_type	Type of assays used for CNV calls, e.g. microarray, WXS		m		✓	✓	✓
feature_type	Type of features used for CNV calls, e.g. probe, exon		m				✓
N_called_CNV	Number of called CNVs in this sample		o				
L2R_smoothness	Log2ratio smoothness score in this sample		o				
study_reference_publication	Reference publication for the CNV study			m	✓	✓	✓
study_reference_websource	Reference website for the CNV study			m		✓	✓
study_contact_person	Whom to contact with for data access			o			
study contact email	Email to contact with for data access			o			
study_contact_phone	Phone to contact with for data access			o			

m: minimum requirement; **o**: optional but highly recommended

4.2   CNV Data Entities of Loaded Public Data Sources

Here, we described two examples of loaded entities from two representative CNV data sources, shown as Fig. 2. Besides of self-contained queries, MongoDB has a series of flexible API for enabling communications with different programming languages, such as C++, Python and R. In particular, we evaluated several solutions and identified "rmongodb" R package as for enabling flexible and complex queries (https://gist.github.com/Btibert3/7751989), with future statistical and visualization considerations.

Fig. 2. Examples of CNV entities retrieved from the genomic services: (A) a CNV event reported at single germline sample level from DGV; (B) a CNV event reported at aggregated population level from ExAC

4.3   Quality Assurance of a PDX CNV Dataset

In order to examine functionality of the CNV-QA module, we performed a case study on an internal CNV dataset of SCNA samples measured from ovarian cancer patient-derived xenograft (PDX) models, which were developed at Mayo Clinic (IRB: 09-008768; IACUC: A60115-15). These PDXs are relevant to ovarian cancer patients because they recapitulate patient disease in terms of histologic, genomic, and tran-scriptomic heterogeneity [20–22]. Most importantly, the PDX response to carboplatin/paclitaxel *in vivo* correlates with the matched patient clinical outcomes and similarly, they demonstrate a high concordance of SCNAs with the matched patient tumor [21]. In particular, SCNAs have been found associated with signaling mecha-nisms mediating chemo-responses in ovarian cancer [23], and with ongoing as well as future studies, these PDX models and their corresponding molecular data will continue to grow. Given the established SCNA knowledge for ovarian cancer, it is of great research interest to not only standardize methods to curate ovarian cancer SCNA data, but also to ensure the quality of such data. Previously, SCNA profiling was performed on 40 PDX models using the Agilent Human Genome CGH microarray kit 244A with matched-patient reference germline DNA as described in [21]. CNV raw data were first normalized to aCGH probe-level L2R signals, and CNV segments were inferred using a circular binary segmentation algorithm [24]. Following related recommendations in calling CNVs in tumor samples [25], L2R values of −0.1 and 0.1were used for CNV loss and gain calling cutoffs, respectively. In practice, we found "smoothness" and "N_called_CNV" are the most informative metrics to identify outlier samples. Shown as Fig. 3(A) and (B), smoothness and N_called_CNV metrics are both of single-peak distributions, while extreme values may indicate problematic samples. Figure 3(C) showed a scatterplot between smoothness and N_called_CNV metrics, highlighting a few representative PDX samples. Shown as Fig. 3(D) and (E), "PH036" and "PH079" are two typical ovarian cancer samples with an expected high degree of genome instability and many SCNA events; moderate smoothness scores suggest they have clean copy number measurements. In contrast, PDX "PH101" was derived from a typical serous ovarian cancer but had very few called CNV events (Fig. 3F), consistent with a diploid genome; after further pathology evaluation, it was found to be an unintended EBV transformed lymphoma rather than the originally implanted ovarian tumor, which happens occasionally from co-transplantation of human tumor infiltrating lymphocytes in the immunodeficient mice [26]. In Fig. 3(G), we further found an extremely noisy PDX sample associated with an ultra-high smoothness score that was later explained by low input DNA from a recurrent ovarian tumor. Together, these examples support the QA module as a useful correlate to PDX validation in addition to the CNV data for which the assay was designed.

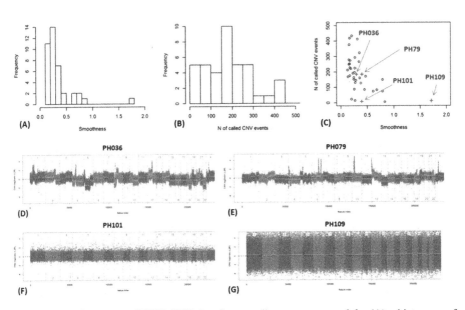

Fig. 3. Example outputs of PDX CNV data from quality assurance module. (A) a histogram of smoothness scores, (B) a histogram of N_called_CNV scores; (C) a scatterplot between smoothness and N_called_CNV scores, with highlighted PDX models. (D–G) whole-genome CNV plots for highlighted PDX models.

5   Discussions

A number of CNV datasets have been generated using various techniques to understand common population diversity, human disease risks and tumor genomic landscapes. These techniques include fluorescence in situ hybridization (FISH), array comparative genomic hybridization (aCGH), SNP microarray and next-generation sequencing techniques [10]. Given large volume of existing CNV data and increasing knowledge around CNVs, there are great incentives to curate and reuse existing CNV data for addressing basic and translational research questions. Several annotation tools and aggregation databases have been developed for the purpose. For examples, using text-mining based approaches to curate CNV with disease phenotype relationships [27], and developing annotation tools to predict likely functional and pathogenic status of CNV events [28]. However, for each CNV study, a series of platform-specific processing and bioinformatics procedures are needed to convert raw data to actual CNV data. The exact CNV calling procedures may significantly differ among various methods, as well as be limited by data platforms. Moreover, basic meta-data are required to make different studies comparable, e.g., projects focusing on health individuals (e.g. 1000 genome project), human cancer models (e.g. cell line and xenograft studies [18, 19]), and patient tumor cohorts (e.g. the cancer genome atlas) [3]. The pilot studies described in this manuscript are based on thorough surveys of existing CNV data sources and phenotype databases, and intended to further leverage existing data and knowledge to overcome the challenges towards efficient CNVs data re-use. In brief, we developed ETL methods that can effectively aggregate different CNV data sources and reconcile CNV data in a common schema, from DGV [11], ExAC [12], and TCGA [3].

From designing stage, our common data schema was intended to accommodate different CNV data sources with heterogeneous formats. Our initial design could be of limited scopes and restricted by our views of required data formats. It is of community interest, we believe, to refine and agree upon such common data schema. During ETL processes of loading different data sources to central database, we often found ambiguous mappings from original terminologies of individual data source to standard attributes we recommended: e.g. DGV does not distinguish "gain" or "amplifications" for increased DNA copy numbers while TCGA has strictly different definitions of different degrees of increased copy numbers. Further, population-level aggregations of CNV reports, such as from ExAC, often impose challenges of checking and assuring qualities of CNV events. All these issues are also obstacles of the FAIR data principles and thereby required future community-based efforts to address. Noticeably, genomic data standards have been separately developed by several major initiatives, including the NCI's Genomic Data Commons (GDC) (https://gdc.cancer.gov/), the Global Alliance for Genomics and Health (GA4GH) (http://genomicsandhealth.org/), and HL7 Fast Healthcare Interoperability Resources (FHIR) (https://www.hl7.org/fhir/). As more genomic CNV data and results being generated, it is critical to reach community-based consensus and develop corresponding CNV API services to standardize CNV data exchange formats, specify quality assurance practices, as well as enable CNV data sharing and collaborations.

As another highly valuable future work, we will integrate the CNV genomic data repository with medical phenotype database, for examining samples with phenotype-implicated CNVs, such as severe clinical syndromes or research-reported phenotype associations. For examples, some large CNV regions have been reported associated with hyperlipidemia [29, 30], essential hypertension of extreme blood pressures [31], type-2 diabetes and extreme obesity [32, 33]. At gene-level, several research observations have also been reported with treatment implications, e.g. amplification of *CCNE1* gene has been reported associated with resistant to chemo-therapies [23, 34]. Noticeably, there already exist several CNV phenotype collections curated by genomic community, such as DECIPHER (https://decipher.sanger.ac.uk/), ISCA (http://dbsearch.clinicalgenome.org/search/) and ClinVar databases (https://www.ncbi.nlm.nih.gov/clinvar/). These would serve as important phenotypic information sources for us to expand our CNV genomic repository in the future.

6 Conclusions

We summarized our preliminary efforts of designing, developing and evaluating a CNV data repository with genomic service for effectively managing storage and enabling flexible queries of various CNV data sources. We will make continuous efforts to expand and share the genomic service as an open-source solution in collaboration with genomic and translational research communities. Currently, we make an open-source project calling for collaborative participants and community-orientated improvements and the project GitHub website is available at: https://github.com/raymond301/CNVdb-Mongo-ETL.

Acknowledgements. The study is supported in part by a NIH BD2KOnFHIR U01 project (U01 HG009450), a NCI U01 Project – caCDE-QA (U01 CA180940), the Mayo Clinic Specialized Program in Research Excellence (SPORE) grant P50 CA136393, R01 CA184502 from the National Institutes of Health, Minnesota Ovarian Cancer Alliance, and Ovarian Cancer Research Fund Alliance.

References

1. Gamazon, E.R., Stranger, B.E.: The impact of human copy number variation on gene expression. Brief. Funct. Genomics **14**(5), 352–357 (2015)
2. Karlsson, J., Larsson, E.: FocalScan: scanning for altered genes in cancer based on coordinated DNA and RNA change. Nucleic Acids Res. **44**(19), e150 (2016)
3. Zack, T.I., et al.: Pan-cancer patterns of somatic copy number alteration. Nat. Genet. **45**(10), 1134–1140 (2013)
4. Bragin, E., et al.: DECIPHER: database for the interpretation of phenotype-linked plausibly pathogenic sequence and copy-number variation. Nucleic Acids Res. **42**(Database issue), D993–D1000 (2014)
5. Zarrei, M., et al.: A copy number variation map of the human genome. Nat. Rev. Genet. **16**(3), 172–183 (2015)
6. Wain, L.V., Armour, J.A., Tobin, M.D.: Genomic copy number variation, human health, and disease. Lancet **374**(9686), 340–350 (2009)
7. McCarroll, S.A., et al.: Integrated detection and population-genetic analysis of SNPs and copy number variation. Nat. Genet. **40**(10), 1166–1174 (2008)
8. Wang, C., et al.: PatternCNV: a versatile tool for detecting copy number changes from exome sequencing data. Bioinformatics **30**(18), 2678–2680 (2014)
9. Wang, W., et al.: Target-enrichment sequencing and copy number evaluation in inherited polyneuropathy. Neurology **86**(19), 1762–1771 (2016)
10. Zhao, M., et al.: Computational tools for copy number variation (CNV) detection using next-generation sequencing data: features and perspectives. BMC Bioinf. **14**(Suppl 11), S1 (2013)
11. MacDonald, J.R., et al.: The database of genomic variants: a curated collection of structural variation in the human genome. Nucleic Acids Res. **42**(Database issue), D986–D992 (2014)
12. Karczewski, K.J., et al.: The ExAC browser: displaying reference data information from over 60 000 exomes. Nucleic Acids Res. **45**(D1), D840–D845 (2017)
13. Wilkinson, M.D., et al.: The FAIR guiding principles for scientific data management and stewardship. Sci. Data **3**, 160018 (2016)

14. Diskin, S.J., et al.: Adjustment of genomic waves in signal intensities from whole-genome SNP genotyping platforms. Nucleic Acids Res. **36**(19), e126 (2008)

15. Staaf, J., et al.: Normalization of illumina infinium whole-genome SNP data improves copy number estimates and allelic intensity ratios. BMC Bioinf. **9**, 409 (2008)

16. Ginsbach, P., et al.: Copy number studies in noisy samples. Microarrays **2**(4), 284–303 (2013)

17. Cooper, N.J., et al.: Detection and correction of artefacts in estimation of rare copy number variants and analysis of rare deletions in type 1 diabetes. Hum. Mol. Genet. **24**(6), 1774–1790 (2015)

18. Barretina, J., et al.: The cancer cell line encyclopedia enables predictive modelling of anticancer drug sensitivity. Nature **483**(7391), 603–607 (2012)

19. Gao, H., et al.: High-throughput screening using patient-derived tumor xenografts to predict clinical trial drug response. Nat. Med. **21**(11), 1318–1325 (2015)

20. AlHilli, M.M., et al.: In vivo anti-tumor activity of the PARP inhibitor niraparib in homologous recombination deficient and proficient ovarian carcinoma. Gynecol. Oncol. **143** (2), 379–388 (2016)

21. Weroha, S.J., et al.: Tumorgrafts as in vivo surrogates for women with ovarian cancer. Clin. Cancer Res. **20**(5), 1288–1297 (2014)

22. Glaser, G., et al.: Conventional chemotherapy and oncogenic pathway targeting in ovarian carcinosarcoma using a patient-derived tumorgraft. PLoS ONE **10**(5), e0126867 (2015)

23. Etemadmoghadam, D., et al.: Integrated genome-wide DNA copy number and expression analysis identifies distinct mechanisms of primary chemoresistance in ovarian carcinomas. Clin. Cancer Res. **15**(4), 1417–1427 (2009). An official journal of the American Association for Cancer Research

24. Olshen, A.B., et al.: Circular binary segmentation for the analysis of array-based DNA copy number data. Biostatistics **5**(4), 557–572 (2004)

25. Mermel, C.H., et al.: GISTIC2.0 facilitates sensitive and confident localization of the targets of focal somatic copy-number alteration in human cancers. Genome Biol. **12**(4), R41 (2011)

26. Butler, K., et al.: Ovarian cancer tumorgraft: viral latency propagates lymphoma. Gynecol. Oncol. **127**(1), S16 (2012)

27. Qiu, F., et al.: CNVD: text mining-based copy number variation in disease database. Hum. Mutat. **33**(11), E2375–E2381 (2012)

28. Zhao, M., Zhao, Z.: CNVannotator: a comprehensive annotation server for copy number variation in the human genome. PLoS ONE **8**(11), e80170 (2013)

29. Pollex, R.L., Hegele, R.A.: Copy number variation in the human genome and its implications for cardiovascular disease. Circulation **115**(24), 3130–3138 (2007)

30. Shia, W.C., et al.: Genetic copy number variants in myocardial infarction patients with hyperlipidemia. BMC Genom. **12**(Suppl 3), S23 (2011)

31. Marques, F.Z., et al.: Measurement of absolute copy number variation reveals association with essential hypertension. BMC Med. Genomics **7**, 44 (2014)

32. Wang, K., et al.: Large copy-number variations are enriched in cases with moderate to extreme obesity. Diabetes **59**(10), 2690–2694 (2010)

33. Prabhanjan, M., et al.: Type 2 diabetes mellitus disease risk genes identified by genome wide copy number variation scan in normal populations. Diabetes Res. Clin. Pract. **113**, 160–170 (2016)

34. Patch, A.M., et al.: Whole-genome characterization of chemoresistant ovarian cancer. Nature **521**(7553), 489–494 (2015)

DEAME - Differential Expression Analysis Made Easy

Milena Kraus[(⊠)], Guenter Hesse, Tamara Slosarek, Marius Danner,
Ajay Kesar, Akshay Bhushan, and Matthieu-P. Schapranow

Hasso Plattner Institute, Prof.-Dr.-Helmert-Str. 2-3, 14482 Potsdam, Germany
{milena.kraus,guenter.hesse,schapranow}@hpi.de
{tamara.slosarek,marius.danner,ajay.kesar}@student.hpi.uni-potsdam.de
https://www.hpi.de

Abstract. Differential gene and protein expression analysis reveals clinically significant insights that are crucial, e.g., for systems medicine approaches. However, processing of data still needs expertise of a computational biologist and existing bioinformatics tools are developed to answer only one research question at a time. As a result, current automated analysis pipelines and software platforms are not fully suited to help research-oriented clinicians answering their hypotheses arising during their clinical routine. Thus, we conducted user interviews in order to identify software requirements and evaluate our research prototype of an application that (i) automates the complete preprocessing of RNA sequencing data in a way that enables rapid hypothesis testing, (ii) can be run by a clinician and (iii) helps interpreting the data. In our contribution, we share details of our preprocessing pipeline, software architecture of our first prototype and the identified functionalities needed for rapid and clinically relevant hypothesis testing.

Keywords: Differential expression analysis · Explorative analysis ·
Rapid hypothesis testing · Web application

1 Introduction

Analysis of differential expression (DE) is the process of identifying genes or proteins that have an altered level of expression in a group of samples, which is statistically significant when compared to another. The differences in expression levels may be the result of a disease or other perturbations of the examined cells or tissues. Therefore, the identification of the differences can lead to biomarkers of a disease [11] or a transcriptomic profile that may be reversed through a new or existing treatment.

The development of next-generation sequencing (NGS) techniques have enabled the usage of RNA sequencing (RNAseq) data as primary source for DE analysis [5]. Processing of raw RNA reads includes a pipeline of quality control, read alignment and quantification, all of which require a sophisticated selection of tools and methods [6]. Byron et al. describe examples for how analysis of

© Springer Nature Switzerland AG 2019
V. Gadepally et al. (Eds.): Poly 2018/DMAH 2018, LNCS 11470, pp. 162–174, 2019.
https://doi.org/10.1007/978-3-030-14177-6_13

RNAseq can benefit clinical practice. However, the great flexibility and resulting complexity for RNAseq have hindered its path to the clinic so far [5].

In recent years, many studies, e.g., in the context of systems medicine, included a detailed clinical examination of patients, supported by a molecular characterization via omics technologies [10]. Oftentimes these studies have an observational, i.e., a non-interventional character and do not include the effect of an active perturbation, e.g., testing a new drug or therapy in a defined environment. Thus, effects on the molecular level, e.g., in gene expression, are the result of many *in vivo* factors. Research-oriented clinicians, i.e., physicians that work in part as a physician but also conduct research on their patients, observe these *in vivo* factors, such as gender or previous diagnoses, but only have a limited understanding and capability to interpret DE results. Contrary, computational biologists have little insights into clinical practice and thus, their research hypotheses are mainly motivated by literature. In order to find and validate a joint research hypothesis the clinician and the computational biologist must interact and communicate efficiently.

In our contribution, we share a software systems architecture as well as our first prototypical web application, which will enable clinicians and computational biologists to rapidly perform exploratory hypothesis testing in the context of observational studies. The hypothesis testing is based on gene as well as protein expression data and results are visualized within the proposed application.

Our contribution is structured as follows: First, we describe the generic process of how differential expression analysis is performed traditionally in Sect. 2 and how it has been implemented in related work so far (Sect. 3). In Sect. 4 we share details of our user research, which results in specific software requirements. The developed software systems architecture and application prototype are described in Sect. 5.

2   The Differential Expression Analysis Process

We provide a generic process model of all steps needed for a DE analysis emanating from an RNA sequencing experiment using Business Process Modeling Notation (BPMN) in Fig. 1. The pipeline is based on Conesa et al. [6] and resembles many of the implemented pipelines described in Sect. 3.

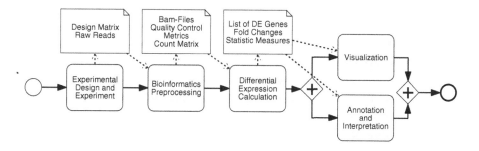

Fig. 1. Generic differential expression process steps and their results.

Experimental Design. Inherent to DE analysis are at least two groups of samples that are assumed to show differences in gene expression. These groups need to be specified before *in vitro* testing in order to plan and design the wet lab process, such as treatment with a specific chemical or drug. In contrast, the clinical context usually assumes *in vivo* experiments, e.g., biopsy analysis for a group of diseased patients as well as a healthy control group. Many of these studies are purely observational and factors that contribute to the differential gene expression are multiple and therefore not defined as clearly as in the *in vitro* setup. Confounding factors, such as batch effects or other patient specific clinical parameters, should be recorded and taken into account when analyzing DE results. As a result, the researcher needs to define a design formula which resembles the research hypothesis and is the basis of any DE experiment. The formula is then provided as input of the pipeline.

Bioinformatics Preprocessing. The sequencing process results in raw reads. Raw reads go through quality control and in some cases need to be trimmed from adapter sequences prior to alignment. All reads are aligned to a reference genome or transcriptome. In the best case all genomic ranges, such as a gene, an exon or coding region, are covered by multiple reads after the alignment step. Counting tools calculate the exact quantity of reads per given genomic range.

Differential Expression Calculation is the statistical process of finding significant expression differences of two or more groups as defined in the experimental design. In short, all counts of a genomic range in one group are compared to the counts of the same range in another group of samples. The calculation provides information about the fold change, i.e., how much more counts where found in one group when compared to the other. Additionally, p-values are given, which are adjusted for multiple testing as many data sets comprise 10–20 k genomic regions to compare.

Visualization of results is a critical part in DE analysis as raw and transformed data as well as DE results are usually high in dimension and therefore need to be displayed in a comprehensive format. Frequently used techniques are principal component analysis and clustering of data. Both give an impression of similarity between the analyzed samples. For example, plotting samples on their corresponding first and second principal component (dimension of largest variation) should result in scatters of samples grouped according to the experimental design formula. Accordingly, clustering algorithms should be able to find clusters and a dendrogram resembling the desired study groups. Clustered heatmaps are specifically popular as they can display sample-to-sample as well as gene-to-gene relationships and the corresponding normalized and log transformed count values in a single diagram. Volcano plots depict the p-value versus expression fold change between two conditions. Differentially expressed genes or proteins are usually marked and therefore the plot gives a good overview of all results. Many more diagnostic plots are used as, e.g., depicted in a bioconductor workflow [17].

Annotation and Interpretation. Annotation and interpretation of results is a critical and complex part of the analysis. Typically, more than 100 genes/proteins are found to be differentially expressed between patient groups. Regarding the most relevant expression changes, a manual search for function and involved pathways is performed. Gene Ontology (GO) annotation and Gene Set Enrichment Analysis (GSEA) help to find perturbed anatomical structures, biochemical processes or pathways in an automated manner.

3   Related Work

Gaur et al. provide an overview about automated RNAseq analysis platforms and a short description of their utility [9]. Four of the tools listed by Gaur et al. show similarities to our approach:

The main aim of RAP [7] is to provide an RNAseq tool that does not need to be installed on the client side. The web interface provides possibility for data submission and a browsing facility for results exploration. While the overall appearance seems more user friendly than command line tools, the platform is suited for users with bioinformatics knowledge that are able to configure pipelines and interpret results. Furthermore, RAP offers a great variety of possibilities for analyzing RNAseq data and thus, no focus on DE analysis. Especially visualizations and plots are not available so far. DE genes are given as lists.

RNAminer [14] provides three different fully parameterized pipelines that work simultaneously and results are consolidated among the pipeline. However, the resulting DE genes are given as text files and any new hypothesis needs an upload of files and a manual specification of two groups of samples at the maximum.

QuickNGS [21] has many options to analyze a variety of NGS data and thus lacks visualizations and functions that are specific for RNAseq analysis. Again, results are only given in lists. Plots are limited to a static clustered heatmap and a PCA plot. Additionally, experimental design is static and as described within the publication only usable for two groups (sample and control) plus batch effects.

Wolfien et al. implemented TRAPLINE for automated analysis of RNAseq data, evaluation and annotation within the Galaxy framework [3,22]. The TRAPLINE workflow was built to enable experimentalists to analyze data without requiring programming skills [22]. In addition to preprocessing and DE calculation, it provides several lists of results and help or links for visualizing data. Additionally, links to annotation and interpretation tools are given. RAP and RNAMiner are both closed source web applications, while QuickNGS and TRAPLINE (as a Galaxy implementation) offer the possibility to setup a private instance.

In general, most state-of-the-art tools are designed for users with some bioinformatics knowledge that is needed to configure the pipelines and interpret the data. Moreover, some applications are built on the assumption that there is only a single experimental design or perturbation to be tested on. As a result, all programs mentioned have at least two of the following drawbacks: (i) No ad-hoc or only static visualization for DE results, (ii) a static experimental design and/or a resulting (iii) cumbersome reconfiguration for any new hypothesis to be tested. Additionally, the complete pipeline including preprocessing is repeated in every analysis of the input data, which results in redundancy when multiple hypotheses are tested on the same or a subset of samples. While the listed tools work well for interventional studies and a single hypothesis, a new approach is needed in the case of observational setups and many hypothesis.

4   Requirements Engineering

The idea and development of the web application has been discussed and evaluated iteratively within the Systems Medicine Approach for Heart Failure (SMART) consortium based on an RNAseq raw data and clinical data raised within an observational study on heart failure patients. Several iterations on mockups and prototypes were conducted within the SMART consortium, which consists of research-oriented clinicians, molecular and computational biologists.

In a literature survey, we identified relevant and state-of-the-art preprocessing tools as well as DE calculation and visualization options. In order to validate the pipeline as described in literature, we conducted informal phone interviews with experts from different research institutes that focus on the analysis of RNAseq data and DE analysis. We discussed all steps of the technical pipeline to determine the acceptance of tools within the user community and shortcomings of selected programs.

In the following, key findings gathered in user research and literature review are assembled to identify concrete user groups of our application.

4.1   User Groups

We identified and characterized two user groups of our application: The **Research-oriented Clinician** who is interested in (i) testing own hypotheses based on daily observations and assessed clinical parameters and (ii) interpretation of DE results in the clinical context, e.g., if results point to a disease, a potential treatment or interesting research directions. All of that should not require any programming skills. The **Computational Biologist** is primarily interested in a statistically accurate preprocessing pipeline and calculation of DE results. The execution of the pipeline should require minimum input and configuration. It should allow ad-hoc exploration and analysis of DE experiment results. Furthermore, the computational biologist would like to get publication-ready result reports.

While the computational biologist has little insights with respect to the patients studied and the resulting hypotheses, the clinician cannot perform bioin-formatic processes and algorithms alone. Frequently, the clinician has no experience with omics data and therefore does not know what information can be obtained from it. Communication on interesting results and strategies on further investigations is therefore hampered. Therefore, both user groups need a platform that provides a common ground for discussion.

4.2 Software Requirements

Based on our user research observations and the shortcomings of related platforms as depicted in Sect. 3, we specified the following software requirements (R) of our DEAME application.

R 1 Automated Preprocessing: Only a single program execution is needed to preprocess raw RNAseq reads to count matrices.

R 2 Pipeline Configuration Options: The pipeline may be altered and configured by the computational biologist, but does not need to.

R 3 Split of Pipeline: Bioinformatics tools within the processing pipeline need to allow a split into preprocessing and experimental design/DE calculation.

R 4 State-of-the-art Tools: All bioinformatics tools need to be well-established and accepted within the scientific community.

R 5 Clinical Information: Clinical data on the samples needs to be readily accessible to setup the experimental design.

R 6 Rapid Experimental Design Creation: The translation of the clinician's hypothesis into an experimental design matrix needs to be easy and fast.

R 7 Interactive Visualization of Results: Results of DE calculation are high in dimensionality and need proper and interactive visualization.

R 8 Actionable Information on Results: Additional information on DE calculation results need to be provided within the application context, i.e., publications on regulated genes may be available.

R 9 Usability: The overall workflow should resemble the research process. The representation needs to be visually appealing but at the same time correct in content. The application provides sufficient features for the computational biologist yet comprehensible for the clinician.

5 DEAME Application

Our DEAME application is part of the systems medicine IT infrastructure (SMART IT platform) described in [12] and uses resources, such as the worker framework and the in-memory database, provided by the AnalyzeGenomes (AG) platform [18]. In Fig. 2, the overall software architecture of the DEAME application as well as relevant parts of the SMART platform are modeled using Fundamental Modeling Concepts (FMC). A thorough explanation of all components will be given in this section.

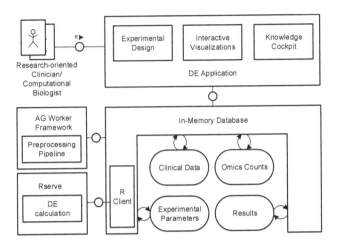

Fig. 2. Software system architecture of the DEAME application including parts provided by the SMART and AnalyzeGenomes IT infrastructure [12,18].

5.1 Data Layer

An in-memory database contains all frequently accessed data: The patient centric star schema of the SMART platform was expanded within the experiment part (please refer to [12] for further details on the clinical data and security aspects). Tables for counts, as they are produced within the preprocessing as well as intensities from, e.g., proteomics data, are added as well as tables for experimental parameters and results of DE calculation. Furthermore, an R client is established to perform DE calculation within an Rserve instance.

5.2 Platform Layer

The platform layer contains the preprocessing pipeline, experimental setup information and DE calculation functionality. The split into preprocessing and experimental design plus DE calculation is a design decision that limited the selection of tools to be used within the pipeline when compared to the traditional setup as in Sect. 2. The split resembles the need given within a clinical setting, where many hypotheses may be tested and thus, the experimental design for DE calculation is not known before preprocessing of raw data. As a result, preprocessing and DE calculation are independent from each other.

Technical Preprocessing Pipeline. In our architecture, the preprocessing is embedded within the worker framework of AnalyzeGenomes, which provides a scalable runtime environment for automatic execution of BPMN pipeline models. In Fig. 3, we describe the pipeline, input and output of the individual steps and the order in which they are executed. The boxes represent applications, i.e., python wrappers around the incorporated bioinformatics tools, e.g., TopHat.

Such programs could be extended and interchanged when new tools need to be introduced.

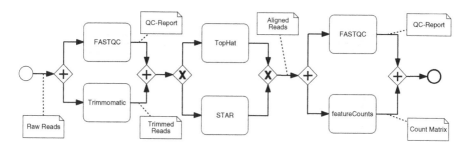

Fig. 3. Specific implementation of our RNAseq preprocessing pipeline

We identified the following tools to be suitable for our first prototype: FastQC [2] for quality control before and after trimming of reads with trimmomatic [4], Tophat [20] or STAR [8] for alignment of reads to the reference genome, and featureCounts [15] for creating count tables from alignment files. In this setup, all samples will be preprocessed only once to avoid redundancies.

DE Calculation and Design Formula Creation. DE calculation as explained in Sect. 2 is done via DESeq2 [16] within our Rserve instance. DESeq2 is called from a stored procedure within our in-memory database and requires the raw count table as generated by our preprocessing pipeline. Furthermore, DESeq2 receives metadata on the selected patients, i.e., user selected features and the corresponding design formula, e.g., gender + age + gender:age. We reduced the number of possible designs to be a two-factorial, two-level design with an interaction term to allow for sufficiently large study groups in small data sets. Factors in the clinical data are of differing statistical types, i.e., they consist of numerical data, e.g., age, binary data, e.g., gender, or categorical data, e.g., race, as given in Table 1. Furthermore, categorial data can be differentiated to be exclusive, i.e., a patient can only be described by one category (blood group), or non-exclusive, i.e., a patient may be assigned to more than one instance of a category (e.g., different medications). The type of data defines how it is handled within in the experimental design procedure.

In this setting, any given **factor** needs to be split into two **levels** as specified by the user and therefore will be reduced to a binary representation (Table 1). While **levels** are natural in the case of binary data, the **levels** of numerical and categorial data need user input. In the case of numerical data the user defines a split point x which divides the values into two groups. For exclusive categorial data, the user chooses at least one instance of the **factor** per **level** or can combine multiple instances into one level. Non-exclusive **factors** need one binary representation per instance. Thus, e.g., the instance "Beta-blocker" of the **factor** "Medications" is split into being present or absent (yes/no). A

Table 1. Description of statistical data types, `factors` and their corresponding binary representation (`levels`).

Data type	Factor full range example	Binary level example
Binary	Gender Male/Female	Male = all male patients Female = all female patients
Numerical	Age 0–90 years	Below_x = [0 – x) AboveAnd_x = [x – 90]
Categorial exclusive	Blood group A, B, AB, 0	Blood_1 = A, B, AB Blood_2 = 0
Categorial non-exclusive	Medication Beta-blocker, Aspirin, Thyroxin	Med_yes = Aspirin yes Med_no = Aspirin no

second instance of the `factor` can be used to create a second factor. `Factors` and `levels` are subsequently translated into the design formula as expected by DESeq2.

Interactive Visualization and Annotation. Many results and intermediate results are of interest for both the clinician and computational biologist. Quality control as done by FASTQC produces an html-file for every sample which is stored and accessed for display within the application. Additionally, results from DESeq2, i.e. the list of DE genes, their test statistics and also the complete normalized and transformed count matrix, are visualized within the application. Interactive heatmaps are implemented via the clustergrammer software and its biology-specific extensions to show gene/protein names, cluster statistics and GSEA [1]. Further plots are implemented as D3 library extensions.

5.3   Application Layer

Our application consists of three parts: (i) the experimental design panel, (ii) a visualization panel and (iii) a knowledge panel.

Experimental Design Panel. The experimental design panel is the main part of the application as it enables to dynamically choose interesting clinical patient data categories to be studied in DE analysis (Fig. 4). The overall goal is to split the patient population into at least two subgroups based on the patients' characteristics. For demonstration purposes, we use data from the SMART study. Patients are characterized by approx. 200 clinical variables (e.g., gender, height, blood pressure) that are grouped in categories (e.g., demographics or ECG measurements). All categories are displayed and may be expanded to show the variables. Binary variables and non-exclusive categorical data can be dragged into the design matrix directly. Continuous variables are split by the user via an interactive slider over the full range of possible values. Exclusive categorical variables

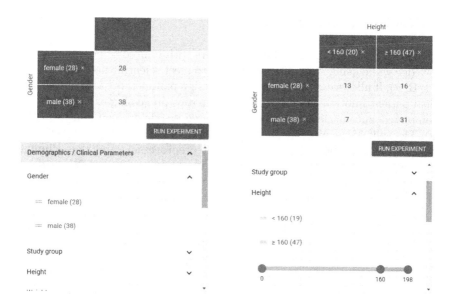

Fig. 4. Screenshot of experimental design panel.

may be combined within one column of the design matrix via drag-and-drop. The design matrix displays `factors` and `levels`, calculates group sizes and provides an estimation on the achieved statistical power at user interaction. After the creation of a valid design, i.e. at least three samples in every group, DeSEQ2 is triggered with the corresponding count tables generated in the preprocessing step via the 'Run Experiment'-button.

Visualization Panel. Within the visualization panel the user may choose between four different tabs to choose plots on quality control of the preprocessing from FASTQC, overall characteristics of the data (e.g., PCA, sample-to-sample heatmap) and DE results (e.g., interactive heatmap, volcano plot, list of Genes/proteins and their statistics). A mouse over on genes/proteins displays a short description and clusters are clickable for statistics and for an update of the literature search. All results can be downloaded into a publication-ready report.

Knowledge Panel. Especially the clinician needs additional external information on analysis results. Instead of querying for mere names of, e.g., a gene, the found relationship, e.g., effects of upregulation of a gene or the disease context, are included in the query to find actionable insights. Examples for external resources that can be leveraged are search engines such as Olelo [13] for intelligent PubMed queries or DisGeNet [19] for gene-disease associations.

6   Evaluation and Discussion

Our DEAME application is designed for users with limited to no bioinformatics knowledge while using state-of-the-art tools to meet scientific needs for accuracy (**R 4**, **R 9**). It allows easy configuration of design parameters based on the actual clinical patient information (**R 5**). Bioinformatics processing of raw RNA reads is completed automatically in the background to yield count matrices (**R 1**, **R 2**). The split of the pipeline (**R 3**) does not necessarily reduce the time to test a single hypothesis, but it avoids redundant preprocessing and thus eliminates computational overhead as soon as multiple hypotheses are tested. We bridge the gap between DE calculations and their clinical interpretation by the experimental design panel. Static design formulation as used in related work is exchanged by a more flexible handling that allows for ad-hoc adaptions (**R 6**). The interactive plots do not require additional experience or tools and display information on the found genes and proteins (**R 7**). Additionally, our knowledge panel shows literature on the found genes/proteins and includes the context of the analysis to provide actionable insights (**R 8**).

Within most of the used tools there are many options to fine-tune the analysis. We purposely do not use many of these options as they most certainly will confuse the clinician as a user. We expect the results set of regulated genes or proteins to be smaller than within a fine-tuned environment. While this is a drawback in a detailed analysis of a computational biologist, the clinicians we spoke to are interested primarily in the strong signals and are pleased with a shorter list of candidate genes/proteins. If a specific hypothesis turns out to be worth more research, the computational biologist may take over or a follow-study can be set up. Our application provides a platform for communication in DE results between the research-oriented clinician and the computational biologist. The concept of DEAME is aimed for use in observational studies, e.g., in the systems medicine context, were study design lacks a strong intervention or treatment factor to test in differential expression analysis.

7   Conclusions and Future Work

For the first time, requirements of a clinicians were included and matched with those of computational biologists in the design of an RNAseq and DE calculation platform. As a result, we planned and implemented a research prototype of an application that (i) automates the complete preprocessing of RNA sequencing data in a way that enables rapid hypothesis testing, (ii) can be run by a clinician and (iii) helps interpreting the data. Our first working prototype will be validated in terms of specificity of the results set and the usability of the application within the SMART systems medicine consortium.

In addition to the RNAseq data, we have also started to use our framework to analyze DE proteins as calculated from shot gun proteomics. We will also extend possible design formulas to enable more complex experimental designs. Currently, our application is only usable within the SMART project, but as soon as the data is published, we plan to provide free of cost access to the web application. Users will then be able to browse the rich SMART data or to create own projects to explore.

Acknowledgement. Parts of this work were generously supported by a grant of the German Federal Ministry of Education and Research (031A427B).

References

1. Clustergrammer's Documentation. http://clustergrammer.readthedocs.io/index.html
2. FASTQC Documentation. http://www.bioinformatics.bbsrc.ac.uk/projects/fastqc
3. Afgan, E., et al.: The Galaxy platform for accessible, reproducible and collaborative biomedical analyses: 2016 update. Nucl. Acids Res. **44**, W537–W544 (2016)
4. Bolger, A.M., Lohse, M., Usadel, B.: Trimmomatic: a flexible trimmer for Illumina sequence data. Bioinformatics **30**, 2114–2120 (2014). https://doi.org/10.1093/bioinformatics/btu170
5. Byron, S.A., et al.: Translating RNA sequencing into clinical diagnostics: opportunities and challenges. Nat. Rev. Genet. **17**, 257 (2016)
6. Conesa, A., et al.: A survey of best practices for RNA-Seq data analysis. Genome Biol. **17**(1), 13 (2016)
7. D'Antonio, M., et al.: RAP: RNA-Seq analysis pipeline, a new cloud-based NGS web application. BMC Genom. **16**(6), S3 (2015)
8. Dobin, A., et al.: STAR: ultrafast universal RNA-Seq aligner. Bioinformatics **29**(1), 15–21 (2013)
9. Gaur, P., Chaturvedi, A.: A survey of bioinformatics-based tools in RNA-Sequencing (RNA-Seq) data analysis. In: Wei, D.Q., Ma, Y., Cho, W., Xu, Q., Zhou, F. (eds.) Translational Bioinformatics and Its Application, pp. 223–248. Springer, Dordrecht (2017). https://doi.org/10.1007/978-94-024-1045-7_10
10. Gietzelt, M., et al.: The use of tools, modelling methods, data types, and endpoints in systems medicine: a survey on projects of the German e: Med-Programme. Stud. Health Technol. Inform. **228**, 670–674 (2016)
11. Han, H., Jiang, X.: Disease biomarker query from RNA-Seq data. Cancer Inform. **13**(Suppl. 1), 81 (2014)
12. Kraus, M., Schapranow, M.P.: An in-memory database platform for systems medicine. In: Proceedings of the 9th International Conference on Bioinformatics and Computational Biology. ISCA (2017)
13. Kraus, M., et al.: Olelo: a web application for intuitive exploration of biomedical literature. Nucl. Acids Res. **45**(W1), W478–W483 (2017)
14. Li, J., et al.: From gigabyte to kilobyte: a bioinformatics protocol for mining large RNA-Seq transcriptomics data. PloS ONE **10**(4), e0125000 (2015)
15. Liao, Y., Smyth, G.K., Shi, W.: FeatureCounts: an efficient general purpose program for assigning sequence reads to genomic features. Bioinformatics **30**(7), 923–930 (2014)
16. Love, M., Anders, S., Huber, W.: Differential analysis of count data-the DESeq2 package. Genome Biol. **15**, 550 (2014)
17. Love, M.I., Anders, S., Kim, V., Huber, W.: RNA-Seq workflow: gene-level exploratory analysis and differential expression. F1000Research **4** (2015)

18. Plattner, H., Schapranow, M.P. (eds.): High-Performance In-Memory Genome Data Analysis: How In-Memory Database Technology Accelerates Personalized Medicine. Springer, Cham (2014). https://doi.org/10.1007/978-3-319-03035-7

19. Queralt-Rosinach, N., Piñero, J., Bravo, A., Sanz, F., Furlong, L.: DisGeNET-RDF: harnessing the innovative power of the semantic web to explore the genetic basis of diseases. Bioinformatics **32**(14), 2236–2238 (2016)

20. Trapnell, C., Pachter, L., Salzberg, S.L.: TopHat: discovering splice junctions with RNA-Seq. Bioinformatics **25**(9), 1105–1111 (2009)

21. Wagle, P., Nikolić, M., Frommolt, P.: QuickNGS elevates next-generation sequencing data analysis to a new level of automation. BMC Genom. **16**(1), 487 (2015)

22. Wolfien, M., et al.: TRAPLINE: a standardized and automated pipeline for RNA sequencing data analysis, evaluation and annotation. BMC Bioinform. **17**(1), 21 (2016)

Author Index

Printed in the United States
By Bookmasters